Agile Odyssey

Unlock Your Inner Leader, Inspire Transformation, and Drive Success

Rama Krishna Rao Tadepalli
Sayali Shintre
Suchinhita

ARCCHIE

Agile Odyssey

Unlock Your Inner Leader, Inspire Transformation, and Drive Success

Editor: Sowmya
Production Manager: Meghna
Cover design by Freepik

First Edition: June-2024

Reference: 2406024

Published by Arcchie Publications

ISBN-13 (paperback): 978-81-974190-2-7
ISBN-13 (ebook): 978-81-974190-4-1

Published by ARCCHIE PUBLICATIONS, Greater Noida, U.P. -201 306
and Printed at Repro India Ltd., Mumbai

www.arcchieonline.com

TABLE OF CONTENTS

JOIN US ON THE ARCCHIE PUBLICATIONS DISCORD SERVER

Connect with fellow readers, authors, and enthusiasts to discuss all things related to our publications and the exciting world of AI, programming, and learning. Share your insights, ask questions, and engage in vibrant discussions to expand your knowledge and inspire creativity. Take advantage of this opportunity to be part of a dynamic community dedicated to exploring the frontiers of technology and innovation. Join our Discord Server today and be part of the ARCCHIE Publications community!

https://discord.gg/z26SenmpEt

FOREWORD

As a Practice leader & Thought leader in the Hybrid Multi Cloud team at IBM, I am responsible for partnering with multiple clients across industries in their Business transformation strategies embracing Agile framework and methodologies; and developing skills, capabilities, tools & assets to facilitate & accelerate their transformation journeys. Through my 27 years of career, I have been a constant innovator, embracing new technologies that have changed & disrupted the IT industry in a positive way. As an IBM Master Inventor with 20+ issued / patents, and 30+ technical publications, I have been an advocate of exploring new technologies to drive efficiencies, productivity, environment sustainability and quality.

The world today is witnessing rapid acceleration of transformation programs and initiatives across industries. There are several innovative as well as disruptive forces that have compelled several businesses to transform themselves in entirety as well. Change is omnipresent and uncertainty is the only certainty, which is pushing organizations to adapt and embrace Agile framework /methodologies as their guiding principle. Agile is not just a framework or methodology, it is a mindset, a culture and a philosophy that empowers teams to adapt, innovate and excel. Agile offers a proven means to not just survive but succeed in an environment defined by complexity, unpredictability and continuous change. As Agile continues to gain momentum across industries, it's imperative that we have accessible resources to guide individuals, teams, and organizations on this transformative journey.

The book that you now hold in your hands is a unique and creative approach to introduce Agile, offering a novel view of how Agile principles and practices can transform the way we work and deliver outcomes.

Agile frameworks are easy to understand, however difficult to master it and adapt to, and a lot of programs get into a troubled state as they are unable to embrace Agile in a correct way. To be able to transform, one has to first transform oneself embracing Agile principles & concepts. This book is a key to this "Transform to transform" need and rightly titled as "Agile Alchemy: Fusing Timeless Wisdom with Triumph in the Digital Era" as it provides an engaging and imaginative way to demystify Agile concepts. It introduces Agile concepts with a storyteller's touch, weaving examples from real life, ancient texts and famous personalities' lives to simplify the concepts. As you progress reading the book, you will notice that the real world scenarios resonate with your understanding of Agile making it easy to adapt it to your programs in your professional and personal lives.

Agile transformation in itself is a continuous journey, and this book promises to be an excellent companion along the way. As you go through the chapters of this book, I encourage you to adapt and embrace the learnings in your day to day life and transform how you approach different programs & initiatives. Whether you are a leader of an organization or a team member, whether you are a seasoned Agile practitioner or someone new to Agile, this book provides valuable insights for one and all.

Cheers,
Deepak Gupta
New Delhi, India
Linkedin:/in/bankush/

DEDICATED TO

This book, "Agile Alchemy," is dedicated to the unsung heroes of transformation, whose resilience and dedication inspire us all. To the Farmers, whose unwavering commitment to nurturing the land and feeding the world reminds us of the power of growth and adaptation.

To the Soldiers, whose courage and sacrifice in the face of adversity demonstrate the essence of transformation, protecting the freedoms we hold dear. To all Transformation enthusiasts, Agile practitioners, and Product enthusiasts who strive for continuous improvement and change, pushing the boundaries of what is possible. We extend our deepest gratitude to the Agile Practice team, Coaches, Subject Matter Experts, and Champions of our present company. Your unwavering support and innovative ideas have played a vital role in delighting our customers and empowering our teams. Your dedication to transformation is truly commendable. We also pay our respects to Sanathana Dharma and its Gurus, the eternal wisdom and guidance that have illuminated our paths and provided timeless insights into transformation. Finally, we honor Nature, the ultimate source of inspiration and change, whose beauty and wisdom remind us of the importance of preserving our planet for future generations. Thank you for being the driving force behind our journey of transformation and for making this book possible.

With immense appreciation.

- Rama Tadepalli,
Sayali Shintre,
Suchinhita

ACKNOWLEDGMENTS

Writing a book is a journey filled with challenges and rewards, and it would not have been possible without the support, guidance, and encouragement of so many wonderful individuals. We extend our heartfelt gratitude to all those who played a significant role in the creation of "Agile Alchemy"

First and foremost, we want to express our deep appreciation for the unwavering support and inspiration provided by our families and loved ones. Your understanding, patience, and belief in our endeavor kept us going during long nights and busy weekends.
To our readers, whose interest and enthusiasm in the subject of Transformations, Agile Transformation and Product development have driven us to share our insights and experiences. Your curiosity fuels our passion.

We would like to express our heartfelt gratitude to Nisar A Rayadurg and Deepak Gupta for their invaluable leadership and guidance, which have played a pivotal role in enhancing our capabilities. The opportunities they have presented, and timely mentorship have truly been a catalyst for transformation. Our gratitude also extends to the team at Arcchie Publishing house, for their dedication, enthusiasm, and unwavering commitment in bringing this book to fruition. Your expertise and tireless efforts have transformed our vision into a tangible reality.

To our colleagues and peers who offered their insights and feedback, thank you for your thoughtful contributions that enriched the content and depth of this book. Your collective wisdom has left an indelible mark. Special thanks to Vivek Kumar for providing few impactful pictures.

We extend our sincere gratitude to Gaurav Arora, whose invaluable support has been instrumental in ensuring the success of this journey.

Finally, we wish to convey our appreciation to our readers, whether they are newcomers or seasoned experts, who are embarking on transformative journey with us. Our hope is that this book sparks your curiosity, expands your horizons, and motivates you to push the boundaries of knowledge, ultimately assisting you in surpassing your aspirations.

With profound appreciation and warm regards.

- Rama, Sayali, Suchinhita

ABOUT THE AUTHORS

Rama Krishna Rao Tadepalli is an Agile Practice Leader and Strategic Product Management Professional at a prominent global IT consulting company. Rama's natural affinity for agility and product-oriented thinking has led to numerous successful transformations that consistently delight customers. With a track record of training over 1,500 individuals in Agile ways of working, Rama is a passionate advocate for people-centric approaches.

Rama is an MBA Gold Medalist with over two decades of experience in Fortune 500 companies, where he has held diverse leadership roles in Business Analysis, Strategic Management, Project, and Program Management, as well as Agile and Product-centric delivery.

Beyond his professional pursuits, Rama is an avid yoga enthusiast, a sought-after speaker in colleges, and deeply committed to community service. In addition to his expertise in Leadership roles, Agile and Product domains, his current focus lies on the spiritual path.

Sayali Shintre as an Energy & Utilities consultant, Sayali is a strong proponent and practitioner of Agile at a leading global IT consulting firm. She has a Computer Science Engineering degree and over 20 years of experience in the IT industry. She has performed multiple roles from Developer to Project Manager to Product Owner. She has witnessed the best and worst of both Agile & Non-Agile approaches.

She has been instrumental in driving several agile transformations for clients. She is a passionate Agile mentor, who has guided hundreds of team members to embrace Agile principles and mindset. She has authored many articles that connect her personal life experiences with Agile principles.

Apart from her professional life, she is passionate about Ashtanga yoga and has a yoga teacher certification. She also enjoys trekking, especially in the Himalayas. The vibes of Himalayan peaks and her yoga practice have inspired her to pursue spiritual exploration, leading her to study various spiritual texts and scriptures.

ABOUT THE AUTHORS

Suchinhita, the pen name for Sandip Sengupta, is an agile enthusiast, an ardent follower and complete believer of Agile mindset and values. With nearly nine years of dedicated experience in multiple roles in the Agile realm, Suchinhita brings a wealth of knowledge and expertise. He has been part of multiple successful transformation programs across numerous global consulting companies. His extensive industry experience of nineteen years, serves as the foundation for his unique perspective on Agile mindset and practices, making him a seasoned guide for those seeking to navigate the complexities of Agile transformations. Suchinhita is a passionate trainer and has trained countless individuals in agile and other different areas and is fully inclined to the spiritual world but is still in a womb, trying to figure out his own duels.

He has written two books in the realm of Bengali Romantic Poems. One of the books was released in the Kolkata International Book Fair 2023 and the other one will be available for sale in the same fair in 2024. This dual passion for both the artistic and the analytical, informs his writing style, offering readers a well-rounded perspective that blends the precision of IT expertise with the elegance of poetic expression and creativity.

ABOUT THE TECHNICAL REVIEWER

Rajiv is an IT Professional having worked with multi-national IT Services companies over last 23 years. In his professional career he has played varied Leadership and Management roles in IT industry. He is a keen technology follower and considers agility literally as his way of life. On personal note, Rajiv is married and has two children, aged 18 and 15. He loves to travel, a fitness freak and an avid sports follower. In his leisure time he likes to watch thriller movies/series or reads anything which seems interesting about current affairs or history.

DISCOVER YOUR WRITING POTENTIAL WITH ARCCHIE

PREFACE

Welcome to "Agile Alchemy: Fusing Timeless Wisdom with Triumph in the Digital Era." This book embarks on a transformative journey that goes beyond the ordinary landscape of agile literature. In a world inundated with guides on how to conduct organizational agile transformations, we felt compelled to delve deeper into the heart of the matter. The real catalysts of change are not flowcharts or methodologies but the leaders who envision, inspire, and steer the transformation journey. This book is dedicated to those leaders – the driving forces behind agile transformation or any transformations. While the primary emphasis was placed on Agile transformation, the methods and strategies provided are adaptable for use in other transformations as well.

What defines a leader? A leader is an individual who motivates and steers others toward a shared objective or vision, frequently leveraging their charisma, competence, and aptitude for making difficult choices. They set a precedent, provide encouragement, and empower their team or colleagues to attain success. This role can be assumed by team members, team leads, project leaders, portfolio managers, or organizational leaders.

As we explore the pages of "Agile Alchemy," you will come to realize that our approach is refreshingly different from what you might have encountered in the agile literature landscape. We believe in the interconnectedness of ancient wisdom and modern agility. In a world where chaos seems to be the new norm, we turn to the timeless teachings of spiritual masters to guide us toward a more agile, adaptable, and sustainable future.

The journey you are about to embark upon transcends the boundaries of time and space. We will venture back through centuries, drawing wisdom from luminaries like Sri Ramakrishna Param Hansa, Swami Vivekananda, Lord Buddha, Sai Baba, Prophet Muhammad, and Jesus Christ. Their teachings offer profound insights into the agile mindset, fostering not only personal growth but also the seeds of change within organizations.

Agility is not merely a concept for software development; it is a way of life. We will explore how these teachings can be applied to transform individuals into true agile leaders. We believe that agile transformation is not a one-size-fits-all journey, and it certainly does not start and end at the organizational level. Real change begins within each leader, spreading its transformative wings outward, touching every corner of the organization. While the transformation process commences with the leader or individual, they need not complete their own metamorphosis before initiating the transformation of their teams and organizations. They can concurrently work on both personal and collective levels of transformation.

What's Inside This Book

Chapter 1: Seeds of Agile – We delve into the essence of Agile framework. It begins by exploring the inception of Agile and its relevance to your life. Furthermore, it traces the evolution of Agile in the realm of software development, providing a comprehensive overview of its origins.

Chapter 2: Unveiling the Mahavakyas for Agile Transformation - Explore the profound teachings of the Four Mahavakyas and their pivotal role in Agile transformation. Discover how these teachings inspire self-awareness and serve as the foundation for personal and organizational evolution.

Chapter 3: Wisdom Vintage- Spreading Ancient Knowledge with a Modern Twist for Agile World – This chapter introduces the age-old concept of agility, tracing its roots back to teachings from spiritual leaders. It invites us to consider whether Agile is a modern manifestation of timeless wisdom and explores the resonating principles in these teachings that emphasize agility and encourage their application in contemporary contexts.

Chapter 4: Know your strength & agility – This chapter delves into the concept of strength, its relevance in the Agile context, and what qualities define a genuinely agile leader.

Chapter 5: Unlocking Agile Success: The Crucial Role of Leader's EQ – It explores the significance of Emotional Intelligence (EI) in fostering effective leadership within agile teams. It covers the fundamentals of EI, its historical context, methods for measurement and enhancement, and practical strategies for leaders to apply EI.

Chapter 6: Know Agile, Know Agile transformation – It provides a comprehensive understanding of Agile, the different approaches to Agile transformation, and how to assess individual and organizational agility.

Chapter 7: Assessment – Transformation Index – This chapter provides guidance on creating appropriate questionnaires to measure and evaluate the reader's strength, emotional intelligence, and agility.

Chapter 8: Industry level challenges & solutions – The chapter highlights industry-wide challenges, focusing on culture, leadership, and consistency as key obstacles to successful Agile implementation. Resistance to change is a significant barrier, emphasizing the need for leaders to shift their mindset.

Chapter 9: Technology level challenges & solutions – This chapter delves into technology-related obstacles in Agile implementation, including legacy tools, broken processes, difficulties in measuring business values, and DevOps challenges and solutions to overcome these challenges.

Chapter 10: The Human Element: Navigating People Challenges and Unlocking Solutions - This chapter explores the transition from traditional work practices to Agile framework & methodologies, emphasizing the transformative power of Agile environments. It underscores the importance of embracing Agile thinking for personal growth and delves into the significance of the human factor in Agile success.

For Whom This Book Is Intended

This book is tailored for the following audiences:

- **Agile Practitioners:** Empower your agile journey with timeless wisdom and practical insights.
- **Organizational Leaders:** Lead agile transformations with a holistic perspective on change and growth.
- **Change Management Professionals:** Transform organizations with the wisdom of the ages and agile framework & methodologies.
- **Technology and IT Professionals:** Unite technology and agility for successful software development.
- **Business Analysts:** Align your analytical skills with agile values for effective project contribution.
- **Leadership Development Programs:** Nurture future leaders with a holistic approach to transformation.
- **Educators and Trainers:** Enrich your curriculum with insights into agile leadership and ancient wisdom.
- **Personal Growth Enthusiasts:** Discover personal and professional growth through ancient wisdom and agile principles.
- **Agile Enthusiasts and Scholars:** Explore the historical and philosophical foundations of agile practices.
- **Spiritual and Philosophy Enthusiasts:** Uncover the synergy between ancient wisdom and modern leadership.
- **Consultants:** Guide clients to agile success with comprehensive insights and strategies.

Download the color images

For color images/diagrams/graphs used in the book,
readers can download from: `https://l1nq.com/color-images`

Sharing Your Perspective and Providing Feedback

Your perspective is invaluable to us, as it helps us enhance our content and gather your feedback. We warmly welcome all forms of feedback. Please feel free to send us an email at feedback@arcchieonline.com, mentioning the book title in the subject line of your message.

Book Review Invitation

We kindly invite you to share your thoughts. After you've read and engaged with this book, consider leaving a review on the platform where you acquired it. Your impartial feedback can greatly assist potential readers in making informed decisions. Your reviews provide valuable insights for us at Arcchie, helping us better understand your perspectives on our products, and they offer authors the chance to appreciate your feedback on their work.

Chapter 1

The Seeds of Agility: Nurturing Transformation in Organizations

Imagine a bustling metropolis where traffic congestion was an everyday nightmare. For years, the city's infrastructure struggled to keep up with its rapid growth, and commuters endured endless hours of gridlock. It seemed like an insurmountable problem that was here to stay.

But then, imagine something remarkable happened. A new city administration took a bold step. Instead of pouring more concrete and widening roads, they decided to embrace an unconventional approach to solving the city's traffic woes. Inspired by principles from an unlikely source – the behavior of flocking birds – they embarked on a transformational journey that would change the city's transportation landscape forever. Hence, we are not even aware, where the genes of transformation might be present. A simple phenomenon of nature or some regular traits or activity which might appear as very common or mundane, might even have seeds of transformation or agility.

This is very similar to the concept of "First Principle". A first principle is a fundamental presumption from which no other conclusions may be drawn. Theoretically, first principles thinking calls on you to dive more and further until you are left with nothing but the situation's fundamental truths.

This chapter is not about birds but about the 'Seeds of Agility' that were sown in the heart of this urban transformation. It's about how an understanding of nature's principles can bring about profound change and agility in even the most complex of human systems. Just as birds effortlessly adapt to their surroundings, organizations, too, can evolve, thrive, and navigate the challenges of change. Join us on a journey to discover the seeds of agility, understand the essence of transformation, and explore how these concepts can revolutionize the way organizations/leaders adapt, evolve, and flourish in the face of change.

In the world of business, change is inevitable. However, implementing successful transformations within organizations can often be challenging due to resistance from individuals and teams. Understanding the reasons behind this resistance and applying effective change management strategies are crucial for ensuring the success of any transformation. Some common reasons can be fear of loss of control, lack of understanding, fear of unknown, threat to personal motivation or interests etc.

Leaders play a vital role in driving and ensuring the success of a transformation. They should exemplify their commitment by actively participating in and embracing the changes themselves. Once leaders have a clear understanding of the transformation, they can provide teams with clear direction. This necessitates effective communication of the vision and the provision of necessary resources and guidance throughout the transformation process. It is important to differentiate between change, transition, and transformation.

Leaders need to recognize that the seeds of agility exist in nature and were present long before the evolution of humans. By understanding this, leaders can gain a deeper insight into the essence of agility and its relevance to organizational transformations. With this understanding, leaders can effectively nurture the seeds of agility within their teams and organizations, allowing them to flourish and drive successful transformations.

The intent of this chapter is:

1. To explore the concepts of transformation, change, transition, and their significance in achieving successful outcomes.
2. To understand the challenges and resistances faced during transformations and the importance of effective change management strategies.
3. To examine the relationship between nature, the seeds of agility, and their relevance to organizational transformations.
4. To provide real-life examples and insights on the principles of agility and their application in various contexts.

In this chapter we will discuss:

- Transformation
- Change Transition to transformation
- Unleashing Agility: Navigating the Transformation Journey
- Transformation – Challenges
- Seeds of Agility in Nature
- Agility in life

Transformation – Why – What – How

We can start with a remarkable familiar childhood example which probably most of us might have experienced. "Don't you want to change yourself?" I think all of us have heard this multiple times when we were kids. During those days, if someone asked us this question, the very first thing coming to our mind was "why to change and change to what?" Once we had some idea on "why" and "what," two things could happen. First is that we dropped the idea of the change because the answer to those questions did not excite us anymore. But if we were interested even after the clarity on "why" and "what," the next question that used to peep in was "How to change?" Once we had clarity on "how" then again there was a fair chance of dropping the idea of the change as we might feel that taking the pain in the process of getting transformed is not worthy of the benefits of the change. After successfully overcoming so many hurdles if our mind believed that "**Gain is more than Pain**" then only we used to move towards an agreed the path of transformation.

To Transform or Not to Transform

Figure 1.1: Why-What-How

Let us start with a simple example. I could remember once my father told me "I think time has come you should change yourself." It was just after the annual results of grade 9. I was little surprised by the question as accidentally my result was good. I asked him quite naively the very same question. "why." What he said was like this, this transformation will help me to live a decent life in future and a good score in 10th and 12th grade boards. I guess every kid of my age then would think of these as their dreams only. And I said that I already got a good score then why I need to change myself. Then came an interesting part. He discussed a bit on the "what" part. I got to know that I need to shift my complete focus to study and learning. It is not that I won't be playing or stopping all my activities but my thinking process, my mindset should evolve around my studies. This somewhat and somehow got me convinced and I asked him the final question, "how you think that I should be doing this?" The details then I got from my father just punched me back. It is like I am thinking or doing something related to studies all the time even between any activities. Like while taking bath I can memorize multiples of 17, 18 etc., while taking breakfast I can recall few laws of physics. Morning walk is the best time for memorizing what I last read in history. It seemed like the entire day I was studying only. I did not say anything to my father, but I decided not to go ahead with any change then. Hence the fear of pain, fear of losing my fun, fear of losing my control over likings, activities and my little life made me completely repellent to the suggested change.

Change – Transition to Transformation

Many years later I could understand that at that age, I really mixed up the difference between a change and transformation.

Change

Change refers to any alteration or modification that occurs in a system, process, behavior, or state. It can be a small adjustment or a significant shift, and it can be planned or unplanned. Change can occur in various areas, such as technology, organizational structure, policies, or personal circumstances. Change often focuses on the outcome or result, highlighting the before and after states.

Transition

Transition is a process of movement from one state, condition, or phase to another. During a transition, there is often a change in focus or priority. Attention may shift from one set of objectives, goals, or tasks to another. It can involve reprioritizing resources, reallocating responsibilities, or adopting new strategies.

Transformation

Transformation is a more profound and comprehensive form of change. It involves a fundamental and often radical shift in the underlying nature, structure, or essence of something. Transformation typically involves a rethinking and reconfiguration of the entire system, resulting in a new paradigm or state. It often involves a notable change in mindset, culture, processes, and strategies. Transformation is typically aimed at achieving long-term and sustainable improvement.

Change	Transition	Transformation
Change refers to the act or process of making something different from its previous state.	Transition refers to the process or period of moving from one state, condition, or situation to another.	Transformation represents a profound and comprehensive shift in form, nature, or character.
It typically focuses on modifying specific elements, processes, behaviors, or aspects within a system or entity.	It involves navigating through a series of adjustments, adaptations, and reorientations during the shift from the old state to the new state.	It involves a holistic and fundamental change that affects multiple dimensions of a system, entity, or individual.
Change can be incremental or transformative, depending on the extent and scope of the modifications.	Transition recognizes the emotional, psychological, and practical aspects of the journey between two states.	Transformation goes beyond surface-level modifications and involves a deep restructuring and reimagining of the underlying beliefs, values, mindset, and fundamental principles.
Change often occurs in response to a specific problem, goal, or external factor, and its purpose is to bring about improvement or adaptation.	It involves managing the impact of change on individuals, organizations, or systems and facilitating a smooth and successful passage from one state to another.	It often requires questioning and challenging existing paradigms, assumptions, and ways of doing things.
Change can be short-term and specific, targeting a particular outcome or objective.	Transition often requires managing people's expectations, supporting them through emotional challenges, and providing the necessary resources and guidance during the period of change.	Transformation aims to create lasting and transformative outcomes, leading to a new state or paradigm that is significantly different from the previous one. Transformation is typically a long-term and ongoing process that involves continuous learning, adaptation, and evolution.

Figure 1.2: Change-Transition-Transformation

To summarize, change focuses on making specific modifications, transition involves managing the process and emotional aspects of moving from one state to another, and transformation entails a profound and holistic shift that affects multiple dimensions and leads to a new state or paradigm. Understanding these distinctions helps in effectively navigating and managing the complexities of change and transformation in various contexts. Let us consider that I followed some changes in my diet plan and routine which helped me to lose my weight in time but once I went back to my old habits then I started gaining weight again. So, I needed an entire shift or the transformation of my diet plan and daily routine which I can adapt sustainably and do not have to adjust temporarily only for some quick results. Let us remember that a caterpillar always transforms into a butterfly, and it goes through a biological transformation including breakdown of tissues, transformation at cellular and molecular levels and this transformation does not stop there. It continues every day in the life of the butterfly guided by the inherent survival instinct.

My father was really referring to a transformation of mindset and thought process but to me it was just a change in my daily activities which makes me have less control over my life and that freaked me out. I was not able to see the better life which could have been if I could go through the transformation then.

Unleashing Agility: Navigating the Transformation Journey

American sociologist James C. Davies introduced J-Curve hypothesis in 1962 to explain the political revolutions.

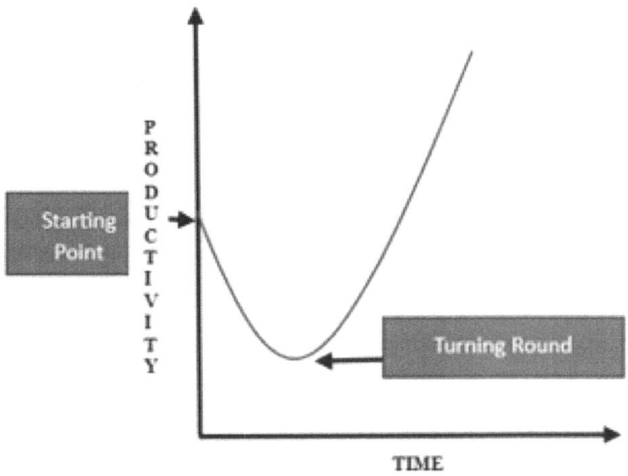

Figure 1.3: J-Curve: Transformation Path

The assertion made by Davies regarding revolutions as a subjective response to a sudden reversal in fortunes after a prolonged period of economic growth, known as relative deprivation, is one perspective on the causes of revolutions. Relative deprivation theory suggests that revolutions occur when there is a perceived gap or discrepancy between expectations and actual achievements or conditions, particularly in relation to economic well-being.

According to this theory, when individuals or groups experience a significant decline in their living standards, opportunities, or social status, despite previous periods of economic growth or relative prosperity, they may feel deprived and aggrieved.

The J-Curve concept is a useful framework that can be applied to understand the progress and challenges involved in Agile transformations. The J-Curve illustrates a common pattern of performance or advancement through time, with a rapid climb following an initial dip or decrease. The J-Curve can be connected to Agile transformations in the following ways:

Initial Dip: There is frequently an initial decline in performance or productivity when a business decides to go through an Agile transformation. The organization is adjusting to new procedures, roles, and working methods, which is why there is a decrease in performance. Teams may experience difficulties during this period understanding and using Agile principles, which may temporarily affect their productivity.

Learning and Adaptation: The organization begins to adopt the Agile mindset and practices after the initial learning curve. The development of Agile procedures, the exchange of knowledge, and the acquisition of new skills characterize this phase. Teams start to notice improvements and positive changes in their productivity and collaboration as they get more experience and familiarity using Agile.

Steep Rise: The J-Curve rises sharply as the organization continues to use Agile principles. The major gains and advancements made possible by the Agile transformation are represented in this phase. Teams become more effective, communication and teamwork increase, and the value of the customer is given more attention. The organization experiences increased adaptability, faster delivery of products or services, and higher customer satisfaction.

Interestingly both transformation and the J-curve involve a temporary decline or setback followed by a subsequent improvement. At the initial phase, transformation may involve a period of disruption, challenges, or temporary decline. However, as the transformation process progresses then gradually improvement in performance, growth, and all the positive outcomes can be seen.

It's crucial to remember that not all Agile transformations will result in the J-Curve. Based on a number of variables, including as the organization's size, culture, level of leadership support, and level of Agile adoption across teams, the curve's shape and duration can change.

The J-Curve concept can also be used in various change efforts or transformations; it is not just applicable to Agile transformations. It aids in illuminating the preliminary difficulties and brief setbacks that frequently happen before to appreciable advancement and achievement.

Transformation – Challenges

"Change is the only constant thing in life." An extremely popular statement but still we all have our instinct to avoid and reject changes and transformation. Accepting and embracing transformations can be challenging due to numerous factors, particularly when it comes to shifting mindsets.

The most important ones are mentioned below:

- **Uncertainty:** Transformation frequently entails foraying into uncharted areas, which can inspire anxiety and apprehension. Resistance to adopting a transformation mentality can be caused by the novelty of the change, potential hazards, and the requirement to venture outside of one's comfort zone. To overcome the fear of the unknown, one must be courageous, open-minded, and eager to try new things.
- **Attachment:** People tend to grow attached to tried-and-true practices, ideas, and frameworks. This attachment may lead to resistance to change and prevent people from accepting changes.
- **Beliefs:** It can be extremely difficult to let go of the past and be open to new possibilities, especially when doing so requires confronting deeply set behaviors or raising doubts about beliefs.

- **Fixed Mindset:** Acceptance of transformation can be hampered by a fixed mindset, in which people hold the belief that their abilities and characteristics are unalterable and immutable. Accepting and embracing shifts requires adopting a growth mindset, which emphasizes the possibility of individual improvement.
- **Loss of Control:** Giving up control of established systems or practices is a common part of transformations. This sense of loss of control can be upsetting and uncomfortable, which can result in resistance and mental difficulties. The difficulties brought on by the fear of losing control can be overcome by acknowledging that transformation necessitates a certain amount of surrender and placing faith in the process.
- **Lack of Awareness:** Sometimes people may find it difficult to accept changes because they are unaware of the causes of the change or the advantages it might have in the future. This barrier can be overcome, and a transformation-embracing mentality can be fostered through increasing awareness, actively seeking out knowledge, and actively participating in learning.
- **Socio-Cultural Factors:** The acceptance of changes by a person can also be influenced by social and cultural factors. It can be difficult to acquire a mindset that favors reforms because of peer pressure, societal conventions, or opposition from others.

It takes self-awareness, a willingness to learn and improve, as well as an initiative-taking attitude to personal growth, to meet these hurdles. It's crucial to understand that accepting changes and developing a change-supportive mentality are continual processes that call for perseverance, effort, and a dedication to both individual and group development.

Since the world is always transforming, transformation is unavoidable. Individuals, organizations, and communities can transform to adapt to changing conditions, technology, and problems. We can adjust to changing circumstances and remain relevant in a world that is changing quickly by embracing transformation. Innovation and progress are frequently driven by transformation. New concepts, methods, and techniques can develop through transformative processes, resulting in improvements in a variety of domains. Transformation fosters growth and development through promoting creativity and problem-solving.

There are several reasons to embrace transformation, including increasing our ability to adapt to change and becoming more agile by identifying and accepting the changes that are most appropriate for our environment. But in order to understand how this evolved to be an intrinsic and essential behavioral feature of survival, we may need to go back millions of years, perhaps even trillions of years, even before the creation of Nature.

The Seeds of Agility in Nature

Nature itself is a testament to constant change and transformation. Life, in its various forms, has also evolved over billions of years, adapting, and responding to changing environments. The nature has demonstrated its ability to transform and adapt from the creation of ecosystems to geological processes shaping landscapes. This inherent characteristic of nature, driven by the instinct for survival, has shaped the diversity and resilience of life on Earth.

The Evolution of Nature: Constant Transformation

The Universe that we can see today started in a vastly different form and over the millions and trillions of years it has changed and is still continuously changing its form.

Nature is no different in this regard when seen as an integral part of the universe. We can say that Nature broadly refers to the physical universe, which includes the Earth and all its ecosystems including both living and non-living creatures. Now, if we want to comprehend how nature was created or evolved then we must investigate the subsequent events or occurrences.

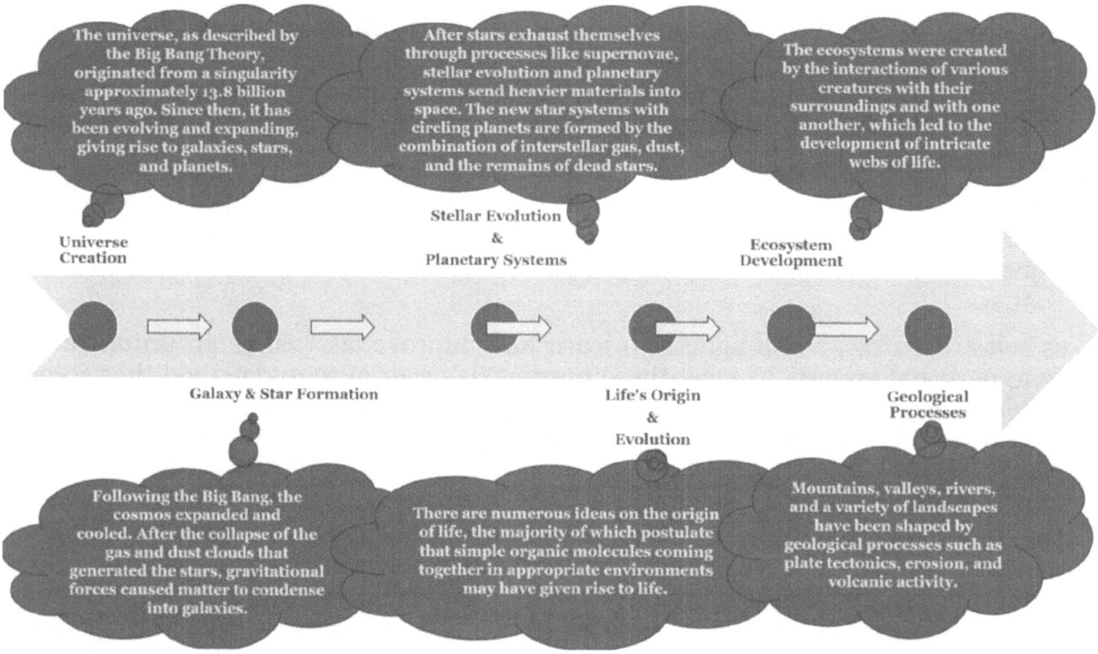

Figure 1.5: Universe Evolution

We all know that the nature is constantly evolving, whether we believe the mentioned chronological events to be genuine or not. If the nature had not gone through such changes, then we are not sure, if we would have 'life'. Probably the entire ecosystem and its inhabitants would also have been different.

The fact that nature and the universe are continually transforming, adapting, and acting in the best manner possible in response to all conceivable disruptions and events surrounding them is one of the reasons we can observe nature in her current state today. This skill is the instinct for survival, which was firmly ingrained even before life itself. Our surroundings might alter in a variety of ways without our ability to influence them. Our natural desire for survival determines how we respond to changes, not always on how we should react to them. An immediate, automatic, or emotional response to an outside stimulus is known as a reaction. After comprehending and analyzing the context, source, and goal of the external disruption, a response is a thoughtful, deliberate, and measured reaction. Hence this inherent nature of survival or the characteristic of understanding external events and responding in the most suitable way is one of the basic MANTRA or PRINCIPLE or LAW (of Nature) or the SEED on which nature or the universe has formed. This is what AGILE is, in it is simple and basic form where we can define "Agility" as the ability to move quickly and adapt to changes.

Let's delve deeper into the concept of adaptation. Life on Earth has seen the emergence of a vast array of creatures, ranging from simple to complex organisms, due to the fascinating process of evolution. Charles Darwin's theory of evolution elucidates how species transform over time, encompassing mechanisms like natural selection, genetic variation, and genetic inheritance. Through billions of years, these mechanisms have enabled life to evolve and adapt to various environments. Nonetheless, history reveals that many of these once dominant life forms have eventually disappeared.

Dinosaurs, for instance, thrived on Earth during the Mesozoic Era, spanning approximately 250 million to 65 million years ago. They reigned supreme over other land-dwelling animals for over 160 million years, giving rise to a diverse range of species with distinct sizes, forms, and behaviors. However, their existence came to an end millions of years ago. The Cretaceous-Paleogene (K-Pg) extinction event, occurring around 65 million years ago, is widely believed to be responsible for their extinction.

This cataclysmic event was marked by a significant asteroid impact, massive volcanic eruptions, and climate changes. It is believed that the Yucatán Peninsula in present-day Mexico served as the epicenter, where a colossal asteroid or comet, estimated to be around six miles (10 kilometers) in diameter, collided with Earth. The collision unleashed an immense amount of energy, resulting in widespread fires, powerful tsunamis, and a global dust cloud. The dust cloud caused by the impact obstructed sunlight, leading to a significant drop in temperatures and reduced photosynthesis. Consequently, the disruption of the food chain and the subsequent decline in photosynthesis triggered a widespread extinction event, affecting not only dinosaurs but also numerous plant and animal species. The extinction of dinosaurs resulted from a combination of immediate destruction and long-term environmental changes. The catastrophic event drastically transformed the ecosystem, paving the way for the extinction of various plant and animal species alongside dinosaurs.

We can observe that life forms that once occupied the highest levels of the food chain suddenly vanished. Nevertheless, this extinction opened doors for the development and evolution of new ecosystems, as well as the rise of new life forms to prominence. The extinction of dinosaurs allowed mammals to thrive and eventually take over as the primary terrestrial animals. Every natural selection and evolutionary process in nature highlights adaptability. Through these mechanisms, organisms gradually adjust to their surroundings, acquiring traits that enhance their survival and reproduction.

The Agile Mindset in Nature

The concept of agility is not only limited to human endeavors; it is deeply rooted in nature itself. Through the process of natural selection and evolution, organisms have developed traits and behaviors that enhance their survival and adaptability. Whether it is the ability of a chameleon to change colors, the speed and agility of a cheetah, or the complex ecosystems that have evolved over time, nature exemplifies agility in its purest form. The agility displayed by organisms allows them to respond effectively to changes in their environment, ensuring their survival and growth.

Embracing Transformation for Growth and Innovation

Embracing transformation is essential for growth and innovation. It enables us to adapt to changing circumstances, technologies, and problems. By embracing transformation, individuals, organizations, and communities can remain relevant and thrive in a rapidly changing world. Transformation leads to the development of new concepts, methods, and techniques, fostering creativity and problem-solving. It is through transformation that progress, and innovation are driven, opening up new possibilities and improving various domains of life. History and Nature has always shown that the strongest have fallen if one fails to understand the changes or challenges in the surroundings.

Let's consider a hypothetical scenario. Humans relied on hunting and gathering for survival during the Paleolithic era. Suppose they continued to do so as their sole source of food throughout the Mesolithic and Neolithic ages. Eventually, all plants and animals would have disappeared, compelling humans to resort to cannibalism to survive, thus regressing back to a dark phase in history. However, in the Neolithic age, humans adapted to domesticating plants and animals, the very ones they previously hunted during the Paleolithic period. This transition was not taught to them but arose from their innate survival instinct. They identified a new and easier way of obtaining food, perhaps even more efficient at times.

The Intrinsic Seed of Agile Thinking

The seed of agility has always been present in nature, even before the creation of life itself. It is the inherent characteristic of understanding external events and responding in the most suitable way for survival. This seed of agility can be traced back to the earliest forms of life on Earth, where organisms exhibited adaptive behaviors to ensure their survival. Humans, too, possess this inherent agility, which enables them to navigate complex and ever-changing environments. By embracing this agile mindset, individuals and organizations can unlock their full potential and drive successful transformations.

Interestingly, aside from essential biological processes such as respiration, excretion, and digestion that are inherent in all forms of life, the instinct of agility has always been a primal characteristic of nature. The problem arises when we deny or fail to align our consciousness with this thought process. The concept of agility, or the mindset underlying the Agile thought process, was present in nature even before the emergence of life. In our daily lives, we are constantly responding or reacting to internal and external events. While we can exert some control over certain events, others remain entirely beyond our control. The Agile thought process or mindset always enables us to provide the best and quickest response. However, do we consistently embody this mindset in our lives?

Agility in Real Life

Few days back I was having "Golgappa or Panipuri," one of the famous street foods in India and was watching the shopkeeper / "Golgappa-wala." He was serving 6-7 customers at a time. He always keeps on serving one panipuri to each of them with a subtle time difference. But somehow, he is serving seven customers together. While one customer was holding the plate, another one was holding the panipuri, while the next was moving the panipuri to the mouth from the plate, the next one was putting it in the mouth and the next one was chewing it and last one was swallowing it. The waiting time for each of the customers was simply in nano seconds.

He is somehow able to assess and maintain the required speed, different tastes with quality, the requirement and hence the customization of the individual customers. He was ensuring that each of the customers keep on getting an increment ("panipuri") at a regular and shortest interval. I am sure he is not aware of the term "AGILE" or "AGILE MANIFESTO." But for survival, nature has made him learn agility.

In **Chapter 3**, Section "**Wisdom Vintage**", we will try to trace the mindset and the thoughts in the "**Agile Manifesto**" back to the ages possible. We will explore if those thoughts were already present in the teachings of the famous spiritual leaders.

Conclusion

This chapter delves into the challenges faced during transformations and the role of effective change management strategies in overcoming resistance. It emphasizes the importance of leaders actively participating in and embracing the changes themselves, providing clear direction, and nurturing agility within teams and organizations. Understanding the difference between change, transition, and transformation is crucial in navigating and managing the complexities of transformation. Transformation is an essential aspect of growth and progress. By understanding the seeds of agility that exist in nature, leaders can nurture and cultivate the agile mindset within their teams and organizations. Overcoming challenges, embracing change, and adapting to new circumstances are crucial for achieving sustainable improvement. Just as nature constantly transforms and adapts, so must we. By embracing transformation and cultivating an agile mindset, we can drive innovation, growth, and success in our personal and professional lives.

In the next chapter we are going to learn the basic teachings of the "**Four Mahavakyas**" and how those teachings help in Agile Transformation.

Test your understanding

Test your knowledge from the chapter by answering the following questions:

Q.1. What are some common reasons for resistance to change during transformations?

Q.2. Why is it important for leaders to actively participate in and embrace the changes during transformations?

Q.3. What is Transition?

Q.4. What is Transformation?

Q.5. How does understanding the difference between change, transition, and transformation contribute to successful transformations?

Chapter 2

Unveiling the Mahavakyas for Agile Transformation

Incorporating the wisdom of the Mahavakyas into Agile leadership can provide a deep understanding of the underlying principles and values that drive successful Agile transformations. By embracing consciousness, interconnectedness, self-realization, and servant leadership, leaders can inspire and guide their teams towards Agile excellence.

In the quest for Agile excellence, leaders often seek inspiration from various sources. One such profound source of wisdom is the Mahavakyas, which are deep spiritual truths encapsulated in the ancient Indian scriptures known as the Upanishads. These timeless teachings offer valuable insights into consciousness, self-realization, and the interconnectedness of all existence. By integrating the principles of the Mahavakyas into Agile leadership, leaders can guide their teams towards Agile excellence, fostering a harmonious and purpose-driven environment. This chapter will explore the significance of the Mahavakyas in the context of Agile transformations and provide practical guidance on how they can address prominent Agile transformation challenges.

The intent of this chapter is:

1. To introduce and explain the concept of Mahavakyas, profound statements found in the Upanishads, and their significance.
2. To explore the four Mahavakyas and their deep spiritual truths, providing insights into consciousness, self-realization, and the oneness of existence.
3. To discuss the relevance and importance of the Mahavakyas in today's corporate world, specifically in the context of Agile transformations.
4. To highlight the potential of the Mahavakyas in guiding and inspiring leaders in Agile

transformations, promoting values, ethics, mindfulness, and personal growth.

5. To provide practical guidance on how each Mahavakya can be linked to prominent Agile transformation challenges and offer solutions to address those challenges.

6. To emphasize the role of the Mahavakyas in transforming leadership in the corporate world and fostering a harmonious and purpose-driven environment.

7. To showcase how integrating the wisdom of the Mahavakyas can guide Agile leadership towards excellence and inspire positive change in organizations, employees, customers, and society.

Understanding the Mahavakyas

Mahavakyas are profound statements or great sayings found in the ancient Indian scriptures known as the Upanishads. The Upanishads are a collection of philosophical and spiritual texts that form the core teachings of Hinduism. They are considered the culmination of Vedic thought and are revered as the highest authority in Hindu philosophy.

The Mahavakyas are specific statements that convey deep spiritual truths and profound insights into the nature of reality and the self. These statements serve as concise summaries of the Upanishadic teachings and encapsulate the ultimate truths that the scriptures aim to convey.

The four Mahavakyas, which are associated with different Upanishads, are as follows:

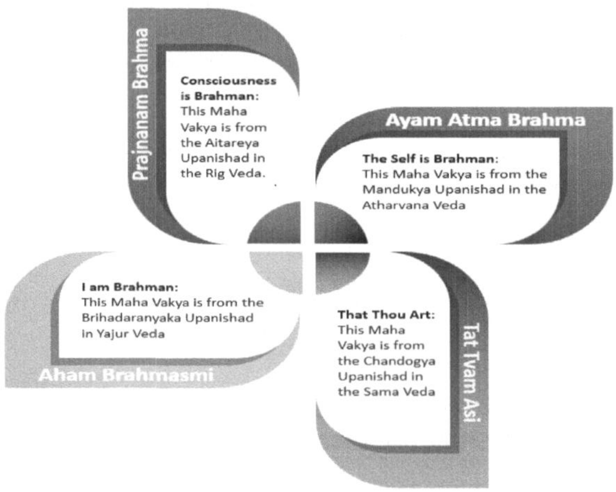

Figure 2.1: Mahavakyas, their meaning and source

- "Prajnanam Brahma" (Consciousness is Brahman): A profound statement from the Aitareya Upanishad in the Rig Veda that emphasizes the importance of consciousness or awareness.
- "Ayam Atma Brahma" (The Self is Brahman): A Mahavakya from the Mandukya Upanishad in the Atharvana Veda that highlights the interconnectedness and intrinsic value of everyone.
- "Tat Tvam Asi" (That Thou Art): This Mahavakya from the Chandogya Upanishad in the Sama Veda signifies the underlying unity between the individual and the universal consciousness.
- "Aham Brahmasmi" (I am Brahman): A Mahavakya from the Brihadaranyaka Upanishad in Yajur Veda that emphasizes the realization of one's own divinity or higher self.

These Mahavakyas have been studied and revered by philosophers, spiritual seekers, and scholars for centuries. They hold immense significance in Hindu philosophy, Advaita Vedanta (non-dualistic philosophy), and the quest for self-realization. The teachings of the Mahavakyas transcend religious boundaries and have influenced various spiritual traditions and philosophical systems beyond Hinduism.

The Mahavakyas offers profound insights into consciousness, self-realization, and the oneness of all existence. They are considered powerful tools for contemplation and meditation, guiding individuals towards the realization of their true nature and the ultimate reality.

Relevance of the Mahavakyas in the Corporate World

The profound teachings of the Mahavakyas hold great relevance and significance in today's corporate world. They offer valuable insights and guidance for leaders and organizations seeking to navigate the complexities of the modern business landscape. Here are a few reasons why the Mahavakyas are important in today's corporate world:

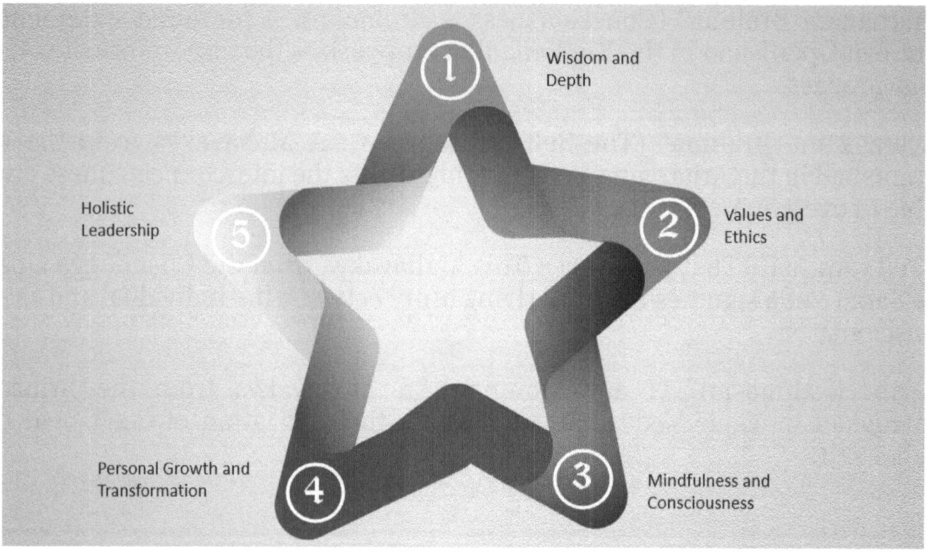

Figure 2.2: Application of Mahavakyas to corporate world

- **Wisdom and Depth**: The Mahavakyas encapsulate profound spiritual wisdom and deep philosophical insights. They address fundamental questions about consciousness, interconnectedness, and self-realization. In the corporate world, where leaders often face challenges and dilemmas, these ancient teachings can offer a broader perspective and a deeper understanding of human nature, purpose, and values. They provide a foundation for ethical decision-making and holistic leadership.
- **Values and Ethics**: The Mahavakyas promote values such as self-awareness, compassion, unity, and service. These values are essential in building a positive corporate culture and fostering trust, collaboration, and employee well-being. By incorporating the teachings of the Mahavakyas, leaders can create a values-driven organization that not only focuses on profitability but also considers the welfare of employees, customers, and society at large.
- **Mindfulness and Consciousness**: The Mahavakyas emphasize the importance of consciousness and mindfulness. In the corporate world, where stress, pressure, and distractions are prevalent, cultivating mindfulness can help leaders make better decisions, manage conflicts effectively, and foster a culture of innovation and creativity. By incorporating mindfulness practices inspired by the Mahavakyas, leaders can create an environment that encourages focus, clarity, and emotional intelligence.
- **Personal Growth and Transformation**: The Mahavakyas offer insights into self-realization and personal growth. In the corporate world, leaders are constantly striving for self-improvement and growth. By reflecting on the teachings of the Mahavakyas,

leaders can embark on a journey of self-discovery, gaining a deeper understanding of their own strengths, weaknesses, and purpose. This self-awareness can lead to personal transformation, enabling leaders to inspire and influence others positively.

- **Holistic Leadership**: The Mahavakyas advocate for a holistic approach to leadership. They emphasize the interconnectedness of all beings and the importance of considering the well-being of individuals, teams, and the larger ecosystem. In the corporate world, where the focus is often on short-term gains, the Mahavakyas remind leaders to take a long-term perspective, balancing the needs of stakeholders and creating sustainable and inclusive organizations.

By integrating the wisdom of the Mahavakyas into the corporate world, leaders can create a harmonious and purpose-driven environment that goes beyond profit-making and embraces values, ethics, mindfulness, and personal growth. These teachings have the potential to inspire leaders to create a positive impact on their organizations, employees, customers, and society.

Mahavakyas: Transforming Leadership in the Corporate World

By integrating the teachings of the Mahavakyas into the corporate world, leaders can create a harmonious and purpose-driven environment that goes beyond profit-making and embraces values, ethics, mindfulness, and personal growth. These teachings have the potential to inspire leaders to create a positive impact on their organizations, employees, customers, and society.

The Mahavakyas, which are profound statements found in Vedic scriptures, can indeed provide valuable insights and inspiration for leaders in Agile transformations.

Let's explore how each of the four Mahavakyas can be related to Agile leadership principles:

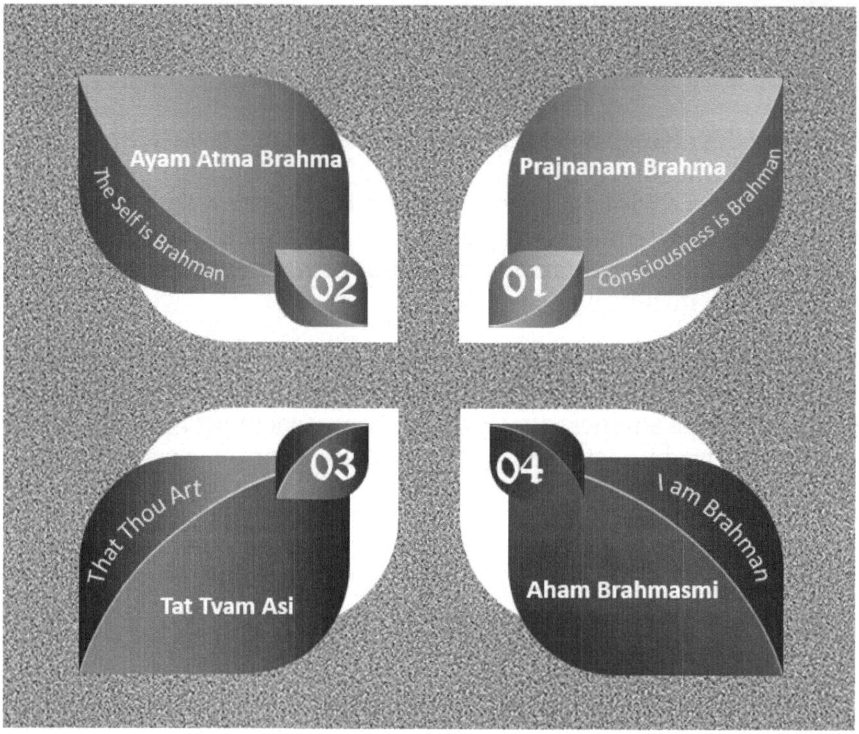

Figure 2.3: Mahavakyas and their meaning

- "**Prajnanam Brahma**" **(Consciousness is Brahman)**: This Mahavakya emphasizes the importance of consciousness or awareness. In the context of Agile transformations, leaders need to develop a deep awareness of the current state of the organization, its culture, and the challenges faced in adopting Agile practices. This awareness allows leaders to make conscious decisions, aligning the organization's values with Agile principles. By being conscious of the need for continuous improvement and fostering a learning mindset, leaders can inspire their teams to embrace Agile practices and adapt to change effectively.

- "**Ayam Atma Brahma**" **(The Self is Brahman)**: This Mahavakya highlights the interconnectedness and oneness of all beings. In an Agile transformation, leaders should encourage collaboration, self-organization, and empowerment within teams. By recognizing the intrinsic value and potential of each team member, leaders can create an environment where everyone feels motivated, engaged, and included. They should foster a sense of belonging and shared purpose, promoting a collective ownership mindset. This Mahavakya reminds leaders to treat individuals as valuable contributors to the overall success of the Agile transformation.

- **"Tat Tvam Asi" (That Thou Art):** This Mahavakya signifies the underlying unity between the individual and the universal consciousness. In the context of Agile transformations, leaders must understand that they are part of the Agile journey themselves. They should lead by example, embodying Agile principles and values. This involves actively participating in Agile practices, such as attending critical meetings, reviewing, and adapting processes, and promoting transparency and trust within the organization. By demonstrating their commitment and embracing an Agile mindset, leaders inspire others to follow suit and create a culture of agility.

- **"Aham Brahmasmi" (I am Brahman)**: This Mahavakya emphasizes the realization of one's own divinity or higher self. In Agile transformations, leaders need to cultivate self-awareness and reflection. They should continuously evaluate their leadership style, seek feedback, and be open to personal growth. This Mahavakya encourages leaders to adopt a servant leadership approach, where they prioritize the needs of the team and enable their success. By empowering others, leaders create an environment that fosters innovation, collaboration, and a sense of purpose.

In this section we have seen how the Mahavakyas relate to Agile leadership principles. In the next section we will see how embodying wisdom from these Mahavakyas can transform Agile leadership.

Wisdom of the Mahavakyas: Guiding Agile Leadership Towards Excellence

Incorporating the wisdom of the Mahavakyas into Agile leadership can provide a deep understanding of the underlying principles and values that drive successful Agile transformations. By embracing consciousness, interconnectedness, self-realization, and servant leadership, leaders can inspire and guide their teams towards Agile excellence.

"Prajnanam Brahma" (Consciousness is Brahman)

One of the prominent challenges in Agile transformations is resistance to change or a lack of awareness about the need for change. The Mahavakya "Prajnanam Brahma" (Consciousness is Brahman) can offer guidance to address this challenge.

In the context of Agile transformations, this Mahavakya reminds leaders that developing consciousness or awareness is crucial for individuals and organizations to embrace Agile principles and practices fully.

Here's how this Mahavakya can be linked to the challenge of resistance to change and provide guidance:

Challenge: Resistance to Change

Many organizations face resistance from employees when introducing Agile methodologies and practices. People may be comfortable with traditional ways of working and may not fully understand the benefits and need for Agile transformation. This resistance can hinder the successful adoption and implementation of Agile practices.

Guidance

Developing Consciousness and Awareness to address the challenge of resistance to change, leaders can draw guidance from "Prajnanam Brahma." They can focus on creating consciousness and awareness among individuals and teams about the reasons behind Agile transformation and its benefits.

Here's how they can approach this:

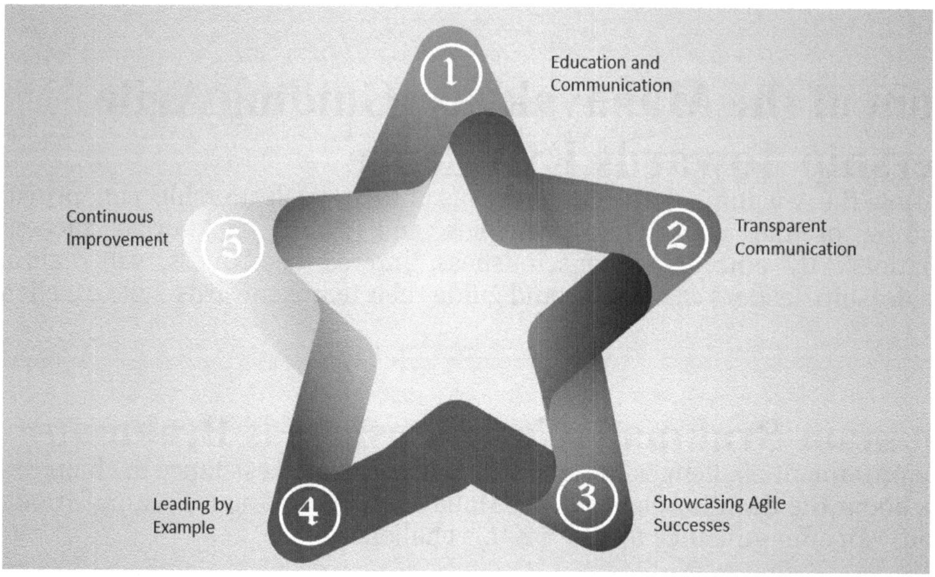

Figure 2.4: Guidance from First Mahavakya

- **Education and Communication**: Leaders can provide education and training sessions to help individuals understand the principles, values, and advantages of Agile methodologies. By explaining the rationale behind Agile and sharing success stories from other teams or organizations, leaders can create awareness and generate interest in Agile transformation.
- **Transparent Communication**: Open and transparent communication channels

should be established to address concerns, doubts, and questions related to Agile transformation. Leaders can foster an environment where individuals feel comfortable expressing their opinions and seeking clarifications. By actively listening and addressing concerns empathetically, leaders can alleviate fears and resistance.

- **Showcasing Agile Successes**: Leaders can highlight examples of successful Agile implementations within the organization or in similar industries. Sharing these success stories can inspire and create awareness about the positive impact Agile practices can have on productivity, collaboration, and customer satisfaction.
- **Leading by Example**: Leaders should embody Agile principles and practices themselves. By demonstrating the benefits of Agile in their own work, leaders can influence others and show how Agile methodologies improve efficiency, adaptability, and customer-centricity. This includes actively participating in Agile ceremonies, using Agile tools, and promoting Agile mindset and behaviours.
- **Continuous Improvement**: Agile is founded on the principle of continuous improvement. Leaders should encourage a culture of experimentation, learning, and adaptation. By promoting a growth mindset and celebrating small wins and improvements, leaders can create a positive environment that motivates individuals to embrace change and contribute to the Agile transformation.

By aligning the guidance of "Prajnanam Brahma" with the challenge of resistance to change, leaders can foster consciousness and awareness, enabling individuals and teams to overcome their resistance and actively participate in the Agile transformation journey.

"Ayam Atma Brahma" (The Self is Brahman)

The Mahavakya "Ayam Atma Brahma" (The Self is Brahman) can be linked to the challenge of fostering collaboration and self-organization in Agile transformations. This Mahavakya reminds leaders of the interconnectedness of individuals and the importance of recognizing the intrinsic value and potential of each team member.

Here's how it can provide guidance to address this challenge:

Challenge: Fostering Collaboration and Self-Organization

Agile transformations require a shift towards collaborative and self-organizing teams. However, individuals who are accustomed to traditional hierarchical structures may struggle to adapt to this new way of working. There might be a lack of trust, hesitancy to take ownership, or difficulty in embracing a collective mindset, leading to challenges in achieving true collaboration and self-organization.

Guidance

"Ayam Atma Brahma" - Recognizing the Intrinsic Value of Each Individual To address the challenge of fostering collaboration and self-organization, leaders can draw guidance from "Ayam Atma Brahma." This Mahavakya emphasizes the interconnectedness of individuals and the recognition that the self (individual) is inherently valuable and capable.

Here's how leaders can apply this guidance:

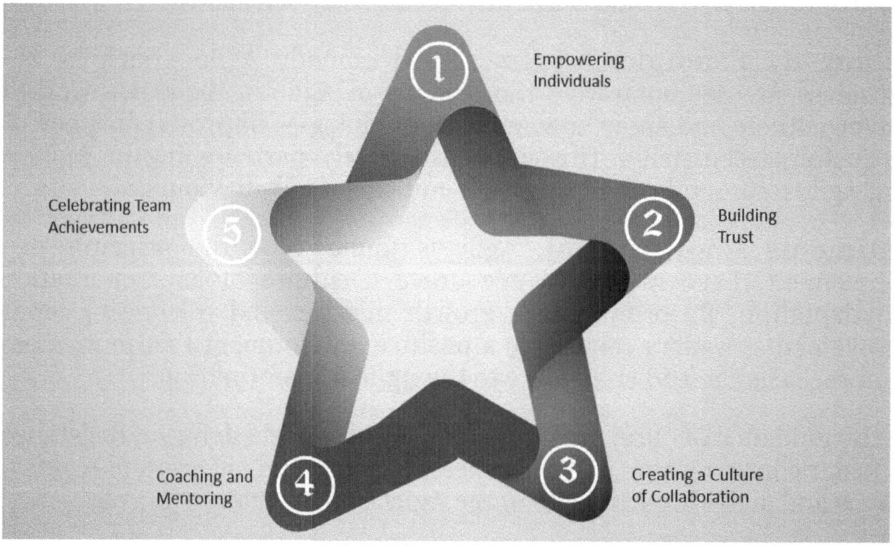

Figure 2.5: Guidance from Second Mahavakya

- **Empowering Individuals**: Leaders should create an environment where individuals feel empowered and valued. They should encourage team members to take ownership of their work, make decisions collectively, and contribute their unique skills and perspectives. By recognizing and appreciating the intrinsic value of each team member, leaders can inspire confidence and motivate individuals to actively participate in collaborative efforts.

- **Building Trust**: Trust is essential for collaboration and self-organization. Leaders should foster an atmosphere of trust by promoting open communication, transparency, and respect. They should encourage individuals to share their ideas, concerns, and feedback without fear of judgment or retribution. By actively listening, addressing conflicts constructively, and supporting the growth and well-being of team members, leaders can build trust and strengthen collaboration.

- **Creating a Culture of Collaboration**: Leaders should promote a culture that values and rewards collaboration. This can be achieved by encouraging cross-functional collaboration, promoting knowledge sharing and learning, and facilitating regular opportunities for teams to work together, such as pair programming, mob programming, or collaborative problem-solving sessions. By highlighting the benefits of collaboration and recognizing collaborative efforts, leaders reinforce the importance of working together towards shared goals.

- **Coaching and Mentoring**: Leaders should serve as coaches and mentors, guiding individuals and teams in developing collaboration and self-organizational skills. They can provide guidance on Agile practices, facilitate workshops on effective communication and teamwork, and encourage continuous learning and improvement. By nurturing the growth and development of individuals, leaders empower them to take ownership of their work and contribute to the success of the Agile transformation.
- **Celebrating Team Achievements**: Leaders should celebrate team achievements and create a culture of collective recognition. By acknowledging and appreciating the collective efforts and accomplishments of teams, leaders reinforce the importance of collaboration and encourage a sense of shared success. This helps in reinforcing the understanding that individual contributions are part of a larger whole.

By applying the guidance of "Ayam Atma Brahma" in the context of fostering collaboration and self-organization, leaders can nurture an environment where individuals recognize their intrinsic value, work together synergistically, and contribute to the success of Agile transformations.

"Tat Tvam Asi" (That Thou Art)

The Mahavakya "Tat Tvam Asi" (That Thou Art) can be linked to the challenge of creating a shared understanding of purpose and fostering a sense of belonging in Agile transformations. This Mahavakya emphasizes the underlying unity between individuals and the universal consciousness.

Here's how it can provide guidance to address this challenge:

Challenge: Creating a Shared Understanding of Purpose and Belonging

In Agile transformations, it is crucial to align teams around a common purpose and foster a sense of belonging. However, individuals coming from diverse backgrounds and with different perspectives may struggle to find a shared understanding of purpose or feel disconnected from the larger goals and objectives. This can hinder collaboration, engagement, and motivation within Agile teams.

Guidance

"Tat Tvam Asi" - Recognizing Unity and Shared Purpose To address the challenge of creating a shared understanding of purpose and fostering a sense of belonging, leaders can draw guidance from "Tat Tvam Asi." This Mahavakya signifies the underlying unity between the individual and the universal consciousness.

Here's how leaders can apply this guidance:

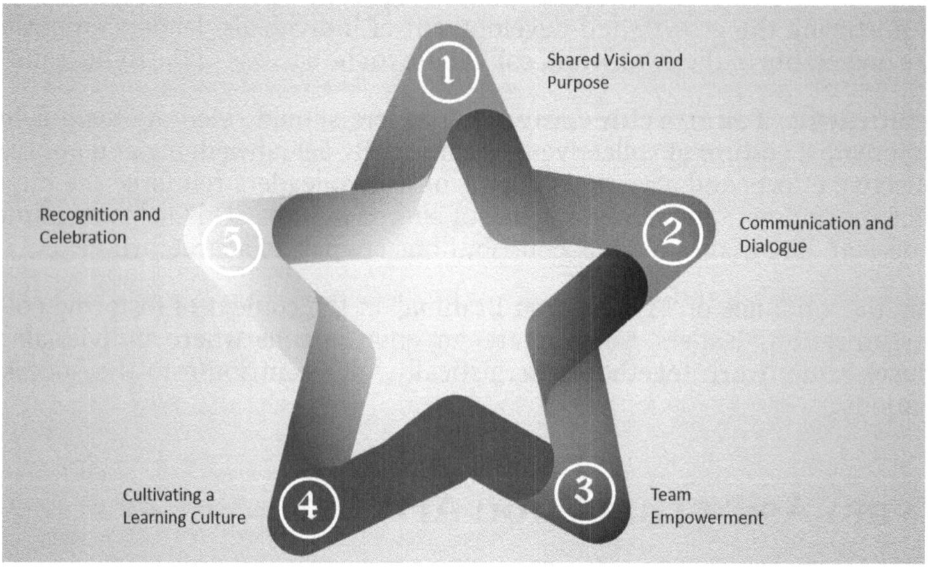

Figure 2.6: Guidance from Third Mahavakya

- **Shared Vision and Purpose**: Leaders should articulate a clear and compelling vision that reflects the organization's purpose and values. By sharing this vision and connecting it to the work of Agile teams, leaders help individuals see the bigger picture and understand how their efforts contribute to the overall goals. This fosters a sense of purpose and aligns everyone towards a common objective.

- **Communication and Dialogue**: Leaders should facilitate open and continuous communication to encourage dialogue and exchange of ideas. By providing opportunities for individuals to express their perspectives and contribute to decision-making, leaders foster a sense of ownership and belonging. This promotes a shared understanding of purpose and encourages collaboration based on mutual respect and trust.

- **Team Empowerment**: Leaders should empower teams to define their own purpose and goals within the broader organizational vision. By involving teams in the goal-setting process and giving them autonomy to make decisions, leaders create a sense of ownership and accountability. This empowers individuals to connect with their work on a deeper level and see themselves as active contributors to the shared purpose.

- **Cultivating a Learning Culture**: Agile transformations thrive on a culture of continuous learning and improvement. Leaders should encourage experimentation, knowledge sharing, and a growth mindset. By fostering a learning culture, leaders create an environment where individuals feel encouraged to explore new ideas, learn from failures, and collectively work towards enhancing their skills and achieving shared goals.

- **Recognition and Celebration**: Leaders should recognize and celebrate achievements and milestones collectively. By acknowledging individual and team contributions, leaders reinforce the shared purpose and foster a sense of belonging. This can be done through regular team retrospectives, public recognition, and rewards that highlight collaborative efforts and the positive impact of Agile practices.

By applying the guidance of "Tat Tvam Asi" in the context of creating a shared understanding of purpose and fostering a sense of belonging, leaders can help individuals connect with the larger purpose of Agile transformations. This promotes collaboration, engagement, and a shared commitment to achieving organizational goals.

"Aham Brahmasmi" (I am Brahman)

The Mahavakya "Aham Brahmasmi" (I am Brahman) can be linked to the challenge of individual empowerment and self-actualization in Agile transformations. This Mahavakya emphasizes the inherent divinity and limitless potential within everyone.

Here's how it can provide guidance to address this challenge:

Challenge: Individual Empowerment and Self-Actualization

Agile transformations require individuals to take ownership of their work, embrace autonomy, and tap into their full potential. However, individuals may face challenges in recognizing their own capabilities, stepping out of their comfort zones, or fully embracing the empowerment that Agile methodologies offer. This can hinder their ability to contribute effectively to the Agile transformation.

Guidance

"Aham Brahmasmi" - Recognizing Inherent Divinity and Potential To address the challenge of individual empowerment and self-actualization, leaders can draw guidance from "Aham Brahmasmi." This Mahavakya signifies the recognition of the divinity and limitless potential within everyone.

Here's how leaders can apply this guidance:

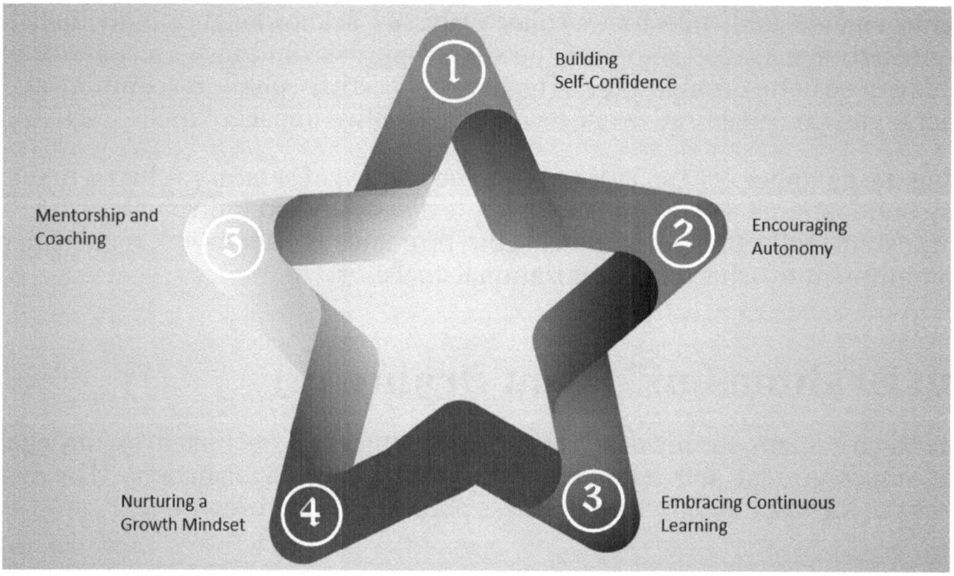

Figure 2.7: Guidance from Fourth Mahavakya

- **Building Self-Confidence**: Leaders should focus on building self-confidence among individuals by providing constructive feedback, acknowledging their strengths, and encouraging them to take on new challenges. By reminding individuals of their inherent potential, leaders help them recognize that they possess the capabilities to contribute meaningfully to the Agile transformation.
- **Encouraging Autonomy**: Agile methodologies emphasize self-organization and autonomy. Leaders should create an environment that encourages individuals to make decisions, take ownership of their work, and experiment with new ideas. By empowering individuals to have a voice and encouraging them to trust their own judgment, leaders enable them to realize their potential and contribute effectively.
- **Embracing Continuous Learning**: Agile transformations are learning journeys. Leaders should foster a culture of continuous learning, where individuals are encouraged

to develop new skills, expand their knowledge, and explore new opportunities. By providing resources, training, and support for personal and professional growth, leaders enable individuals to realize their potential and contribute at their best.

- **Nurturing a Growth Mindset**: Leaders should promote a growth mindset that embraces challenges, sees failures as opportunities for learning, and encourages continuous improvement. By celebrating efforts, providing constructive feedback, and promoting a culture of psychological safety, leaders create an environment where individuals feel empowered to experiment, learn, and grow.

- **Mentorship and Coaching**: Leaders should act as mentors and coaches, supporting individuals in their personal and professional development. By providing guidance, offering mentorship programs, and creating opportunities for skill-building and career advancement, leaders help individuals unlock their potential and contribute to the Agile transformation in meaningful ways.

By applying the guidance of "Aham Brahmasmi" in the context of individual empowerment and self-actualization, leaders can help individuals recognize their inherent divinity and tap into their limitless potential. This promotes a sense of ownership, confidence, and engagement, enabling individuals to contribute effectively to the Agile transformation.

By embracing the teachings of the four Mahavakyas, leaders and teams can realize the essence of agility - the ability to adapt, innovate, and thrive in an ever-changing landscape. These ancient principles guide us towards a holistic approach to leadership and teamwork, rooted in interconnectedness, self-realization, consciousness, and introspection.

Conclusion

The Mahavakyas, with their profound teachings, offer valuable insights and inspiration for leaders in Agile transformations. By integrating the principles of the Mahavakyas into Agile leadership, leaders can create purpose-driven organizations that embrace values, ethics, mindfulness, and personal growth. The teachings of the Mahavakyas remind leaders to cultivate awareness, foster collaboration, recognize the intrinsic value of individuals, and create a shared understanding of purpose. By aligning their leadership practices with the wisdom of the Mahavakyas, leaders can guide their teams towards Agile excellence and create a positive impact on their organizations and society.

In the next chapter we are going to look at various teachings of spiritual leaders.

Test your understanding

Test your knowledge from the chapter by answering the following questions:

Q.1. What are the four Mahavakyas?

Q.2. What is the source of the Mahavakyas?

Q.3. Is deepening awareness and holistic perspective a way to enhancing understanding of Agile practices and principles?

Q.4. Will the concept of oneness have emphasized and inspired towards collaboration and collective success?

Q.5. What guidance is provided by each of the Mahavakyas for solving industry challenges?

Chapter 3

Ancient Wisdom Unveiled: A Modern Twist for the Agile Era

Transmitting traditional knowledge in a contemporary context can effectively bridge the gap between conventional wisdom and our fast-paced society. By incorporating agile concepts and practices into the dissemination of this knowledge, we can continually enhance its accessibility, relevance, and practicality.

To truly grasp and embrace the agile transformation, leaders must develop a thorough comprehension of the Agile mindset. This understanding ultimately leads to recognizing the necessity for transformation. Let us take a moment to reflect on the Agile mindset and its presence throughout history, passed down through the teachings of great spiritual leaders over the centuries.

The intent of this chapter is:

- To understand the need for the development of agile mindset.
- To know the evolution of the agile mindset.
- To get a deep dive into the Agile Manifesto (Agile values & principles)
- To understand the concept of self-organizing team and its significance in transformation.
- To understand the meaning of the cross-functional team.
- To understand what empiricism is.

- To understand what is meant by doing agile and being agile.
- To understand the importance of inspect and adapt.
- To understand how the birth of the Agile wisdom and embracement of transformation is traced back to centuries ago in the teachings of the famous spiritual gurus.

In this chapter we will cover:

- Evolution of the Agile Mindset: Shaping Software Development
- Agile Manifesto (Values & Principles)
- Empowering Self-Organizing Teams: Unleashing Innovation and Collaboration
- Cross-Functional Teams: Collaborative Excellence for Innovative Results
- Embracing Agile Transformation - Empiricism - A Journey to Future from Past Within
- Exploring the Essence of Agile: Beyond Doing to Being Agile
- Inspect and Adapt – Awareness is Pivotal
- Wisdom Vintage

Evolution of the Agile Mindset: Shaping Software Development

Understanding the need for the rise of Agile mindset is essential before delving deeply into the specifics of such thought process. To effectively respond to the changing dynamics of the market and satisfy evolving client expectations, one must have and adhere to an agile mind frame.

Figure 3.1: Embracing Agile Mindset

Following the concepts of Agile, the organizations can improve their capability to offer value, maintain competitiveness, and respond quickly in the fast-paced business climate of today which triggered a formation of Agile mindset and prompted the enterprises in the transformation towards it.

Below are some of the specific reasons which prompted the necessity for the development of agile mindset in response to the changing market conditions and evolving customer needs.

- **Increasing Complexity:** Recent years have seen an increase in the complexity and volatility of market situations. Traditional methods of project management and product development frequently find it difficult to handle this degree of complexity. Agile approaches offer a framework that is more adaptable and flexible for coping with volatile and quickly changing market realities.

- **Accelerated Pace of Change:** Globalization and technological breakthroughs have accelerated the change in practically every sector of the economy. Customers today demand items and services to be delivered more quickly. Agile approaches allow businesses to release products in smaller batches, giving them a competitive advantage and the ability to respond to market demands more quickly.

- **Customer-Centric Approach:** In today's business environment, the move toward client centricity has become crucial. Agile development approaches place a strong emphasis on close customer collaboration. Businesses may make sure that their goods better match customer needs by including clients early on and getting their input repeatedly.

- **Continuous Improvement:** A culture of continuous improvement is embraced by the agile frameworks. Teams can learn from their experiences and make required improvements in subsequent iterations by breaking projects down into smaller iterations or sprints. Organizations can respond to shifting market conditions, streamline their operations, and produce superior products with the aid of this recurrent feedback loop.

- **Flexibility and Adaptability:** Agile approaches place a strong emphasis on adaptability and flexibility. They enable businesses to quickly adjust if market circumstances or client demands change. Businesses can more successfully grab new opportunities or manage arising obstacles owing to their capacity to respond quickly.
- **Collaboration and Empowerment:** Team empowerment and collaboration are encouraged by agile mindset. They place a strong emphasis on interdepartmental cooperation, self-organizing teams, and shared accountability for project success. Utilizing the varied knowledge of their teams in this collaborative manner enables firms to promote innovation and creativity.
- **Risk Mitigation:** Conventional methods may involve lengthy development cycles before obtaining client input. This raises the possibility of spending a lot of time and money on something that may not live up to expectations. Agile approaches assist to reduce this risk through their iterative and incremental approach by regularly verifying and modifying the product based on client feedback.

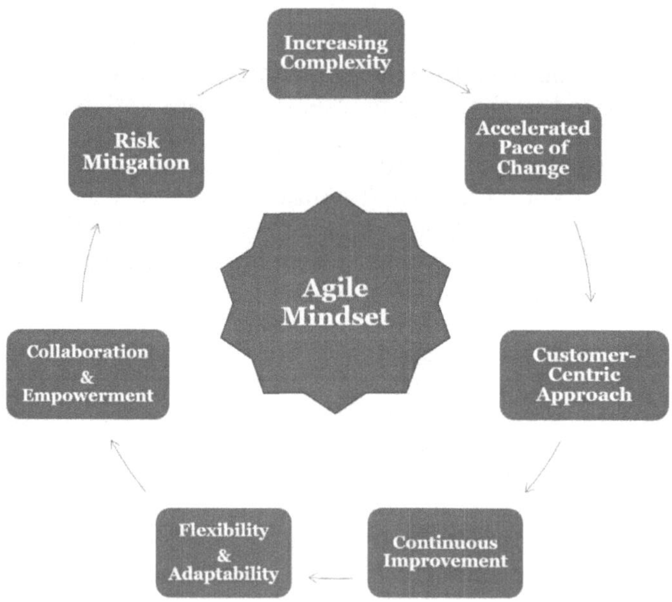

Figure 3.2: Agile Mindset

Although closely related to the Agile Manifesto, the Agile mindset evolved through time because of the collective experiences and views of software professionals. It came into being as a response to the challenges and limitations of conventional, plan-driven approaches to software development. Multiple factors and influences contribute for the development of the agile mindset.

Evolution of Agile Mindset

The dynamic process of the Agile mindset's evolution has changed how people and organizations approach their work and problem-solving. Agile began as a strategy for developing software but has since expanded into a philosophy that places a strong emphasis on teamwork, customer focus, and adaptability.

It promotes teams' use of brief iterative cycles, constant feedback gathering, and data-driven decision making.

- **Evolution of Software Practices:** Software developers have evolved their methods over time, realizing that strict, sequential procedures frequently resulted in delays, inefficiencies, and unsuccessful initiatives. They therefore began looking into different strategies that would enable greater flexibility and responsiveness to consumer needs.
- **Iterative and incremental methodologies:** Iterative and incremental methodologies have been exemplified by various approaches to software development such as Scrum, Extreme Programming (XP), and Lean Software Development. These early techniques emphasized the production of usable software through a series of iterations, with a strong emphasis on regular feedback and modifications. Scrum, Extreme Programming (XP), and Lean Software Development were pioneers in adopting iterative and incremental practices. Instead of attempting to deliver a fully completed product in a single effort, these methodologies advocated for breaking down the development process into smaller, manageable iterations. Each iteration aimed to deliver a working piece of software, allowing for early feedback from stakeholders and users. By embracing iteration and incremental development, these methodologies acknowledged the inherent complexity and uncertainties in software projects. They recognized that requirements and priorities can change over time, and that it is often difficult to fully understand all aspects of a project at the outset. Therefore, they encouraged a flexible and adaptable approach to development, where modifications and adjustments could be made based on ongoing feedback and evolving needs. These methodologies promoted regular communication and collaboration among team members, as well as with stakeholders. They fostered an environment where feedback was actively sought, enabling developers to refine and improve their software in response to user needs and changing requirements. This iterative and incremental approach allowed for continuous refinement and optimization, leading to the creation of higher-quality software. Overall, the early examples of iterative and incremental methodologies, such as Scrum, Extreme Programming (XP), and Lean Software Development, played a crucial role in shifting the software development paradigm. They emphasized the importance of frequent feedback, collaboration, and flexibility, setting the stage for the modern iterative and incremental development practices that are widely adopted today.

- **Collaboration and cross-functional teams:** As developers, testers, business analysts, and other stakeholders realized they had to work closely together to complete the project, the value of collaboration and cross-functional teams became clear. This mindset transformation promoted the importance of collaboration, clear communication, and shared accountability.

- **Lean and quality-focused methodologies:** The development of the Agile mindset is also benefited from the influence of lean manufacturing concepts and quality-focused methodologies like Total Quality Management (TQM). Agile thinking incorporated ideas like reducing waste, pursuing continuous improvement, and providing value to customers.

- **The Agile Manifesto's manifestation:** The Agile Manifesto served as a turning point in the evolution of the Agile mindset. It gathered a group of professionals with similar viewpoints who expressed dissatisfaction with conventional methods and created a set of values and guiding principles that reflected their combined knowledge and experiences. Noting that the Agile approach is not exclusive to software development is crucial. The domains of project management, product development, marketing, and others have accepted and applied its concepts and values. As practitioners modify and refine its ideas to fit the unique requirements and settings of many domains, the agile mindset continues to develop. Overall, the development of the agile mindset may be understood as a response to the shortcomings of conventional methodologies, an accumulation of real-world experiences, and a desire to establish a more collaborative, adaptable, and value-driven mode of operation.

The Agile mindset has expanded beyond its original uses and finds use across many industries, encouraging an environment of adaptability and resilience. It has come to be seen as a representation of innovation, encouraging a sharp awareness of the need to scrutinize and modify plans in the face of ongoing change, ultimately leading to improved results and client satisfaction.

Agile Manifesto (Values & Principles)

The essential values and guiding principles of agile software development are outlined in the Agile Manifesto which was created by a group of seventeen software professionals in February 2001 with the goal of advancing a more adaptable and flexible method of software development. The manifesto places a strong emphasis on people and relationships, functional software, client participation, and adapting to change.

This group collaborated to write the Agile Manifesto, rather than one person. At a meeting in February 2001, the group, which was made up of well-known professionals in the field, discussed their experiences, learnings, and disappointments with conventional approaches to software development.

The meeting was held in Snowbird, Utah, in the US. The participants gathered at a ski resort in Snowbird to reflect, talk about, and consider alternative solutions to the problems they were facing with software development. The event provided an atmosphere of support for participants to share thoughts, debate various points of view, and distill their collective wisdom into the Agile Manifesto.

Together with other participants, these individuals gathered in Snowbird to create the Agile Manifesto, which encapsulates the values and guiding principles of agile software development. Since then, countless software development teams and companies all around the world have adopted the Agile Manifesto as their guiding framework.

Manifesto for Agile Software Development

The Agile Manifesto consists of four key values and twelve principles that provide a foundation for agile software development.

For more information, refer to **https://agilemanifesto.org**

One very important point is that the agile mindset never says that whatever is mentioned as text in the right side of the agile values are not needed. It simply emphasizes more on whatever is mentioned in the left side. To simplify the agile manifestoes give higher importance to the values mentioned in the left compared to what is mentioned in the right.

As an example, while referring to the point 2 of the agile values i.e., "Working software over comprehensive documentation", it is never being said that the document is not needed. It is needed to the extent which is needed but more importance and significance is given to the working software which the customer can use and by means of which customer and the team can understand the progress.

Agile Values

The Agile value, which emphasizes a preference for people and relationships, practical solutions, customer collaboration, and adapting to change over rigid processes and documentation, is a fundamental tenet of the Agile methodology.

All the four agile values are summarized below.

1. **Individuals and interactions over processes and tools**

Figure 3.3: Individuals Over Processes

This value places an emphasis on the significance of people and successful communication within a team. It encourages teamwork, collaboration, and the understanding that software development is a human activity.

2. **Working software over comprehensive documentation**

Figure 3.4: Working Software Over Documentation

This principle emphasizes the necessity to concentrate on providing consumers with real value through working software. Although documentation might be needed, user-accessible functionality is the main indicator of development.

3. **Customer collaboration over contract negotiation**

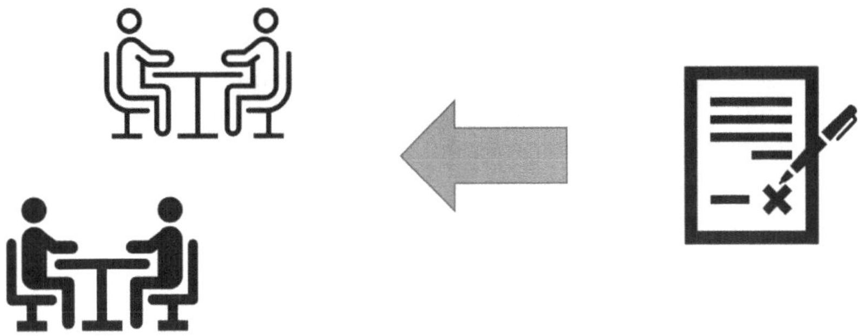

Figure 3.5: Customer Collaboration Over Contract

This concept highlights the benefit of involving customers and stakeholders in the development process over contract negotiations. Teams can produce greater results by working closely with clients to understand their needs and objectives.

4. **Responding to change over following a project plan**

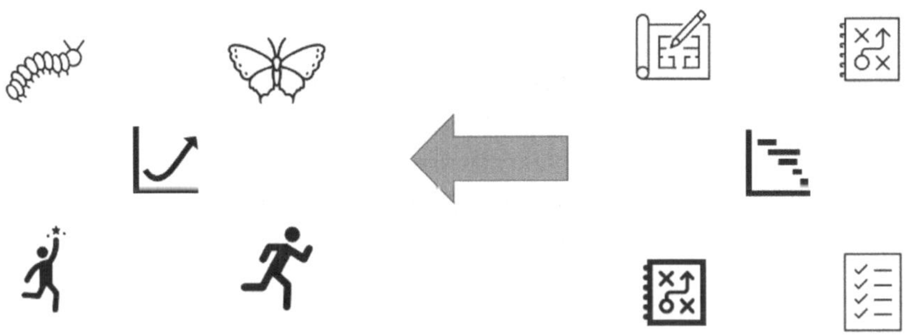

Figure 3.6: Responding To Change

This value acknowledges the fact that change is an inevitability, and that software development should be adaptable and flexible. Agile teams adapt to new circumstances, respond to requests, and embrace change. More detail discussion on agile values is present in chapter 6 section “Implementing Agile Values”.

Agile Principles

The Agile Manifesto's 12 guiding principles serve as an exhaustive guide for efficient software development. They encourage a departure from traditional, process-driven techniques by highlighting the importance of customer collaboration, adaptability, and incremental development.

They are as follows:

1. **"Our highest priority is to satisfy the customer through early and continuous delivery of valuable software.":** This guiding principle highlights the benefits of early and frequent delivery of usable software to customers, feedback gathering, and continual value creation throughout the development process.
2. **"Welcome changing requirements, even late in development. Agile processes harness change for the customer's competitive advantage.":** Agile teams welcome change and are aware that specifications vary over time. By encouraging flexibility and adaptability to shifting client needs, this principle enables teams to modify their plans and priorities as necessary.
3. **"Deliver working software frequently, from a couple of weeks to a couple of months, with a preference to the shorter timescale.":** This approach encourages frequent delivery of functional software with a preference for shorter timeframes to reduce the lag between development and user feedback. To ensure a quick and continual flow of value, it encourages iterative and incremental development.
4. **"Business-people and developers must work together daily throughout the project."**: It is essential that individuals who understand the business area and those who design and develop the software work together effectively. The importance of ongoing communication, common understanding, and close cooperation amongst all parties is emphasized by this principle.
5. **"Build projects around motivated individuals. Give them the environment and support they need and trust them to get the job done.":** This principle acknowledges the importance of motivated people and their innate desire to produce excellent results. Agile teams develop an atmosphere that encourages self-organization, autonomy, and empowerment, empowering people to perform at the top of their game at work.
6. **"The most efficient and effective method of conveying information to and within a development team is face-to-face conversation.":** This principle encourages direct, and in-person contact as the preferred method of distributing infor-

mation within the team because it is the most efficient and effective way to deliver information. Real-time cooperation, lesser misunderstandings, and quick decision-making are all benefits of face-to-face communication. Adapting to the current scenarios (post covid pandemic), face-to-face communication only includes the individuals to be present in the same location but also the communications through different online platforms of meetings which have both the audio and visual interaction mode. Any such mode of interaction needs to be accepted by your organization as means of formal communication like Webex, teams, zoom etc.

7. **"Working software is the primary measure of progress.":** This principle emphasizes the significance of tangible outputs rather than concentrating only on documentation or intermediate objects. The creation of functional software that satisfies user needs and adds value is the true test of advancement. This is not indicating that documentation is not needed. It is always necessary to the extent in which is needed. But to measure the progress of the work or the value delivered only the working software needs to be considered.

8. **"Agile processes promote sustainable development. The sponsors, developers, and users should be able to maintain a constant pace indefinitely.":** Agile methodologies support sustainable development by encouraging teams to work at a pace that prevents burnout and excessive stress. By establishing a steady rhythm of development that can be sustained over time, this notion acknowledges the need for balance.

9. **"Continuous attention to technical excellence and good design enhances agility.":** This principle emphasizes the need of giving technical excellence, quality, and good design practices a high priority. Continuous attention to technical excellence and excellent design practices increases agility. Teams are encouraged to embrace relevant technologies, maintain their technical proficiency, and make investments in strong foundations for future growth.

10. **"Simplicity—the art of maximizing the amount of work not done—is essential.":** The art of simplicity is to maximize the quantity of effort not done. Agile teams put an emphasis on simplicity and aim to get rid of extraneous complexity. The team is urged by this principle to concentrate on delivering the most beneficial features while avoiding over-engineering and pointless work.

11. **"The best architectures, requirements, and designs emerge from self-organizing teams.":** This principle acknowledges the importance of self-organizing teams and their capacity to decide on architecture, requirements, and design in an educated manner. Agile teams work together to develop original and practical solutions

using their combined knowledge and skills.

12. **"At regular intervals, the team reflects on how to become more effective, then tunes and adjusts its behavior accordingly.":** Reflect frequently on how to be more productive, then change your behavior as necessary. This notion is built on the idea of continuous improvement. Agile teams routinely evaluate their behaviors, interactions, and work in search of ways to improve their effectiveness. Based on feedback and lessons learnt, they modify their procedures and actions.

    The interrelated Agile values and principles help both organizations and people to successfully embrace an agile mindset, apply agile practices, and go through transformation. These relationships between the Agile values and principles form the foundation for adopting an Agile mindset and implementing Agile methodologies successfully. Organizations can enhance their capacity to deliver value, adapt to change, and meet customer needs more effectively by aligning their actions and practices with these values and principles. These also helps an individual in their personal life in context of personal growth, relationships, and mental stability. Consider how the agile principle of "Embrace and Adapt to Change" can have a significant effect on a person's daily life. The only thing that is constant in life is change, therefore we must embrace it and approach it with an open mind. We should make changes to our plans after setbacks and seize any new chances that fit with our goals and ideals.

These principles encourage a people-centered and customer-centric strategy by placing an emphasis on communication, motivated people, and offering practical solutions. The ability to embrace change, self-organizing teams, and regular reflection all contribute to better project outcomes and greater customer satisfaction. The Agile Manifesto's 12 guiding principles essentially serve as the basis for a flexible, adaptive, and value-driven methodology that has completely changed the landscape of software development.

One interesting fact about these statements are that they are written 22 years ago and has evolved continuously according to the everchanging landscapes. Like when we are saying that "Working software is the primary measure of progress.", focus is given on the working software rather than any other things. But today, focus is most on the values we are delivering. Remember that values cannot be measured unless we have a working software. Also, these statements frequently talk about outputs. Outputs, by definition, are something which is created at the end of a process. But it does not that add any value for whom we are building the software. So instead of such outputs, the agile team needs to focus on outcomes, the value which it needs to provide the customers by implementing agility in their workflow.

GEN AI – Impact and Augment

Gen AI, or the use of AI and advanced automation in general, can significantly impact and augment Agile principles in several ways:

1. Automation of Repetitive Tasks: AI can automate repetitive and mundane tasks, allowing Agile teams to focus more on valuable work. This aligns with the Agile principle of "Simplicity" (doing the simplest thing that could possibly work) and helps in reducing waste.
2. Faster Decision-Making: AI can provide data-driven insights and recommendations, enabling quicker and more informed decision-making. This supports the Agile principle of "Responding to Change" as teams can adapt to new information or requirements more rapidly.
3. Enhanced Collaboration: AI can facilitate better collaboration within Agile teams by providing tools for real-time communication, project tracking, and knowledge sharing. This complements the Agile principle of "Individuals and Interactions."
4. Predictive Analytics: AI can help forecast project timelines, identify potential bottlenecks, and estimate resource requirements more accurately. This aligns with the Agile principle of "Working at a Sustainable Pace" by reducing overloading and burnout risks.
5. Continuous Improvement: AI can analyze data from past sprints or iterations to suggest improvements in processes and practices. This supports the Agile principle of "Reflecting at Regular Intervals" and the focus on continuous improvement.
6. Enhanced Testing and Quality Assurance: AI can automate testing, identify defects early, and ensure a higher level of product quality. This aligns with the Agile principle of "Working Software" and the emphasis on delivering a potentially shippable product at the end of each iteration.
7. Customer-Centric Development: AI can help gather and analyze customer feedback, enabling more customer-centric product development. This aligns with the Agile principle of "Customer Collaboration" and the goal of delivering value to the customer.
8. Efficient Resource Allocation: AI can help allocate resources optimally, ensuring that the right skills are available when needed, which aligns with the Agile principle of "Self-Organizing Teams" and empowering teams to make decisions about how to accomplish their work.
9. Risk Management: AI can identify potential risks early in the project, allowing Agile teams to plan and mitigate them effectively. This is in line with the Agile principle of "Welcome Changing Requirements" by providing a proactive approach to managing changes.
10. Personalized Task Assignments: AI can help assign tasks to team members based on their skills and capacity, optimizing work distribution and team productivity. This complements the Agile principle of "Motivated Individuals" and ensuring that teams are

empowered and motivated.

While Gen AI can augment Agile principles in numerous ways, it's essential to use AI technologies thoughtfully and not let it replace critical human interactions and decision-making. Agile principles stress the importance of individuals and interactions, and these should always be at the forefront of Agile practices. AI should be used to support and enhance the Agile process, not to replace the core values and principles that underlie it.

Empowering Self-Organizing Teams: Unleashing Innovation and Collaboration

A self-organizing team refers to a group of individuals capable of independently managing and organizing their own work. Unlike traditional hierarchical structures, self-organizing teams operate cooperatively and autonomously, without direct supervision or control from a manager or external authority.

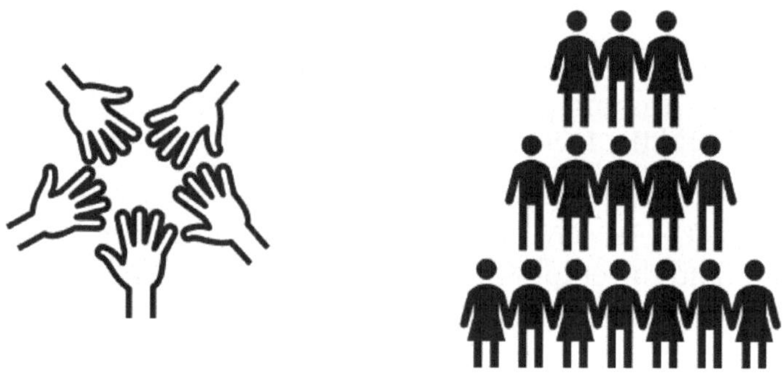

Figure 3.7: Self Organizing Teams

Key Traits of Self-Organizing Teams

The key traits of self-organizing teams are as follows:

1. **Autonomy:** Self-organizing teams possess an elevated level of autonomy in decision-making. They have the freedom to assign tasks, organize their workflow, and tackle problems in a manner that best aligns with their objectives.

2. **Shared Leadership:** Leadership responsibilities are distributed among team members within self-organizing teams. This decentralization of leadership encourages knowledge sharing and the utilization of individual strengths to propel the group forward.

3. **Collective Responsibility:** Each team member is accountable for the achievement of the group's objectives. They collaborate and support one another to accomplish common goals.

4. **Collaboration and Communication:** Effective collaboration and communication are crucial in self-organizing teams. Regular communication, sharing updates, and open discussions facilitate alignment and a shared understanding among team members.

5. **Adaptability and Flexibility:** Self-organizing teams exhibit adaptability and flexibility in responding to changing circumstances. They can modify plans, adjust priorities, and make decisions as a cohesive unit to meet evolving demands.

6. **Continuous Improvement:** Self-organizing teams foster an environment conducive to ongoing learning and progress. They reflect on their work, identify areas for growth, pinpoint improvements, and experiment with innovative ideas to enhance efficiency and output.

7. **Accountability and Commitment:** Each team member assumes personal responsibility for their commitments and the quality of their work. They hold themselves accountable to their group and stakeholders.

The Importance of Self-Organizing Teams in Agile Methodologies

Agile methodologies like Scrum and Kanban recognize the value of self-organizing teams. These approaches emphasize granting teams the freedom to manage themselves, make decisions, and take ownership of their work. By encouraging self-organization, teams are more likely to foster innovation, collaboration, and adaptability, which increases engagement and produce better results.

In conclusion, self-organizing teams empower individuals to take charge of their work, promoting autonomy, shared leadership, collaboration, adaptability, continuous improvement, and accountability. By embracing self-organization, organizations can unlock the full potential of their teams, fostering a culture of innovation and achieving superior outcomes.

Cross-Functional Teams: Collaborative Excellence for Innovative Results

A cross-functional team refers to a dynamic group of individuals with diverse responsibilities, experiences, and skill sets who collaborate to achieve a shared objective or deliver valuable outcomes.

Figure 3.8: Cross Functional Teams

Key Traits of Cross-Functional Teams

Unlike traditional teams organized within functional departments or specialized positions, cross-functional teams bring together professionals from various disciplines and areas of expertise. The key traits of the cross functional teams are as follows:

1. **Embracing Diverse Skill Sets:** Cross-functional teams thrive on the diversity of backgrounds, skill sets, and knowledge among their members. By incorporating multiple perspectives, team members approach tasks and challenges from various angles, enabling comprehensive problem-solving.

2. **Collaborative Decision-Making:** Collaborative decision-making techniques form the foundation of cross-functional teams. Instead of relying on a single authority figure, team members pool their knowledge, skills, and expertise to make well-informed decisions collectively.

3. **Shared Responsibility:** In a cross-functional team, every member shares responsibility for achieving the team's objectives. There is a collective commitment to the team's goals, fostering a sense of collaborative accountability for the outcomes.

4. **Holistic Problem Solving:** Cross-functional teams possess the capabilities to tackle complex problems by leveraging the diverse expertise within the team. They consider multiple aspects of a problem, addressing challenges from different angles, and developing comprehensive solutions.

5. **Breaking Silos and Bottlenecks:** Cross-functional teams play a crucial role in dismantling silos and bottlenecks that often emerge in organizations with rigid departmental hierarchies. By integrating members from divergent functions, these teams work more productively and efficiently, free from organizational constraints.

6. **Iterative and Incremental Progress:** Cross-functional teams embrace an iterative and incremental approach to their work. They prioritize delivering value in small increments, actively seeking feedback, and adapting their approach based on lessons learned. This iterative process enables faster learning and adaptation.

Agile methodologies such as Scrum and Kanban commonly employ cross-functional teams due to their emphasis on cooperation, adaptability, and customer-centricity. By harnessing the collective intellect of the group, cross-functional teams foster innovation, solve complex challenges, and deliver high-quality results, leveraging the integration of multiple talents and viewpoints.

Embracing Agile Transformation - Empiricism - A Journey to Future from Past Within

Empiricism is a method of learning and understanding things via personal experience and direct observation. It places a strong emphasis on the value of using data, statistics, and individual experiences as the foundation for views, choices, and world knowledge. Empiricism is crucial in the context of Agile frameworks like Scrum.

The three pillars of empirical process control—transparency, inspection, and adaptation—serve as the basis for the Agile principles.

- **Transparency:** All stakeholders have access to and should be made aware of information about the project, its status, and any upcoming impediments or difficulties. This openness encourages candid conversation and develops a common knowledge of the project's state.
- **Inspection:** The work, procedures, and results are routinely examined to gauge progress and spot potential improvement areas. In Agile methodologies, teams regularly assess the product increment and collect feedback through processes like Sprint Reviews in Scrum.
- **Adaptation:** Teams and stakeholders make the appropriate tweaks and adaptations based on the findings of the inspection to improve the final product, the procedures involved, or even the overall strategy. This cycle of continual development enables adaptability and reactivity to situations or requirements that change.

In conclusion, empiricism supports learning from first-hand experience, data-driven decision-making, and a focus on continuous improvement in the context of Agile techniques. It promotes teams and organizations to be more adaptable, agile, and responsive to the challenges of contemporary project management and product development.

Empiricism - Pathway to Transformation

Empiricism needs a methodical and conscientious approach to successfully navigate the intricacies of Agile transformation.

To effectively use empiricism during their Agile transformation, organizations can employ the following essential strategies:

- **Create a Sense of Purpose:** Create a compelling and well-defined vision for the Agile transformation. Make sure all stakeholders are aware of the transformation's objectives and purpose, and that they comprehend the advantages and justifications for the change.
- **Identify Pain Points and Goals:** Begin by figuring out the problems and difficulties with the existing procedures. For the Agile transformation, establish clear objectives to address these problems and produce noticeable gains.
- **Analyze Current Situation:** Perform a comprehensive analysis of the organization's present procedures, culture, and structure. This evaluation will function as a starting point for tracking development and pinpointing problem areas.
- **Educate and Train:** Give thorough instruction on Agile concepts, practices, and the empirical process to all team members, leaders, and stakeholders. Make sure everyone is aware of the mentality change necessary for a successful transformation. Promote a learning environment that values experimentation and taking lessons from mistakes. Celebrate accomplishments and disseminate lessons learned to encourage ongoing development.
- **Promote Transparency:** Create open and honest channels of communication to discuss transformational progress, obstacles, and results. Between team members, this transparency fosters collaboration and helps to create trust.
- **Emphasize Continuous Improvement:** Stress continuous improvement by monitoring and adjusting the Agile implementation on a regular basis. Regularly solicit input from the team's stakeholders and team members to make wise judgments for continuous improvements.
- **Leadership Support & Honor Achievements:** Effective leadership support is necessary for agile transitions. Leaders should show their dedication to the Agile values and take an active role in the transformation. Recognize and honor the accomplishments made during the Agile transformation. Encourage the positive effects of Agile techniques by praising the work of people and teams.
- Organizations can successfully negotiate the intricacies and position themselves for long-term success in their adoption and implementation of Agile by embracing empiricism and incorporating these strategies into the Agile transformation process.

In conclusion, empiricism is a foundational principle that emphasizes the importance of observation, experimentation, and tangible evidence in the quest for knowledge and understanding. It is the lynchpin of the scientific process and the engine of advancement in many disciplines. Empiricism encourages an evidence-based approach to decision-making and problem-solving by prioritizing real-world experiences and consequences. This ultimately results in more informed and successful decisions in both software development and daily life.

Exploring the Essence of Agile: Beyond Doing to Being Agile

When it comes to Agile, it's crucial to move beyond the surface-level implementation of practices and delve into the true essence of being Agile.

Let's take a closer look at the concepts of doing Agile and being Agile.

- **Doing Agile:** Superficial Application of Practices Doing Agile refers to the mere utilization of Agile practices and procedures without a comprehensive understanding of the underlying principles. It often involves implementing popular Agile frameworks like Scrum or Kanban and adhering to their prescribed rituals, roles, and artifacts. However, this approach can be superficial, lacking a genuine embrace of Agile's core values. For example, a team may adopt a Kanban board, participate in daily stand-up meetings, and maintain a product backlog. While these practices are indeed part of Agile, blindly following them won't guarantee project success. Without a deeper comprehension of Agile's guiding principles and ideals, teams may struggle to fully reap the benefits.

- **Being Agile:** Embracing Ideals and Mindset Being Agile goes beyond merely following Agile principles. It involves embracing Agile ideals and adopting an Agile mindset, as well as understanding the fundamental concepts that drive Agile approaches.

While Agile initially gained popularity in software development, its principles can be applied in various domains, such as project management, marketing, product development, and even personal life. In these contexts, being agile means adhering to the core Agile mindsets and customizing Agile practices and thought processes to meet the unique requirements of each situation.

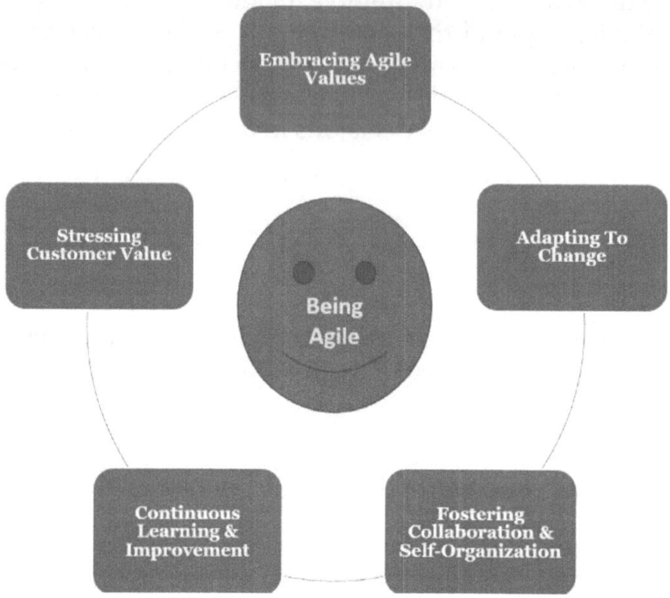

Figure 3.9: Being Agile

To be truly Agile means embracing a mindset and approach to work that goes beyond following specific methodologies. It's about fostering a culture of collaboration, adaptability, and continuous improvement. Being truly Agile involves valuing customer feedback, responding to change, and prioritizing working solutions over exhaustive documentation. It means empowering self-organizing teams and promoting open communication. Being Agile is not merely about adhering to a set of rules but rather about embodying a set of principles and values that guide individuals and organizations towards delivering greater value, enhancing customer satisfaction, and thriving in an ever-changing business environment. It's a commitment to embracing the spirit of Agile, promoting flexibility, and a relentless focus on delivering the highest quality products and services.

- **Embrace Agile Values:** Prioritize people over processes and tools, value working software over exhaustive documentation, emphasize customer collaboration over rigid contracts, and favor adaptability over rigid schedules. Being Agile involves integrating and embodying these ideals across all aspects of work, operations, thinking, and planning.

- **Adapt to Change:** Agility places a strong emphasis on the ability to quickly respond and adapt to change. Being Agile means embracing change as an opportunity and remaining open to continuous iteration and improvement based on feedback and new insights.

- **Foster Collaboration and Self-Organization:** Being Agile involves fostering a culture that values teamwork, trust, and self-organization, allowing teams to reach their full potential. Agile promotes cross-functional collaboration and empowers teams to make decisions and take ownership of their work.

- **Pursue Continuous Learning and Improvement:** Cultivating a culture of learning and improvement is a vital aspect of agility. Teams and individuals actively seek feedback, reflect on their practices, and experiment with latest ideas to continually enhance their processes and deliver greater value.

- **Stress Customer Value:** Agile emphasizes providing frequent and early value to the customer. Being Agile means understanding and prioritizing customer demands, incorporating their feedback into the development process, and delivering incremental value throughout the project's duration.

In conclusion, being Agile requires a profound understanding and adoption of Agile ideals, mindset, and principles. Merely doing Agile is about adhering to Agile practices, while being Agile encompasses embracing teamwork, adaptability, continuous improvement, and a customer-centric approach to achieve better results.

Inspect and Adapt – Awareness is Pivotal

"Inspect and adapt" is a phrase commonly used in agile methodologies, particularly in the context of software development and project management. It refers to the iterative process of evaluating progress, gathering feedback, and adjusting or improvements based on that feedback.

In an agile approach, such as Scrum, teams work in short iterations called sprints. At the end of each sprint, there is a sprint review where the team demonstrates the work completed and receives feedback from stakeholders. This feedback is crucial for inspecting the product and the development process.

The team also conducts a sprint retrospective, where they reflect on their work, discuss what went well, what didn't, and identify areas for improvement. This retrospective allows them to adapt their practices and processes, adjusting enhance productivity and quality in subsequent sprints.

The phrase "awareness is pivotal" suggests that being mindful and conscious of the current situation, both in terms of the product being developed and the team dynamics, is essential. By actively inspecting the work being done and adapting based on the feedback received, the team can continuously improve and deliver better outcomes.

In summary, "inspect and adapt" means regularly reviewing progress, seeking feedback, and making necessary adjustments or adaptations to improve the product and the development process. It emphasizes the importance of awareness, feedback, and continuous improvement in agile methodologies.

Wisdom Vintage

Although the Agile Manifesto, its values, and principles were formally documented in 2001, the core ideas they express have roots in the teachings of ancient spiritual gurus. These timeless teachings have emphasized the importance of agile sentiments, mindsets, and the embracing of transformation long before the structured Agile methodologies we know today even existed. The alignment between the principles and concepts of these teachings and Agile values and mindset is evident.

let's take a closer look at the wisdom imparted by few renowned spiritual leaders throughout history to gain a deeper understanding of the relationship between the teachings of spiritual gurus and the concept of Agile.

Sri Adi Shankaracharya - Unifying Non-Dualism and Spiritual Wisdom!

In the 8th century CE, a notable Indian philosopher and theologian named Sri Adi Shankaracharya emerged as a prominent figure. He is renowned for his profound contributions to Advaita Vedanta, a philosophy that emphasizes the unity between the individual self (Atman) and the ultimate reality (Brahman), highlighting the concept of non-dualism. Adi Shankaracharya's teachings encompassed a diverse array of subjects, encompassing philosophy, spirituality, and practical guidance for everyday life.

In Shankaracharya's philosophy of Advaita, the concept of non-duality emphasizes the fundamental oneness or unity of all existence. It posits that the ultimate reality is Brahman, an unchanging, indivisible, and eternal essence that permeates everything in the universe. From this perspective, all distinctions, and dualities, such as subject-object, self-other, or good-evil, are considered illusory and products of ignorance.

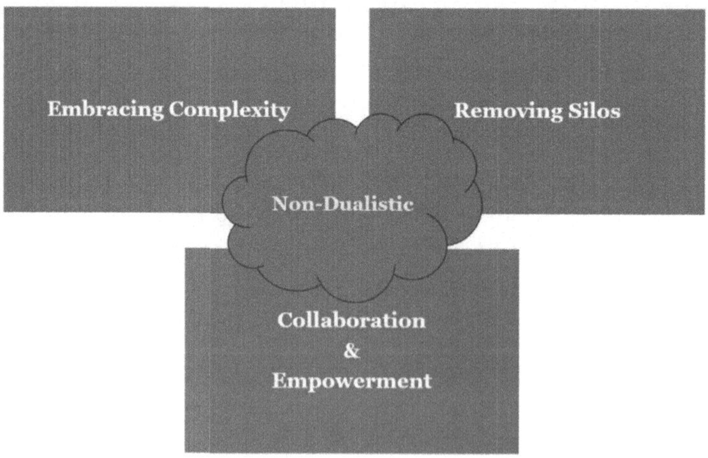

Figure 3.10: Non-Dualistic

When we relate this non-dualistic perspective with Agile ways of working, few interesting parallels can be drawn:

- **Embracing Complexity:** In Agile methodologies, there is a recognition that software development and problem-solving processes are complex and uncertain. Non-duality acknowledges the interconnectedness of all things, and in Agile, complexity is embraced rather than avoided. The focus is on adaptability, continuous learning, and responding to change rather than trying to control every aspect of a project.

- **Collaboration and Empowerment:** Non-duality blurs the lines between self and other, promoting the idea that we are all interconnected. In Agile, the emphasis on collaboration and self-organizing teams resonates with this notion. Agile teams work together as a single unit, leveraging collective intelligence and empowering each team member to contribute their unique skills and perspectives.

- **Removing Silos:** In a non-dualistic perspective, there are no inherent boundaries between entities. Similarly, Agile methodologies strive to break down traditional silos between different departments or roles within an organization. This promotes better communication, shared responsibility, and a more holistic approach to problem-solving.

Agile encourages a culture of continuous improvement, in which people and teams learn from their mistakes and modify their methods as necessary. According to Shankaracharya's teachings, the pursuit of knowledge (vidya) and self-inquiry ("Atma Vichara") are necessary steps on the way to freedom (Moksha). This demonstrates a similar focus on development of the self, introspection, and the search for wisdom. His interpretations of classical texts including the Upanishads, the Bhagavad Gita, and the Brahma sutras continue to be revered and studied by both academicians and spiritual seekers.

Sri Ramakrishna Paramhansa – Old Wisdom Embracing Agile Journey!

Sri Ramakrishna Paramhansa, an Indian saint and mystic of the 19th century, dedicated his life to the pursuit of spiritual enlightenment and the path to unity with the divine. Within his teachings lie profound insights that resonate with the guiding principles and ideals of an Agile mindset

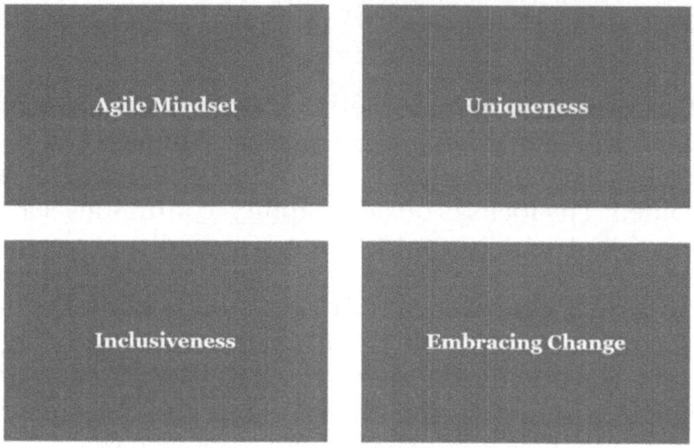

Figure 3.11: Old Wisdom

Though the contexts and terminology of Sri Ramakrishna's teachings are different from the specific practices and procedures connected with Agile frameworks. there are underlying ideas and values in Sri Ramakrishna's teachings that have strong resemblance with the Agile values and principles. Both place a strong emphasis on flexibility, teamwork, ongoing learning, and a comprehensive strategy for development. Some resemblances are summarized below.

- **Agile Mindset**: Emphasizing the significance of spiritual awakening, Sri Ramakrishna encouraged individuals to transcend the boundaries of the material world and connect with a higher reality. Similarly, an Agile mindset advocates for continuous improvement and self-reflection, encouraging teams and individuals to elevate their understanding and adapt their approaches to achieve greater effectiveness.

- **Uniqueness:** Sri Ramakrishna's belief in the universality of religious experiences echoes the core Agile value of "Individuals and interactions over processes and tools." Just as he recognized that various paths could lead to spiritual realization, Agile acknowledges the uniqueness of each team member, valuing their contributions and interactions to foster collaboration and productivity.

- **Inclusiveness:** The saint's teachings on open-mindedness and inclusivity align with the Agile principle of "Customer collaboration over contract negotiation." Sri Ramakrishna welcomed people from all walks of life to his spiritual abode, emphasizing the importance of embracing diversity and learning from different perspectives. In an Agile environment, teams prioritize customer feedback and collaboration, valuing the input of stakeholders to create better products and solutions.

- **Embracing Change:** Furthermore, Sri Ramakrishna's message of perseverance and dedication finds resonance with the Agile value of "Responding to change over following a plan." As he encouraged disciples to persist on their spiritual journey despite challenges, Agile teams are encouraged to become more adaptable, embracing change and learning from setbacks to achieve their objectives effectively.

The importance of being fully present and involved in the present moment was always stressed by Sri Ramakrishna. This is in accordance with the Agile philosophy of emphasizing the importance of mindfulness and being present completely in the present, which encourage teams to concentrate on the work at hand. This thought process probably gave the birth of the concept of "LIMIT WORK IN PROGRESS" in "KANBAN".

In conclusion, the teachings of Sri Ramakrishna Paramhansa, centered around spiritual enlightenment and unity with the divine, hold valuable parallels with the guiding principles of an Agile mindset. By recognizing the importance of continuous improvement, inclusivity, adaptability, and collaboration, individuals and teams can draw inspiration from these timeless teachings to flourish in their personal and professional growth.

Timeless Wisdom: Swami Vivekaṇanda's Teachings and the Agile Mindset

In the late 19th and early 20th centuries, Swami Vivekananda, a devoted follower of Sri Ramakrishna and a renowned spiritual figure, emphasized the practical application of spirituality for individual and societal development. While he didn't explicitly address the term "Agility," but the aspects of his teachings align with the principles of an agile mindset and transformation.

Let's briefly explore the life and teachings of this revered saint, philosopher, and teacher. Two defining characteristics were evident throughout his life: his deep compassion and his unwavering courage.

An interesting incident occurred in Varanasi, where Vivekananda encountered a group of aggressive monkeys outside a temple. Instead of running away, an elderly woman advised him to face the monkeys with courage. Following her advice, the monkeys disappeared as if by magic. Years later, Vivekananda shared the lesson he learned: "Always turn around and face whatever makes you fearful. Never consider running away. Have the courage to confront your challenges and stay focused on your goals."

He believed that youth is a critical period in life where the foundation is laid, and challenges are inevitable. According to Swami Ji, struggle is essential for growth, and stagnation leads to demise. He placed his trust and respect in the strength of ordinary people, considering them the true pillars of a nation, and envisioned a great India built on their capabilities.

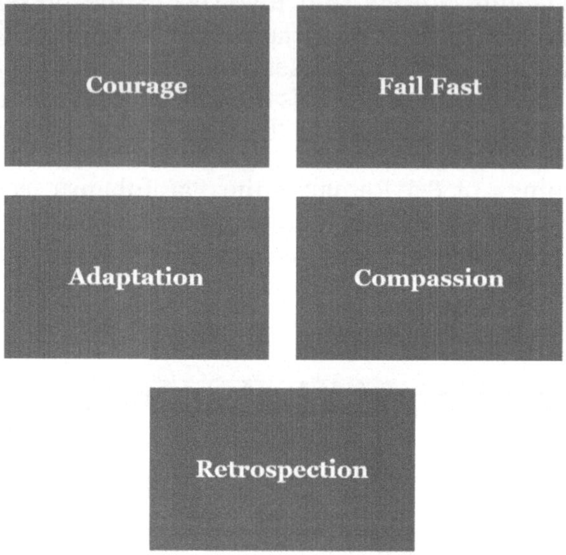

Figure 3.12: Timeless Wisdom

Don't these values resonate with the principles we follow in Scrum? Swami Ji's advice to focus on one task entirely, giving it your whole soul, aligns with the concept of "Limit Your Work in Progress" in Kanban, which emphasizes completing the existing tasks before starting new ones.

Swami Ji's insistence on taking risks and seeing both success and failure as opportunities to gain experience and grow reflects the agile notion of failing fast, adapting, and retrospectively improving. Just as we conduct regular retrospectives in Agile to learn from both successes and failures, Vivekananda's emphasis on introspection and talking to oneself mirrors the idea of self-retrospection and the importance of motivated individuals in Agile.

By connecting with our inner selves and seeking answers within, we can find the motivation to excel and continuously improve, which are vital aspects of Agile principles. Swami Vivekananda's teachings, though from a different time and context, hold a similar flavour to the concepts in Agile and serve as timeless wisdom for personal and collective growth.

Prophet Muhammad's Timeless Teachings: Embracing Agility and Transformation

One of the most renowned spiritual leaders in history is Prophet Muhammad, whose teachings encompassed a wide range of topics, including social justice, ethics, and matters of faith. His profound wisdom and guidance hold relevance even in contemporary times, as they resonate with values and principles of agility and transformation.

Prophet Muhammad's teachings emphasized the importance of social justice, promoting fairness and equality in society. He advocated for the rights of the marginalized, encouraged the support of the less fortunate, and urged the establishment of a just and compassionate community. These principles align with the modern concept of agility, which involves adaptability and responsiveness to changing circumstances while ensuring inclusivity and fairness for all.

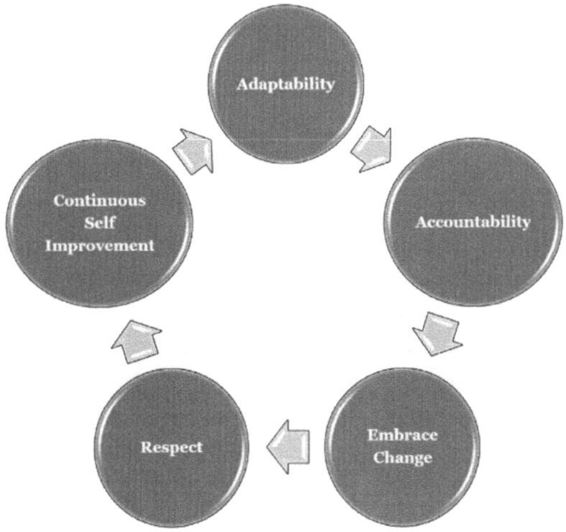

Figure 3.13: Embracing Agility

In matters of ethics, the Prophet's teachings emphasized honesty, integrity, and accountability. He encouraged his followers to uphold strong moral values, treating others with kindness and respect. These ethical guidelines are foundational to building trustworthy and effective relationships, essential aspects in any transformational process.

Furthermore, Prophet Muhammad's teachings on faith embraced the idea of continuous self-improvement and personal growth. He emphasized the importance of seeking knowledge and encouraged his followers to be open to change and growth. This resonates with the principles of transformation, where individuals and societies evolve positively and embrace change to progress.

It is important to note that while acknowledging the historical context in which these teachings were present, their universal and timeless messages continue to inspire and guide people from diverse backgrounds. As we interpret and apply these teachings in our contemporary world, we can find valuable connections to the principles of agility and transformation, fostering a more just, ethical, and dynamic society.

Eternal Wisdom: Embracing Agility and Transformation in the Teachings of Jesus Christ

The teachings of Jesus Christ, as recorded in the New Testament of the Bible, centres around matters of faith, spirituality, ethics, and the concept of the kingdom of God. His profound teachings are highly relevant even in contemporary times and is seen as embodying principles of agility and transformation.

In the New Testament, Jesus imparts invaluable wisdom and guidance on various aspects of life. His emphasis on faith encourages believers to trust in God's plan and divine providence, fostering a deeper connection with the spiritual realm. Moreover, Jesus' ethical teachings promote love, compassion, forgiveness, and empathy towards others, forming a solid foundation for harmonious and compassionate interactions among individuals and within communities.

The kingdom of God, as taught by Jesus, represents a higher realm of existence which is not confined to the afterlife but is accessible in the present through a spiritual transformation. This transformative aspect of his teachings is particularly relevant to the concept of agility, which emphasizes adaptability, responsiveness, and continuous improvement. In embracing Jesus' teachings, individuals are encouraged to be open to change, to grow spiritually, and to align their lives with the values of the kingdom of God.

Furthermore, Jesus' parables and lessons often emphasize the importance of personal transformation and renewal. The notion of being "born again" signifies a radical change in perspective and lifestyle, symbolizing a departure from old ways and embracing a new, more spiritually attuned path.

Figure 3.14: Eternal Wisdom

In contemporary contexts, the principles drawn from Jesus' teachings can inspire individuals and organizations to embrace agility and transformation in various aspects of life. Whether it be in personal growth, relationships, or decision-making, the teachings of Jesus Christ provide a timeless and profound framework for positive change and spiritual development.

In summary, the teachings of Jesus Christ, as recorded in the New Testament, encompass matters of faith, spirituality, ethics, and the kingdom of God. They carry enduring relevance and can be seen as embodying principles of agility and transformation, encouraging believers to be open to change, grow spiritually, and align their lives with the values of love, compassion, and divine guidance.

It is essential to note that while there are some interesting parallels, philosophy and Agile are distinct domains. Agile methodologies are practical frameworks designed for project management and software development, whereas non-dualistic philosophy is a broader and more metaphysical concept. However, exploring the connections between these perspectives can offer valuable insights into how we approach work, collaboration, and the ever-changing nature of reality.

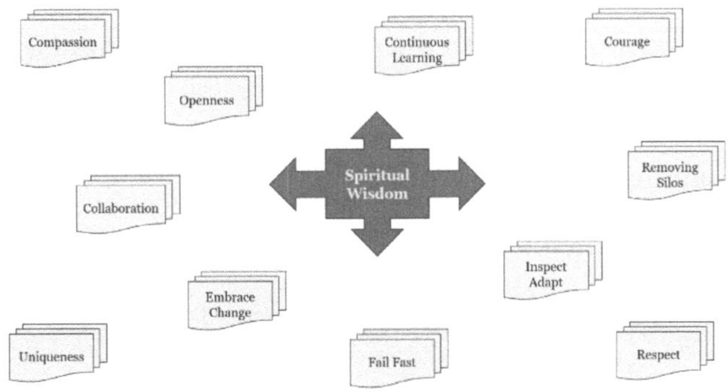

Figure 3.15: Spiritual Wisdom

Conclusion

In this chapter we have learnt about what is meant by agile mindset, what necessitated the evolution of the agile mindset, meanings of the values and principles of agile manifesto, significance of self-organizing and cross-functional team in essence of the agile implementation and transformation, the significance of going beyond doing-agile to being-agile, understanding and implementation of empirical process in transformation, importance of inspection and adaptation and finally the beauty of the fragrance of agility and transformation present within the vintage wisdom of the teachings of our great spiritual leaders from centuries ago.

Following are the key points to remember:

- Agile Mindset
- Conditions catalyzing the evolution of Agile mindset.
- Agile Manifesto
- Cross-Functional & Self-Organizing team
- Fragrance of Agility within teachings of spiritual leaders.

In the next chapter we are going to know how to understand how to know our strength and agility emphasizing on what is strength in Agile and what makes a leader truly agile.

Test your understanding

Test your knowledge from the chapter by answering the following questions:

Q.1. What is agile mindset?

Q.2. What are the factors contributing to the evolution of agile mindset?

Q.3. What is agile manifesto?

Q.4. When was agile manifesto formed?

Q.5. How many values and principles are present in agile manifesto?

Q.6. What do you mean by self-organizing team?

Q.7. What is doing agile and being agile?

Q.8. What relevance you can draw from the teachings of Swami Vivekananda with the agile mindset?

Chapter 4

Know your Strength & Agility

The cheetah is the unrivaled speedster in the vast Savannah grasslands, renowned for its exceptional velocity. Yet, intriguing studies reveal a peculiar finding - the cheetah seldom reaches its maximum speed while pursuing prey. Hunting for this majestic predator is far from a simple sprint; it encompasses a complex pursuit marked by continual shifts in direction and movement. Curiously, one cannot help but draw parallels between this fascinating challenge and the trials delivery teams face.

The cheetah possesses remarkable attributes, such as a powerful grip and a long tail, enabling it to swiftly change direction, even at 50 miles per hour, without compromising balance. Undoubtedly, this demonstrates agility. However, is agility alone sufficient?

To navigate its pursuit effectively, the cheetah relies on its strong bones, acting as shock absorbers during rapid deceleration and turns. Here lies an important lesson - strength and agility are not contradictory traits but complementary. A cheetah's robust skeletal structure is vital in absorbing the impact of sudden braking and rapid maneuvers.

In today's rapidly evolving world, where technology adaptation cycles shrink from year to month, organizations and delivery teams must be both strong and agile. Just as the cheetah swiftly adapts to changing circumstances, these teams must possess the fortitude to change direction promptly, guided by the shifting tides of the market.

We delve into the intriguing fusion of agility and strength, drawing inspiration from the cheetah's remarkable abilities and applying these insights to the realm of delivery teams. We will uncover the keys to navigating the dynamic landscape of modern project execution.

This chapter explores strength and agility concepts. How can we identify our strong and weak points? It shows leaders the advantages of being aware of one's strength in agile transformations. It gives insight into the characteristics of truly agile leadership.

In this chapter we will discuss:

- What is strength?
- Assessing strengths and its benefits in Agile transformations.
- What is Agility?
- What are the traits of a true agile leader?
- Agility in practice.

An Introduction to Strength

Being strong is important for animals, humans and organizations alike. Strength helps us to perform our daily tasks and to survive in challenging situations. Strength can be of two types for humans: physical or mental. We can improve our physical strength by doing exercises and eating healthy food. We can enhance our mental strength by cultivating good habits or practicing methods like meditation or mindfulness.

Organizations are subject to market forces and their ability to withstand these market forces shows their strength. Strength for organizations can mean strong brand loyalty, high efficiency/productivity, Quick time to market, high adaptability.

Strong leaders can change the destiny of the organizations. This is evident from many examples in the industry. Lee Iacocca of Chrysler, Louis Gerstner of IBM, Andy Groove of Intel showed tremendous strength when they not only turned around their companies from the brink of extinction but also made them thrive in the new marketplace. All these leaders share common strengths like Self-awareness, Situational awareness, Decision making, Effective communication skills.

Children are often told to work on their weaknesses and overcome them. But nobody in this world can be perfect at everything. Instead, it would be better to use our productive lifetime to leverage our strengths to be efficient at whatever we do. This doesn't mean we can completely ignore our weaknesses. We need to manage them so that they are not a hindrance to our progress. But we need to focus more on our strengths.

Find your strengths

You can observe yourself, your life patterns, key decisions taken, what do you enjoy doing most, which situations make you uncomfortable, in which situations you are comfortable, etc. You can also take feedback from others. Self-analysis or personal feedback is a great starting point. But in these methods, you may have distortions in analysis due to selective memory and biases. There are many online resources available to gauge your strengths. One such resource is Cliftons Strength Finder assessment by Gallup. Remember, strengths are not limited to specific skills or expertise. They can also encompass qualities like creativity, empathy, leadership, adaptability, or problem-solving.

Role of Strength assessments in Agile transformations

For any Agile transformation to succeed, the leaders should possess an agile mindset. High emotional intelligence (EI) will help leaders have an agile mindset. Self-awareness is the first step in improving your emotional intelligence.

Following are some of the benefits of strengths assessments for agile transformations.

- **Identifying Individual Strengths**: Strength assessment tools can help individuals understand their natural strengths and talents. When individuals are aware of their strengths, they can better align their work and roles within the Agile transformation. This self-awareness enables individuals to contribute their best and find ways to leverage their strengths in their Agile practices. These individuals will also have more fun in their work and will be more engaged in the work, leading to high quality output.

- **Building Complementary Teams**: Don Clifton author of StrengthsFinder 2.0 firmly believed it is better to have well rounded teams than well rounded individuals. A team is more likely to succeed if its team members' strengths complement each other. Agile transformations often require cross-functional teams that can collaborate effectively. Strength assessment can help identify the diverse strengths and talents of team members. By intentionally forming teams with complementary strengths, organizations can foster collaboration, enhance problem-solving capabilities, and encourage mutual support among team members.

- **Empowering Self-Organizing Teams**: Agile methodologies promote self-organizing teams that take ownership and make autonomous decisions. By understanding their strengths, team members can leverage their unique abilities to contribute meaningfully to the team's goals.

  Strengths-based self-organizing teams can foster a sense of ownership, empowerment, and accountability, leading to more effective Agile practices.

- **Encouraging Growth and Learning**: Strength assessment is not limited to identifying existing strengths but also provides a roadmap for growth and development. Individuals can focus on leveraging their strengths while also developing new skills and capabilities. This growth mindset is essential in Agile transformations, as it encourages individuals and teams to continuously learn, adapt, and improve.

- **Enhancing Team Collaboration and Communication**: Strength assessment can improve team dynamics by enhancing communication and understanding among team members. When individuals are aware of each other's strengths, they can appreciate and value the diverse perspectives and contributions of each team member.

This understanding facilitates effective communication, collaboration, and empathy, fostering a positive and productive team environment.

- **Supporting Agile Leadership Development**: Strength assessment can also benefit Agile leaders by providing insights into their own strengths and areas of development. Agile leaders can leverage their strengths to inspire and motivate their teams, delegate tasks effectively, and create an environment conducive to Agile practices. They can also identify areas where they may need support or seek team members with complementary strengths to fill gaps.

Overall, strengths assessment in Agile transformations helps individuals and teams unlock their full potential, foster collaboration, and drive innovation. By understanding and leveraging their strengths, organizations can create a culture of engagement, continuous improvement, and adaptability—key elements for successful Agile transformations.

An Introduction to Agility

Agility means being able to shift quickly and smoothly in a position or direction. It involves both the body and the mind. While physical agility is about moving effectively, mental agility is about adapting one's views based on new evidence.

Organizational agility means being able to respond quickly to changes in the environment. In the capitalist world, this is essential for survival and success. It is like a jungle where only the fittest can survive & thrive. Even large and established organizations can fail if they do not adapt to the shifting market conditions. A case in point is Kodak, which dominated the photography market in the 20th century. It opened the photography market to domestic customers by making the products portable and economical. However, it ignored the potential of digital photography, which was invented by one of its own engineers. This led to its bankruptcy in 2012.

The photography market underwent a transformation that Kodak's leaders failed to grasp. They depended on a strategy of selling cameras at a low price and making profits from consumables like film rolls and printing papers. This strategy was jeopardized by the rise of digital photography, which made film rolls obsolete and decreased the need for printing papers. The team at the ground level attempted to convince the management to change their strategy according to the new market conditions, but they were ignored. The management stubbornly believed that the old strategy would continue to work. By the time they changed their mind and began to produce digital cameras, it was too late. Other companies like Fujifilm had already established themselves in the market and Kodak could not compete with them.

The lesson to be learnt from the Kodak story is that there was no dearth of innovation or funding for Kodak. But the lack of agility in business strategy and mindset caused the downfall of Kodak.

In contrast, Intel's primary business was focused on DRAM manufacturing initially. New Japanese players started to bite into its market share and its profits started falling. But it shifted itself to a higher profit margin microprocessor business which saved it from doom. As the CEO mentioned in his book, the ground level staff have already adjusted the manufacturing outputs based on the feedback received from its distributors. So, it was easy to change the direction to focus on microprocessors when the strategic policy decision was taken at management level. This showcases how the agile principle of decentralization of ownership helped Intel.

The ability of Intel management to change the direction per market conditions and their empowered team members helped them come out on top of the DRAM crises.

These stories show us that agility is essential for leaders. But what does agility entail? Is it about using agile tools or following agile methods? Agility goes beyond a toolset. It requires leaders to adopt an agile mindset. Having an agile mindset matters more than doing agile with tools. The leaders should exhibit qualities that make them agile. These qualities can relate to how they adjust to rapidly changing market situations, and how they enable or leverage their teams for success.

From Market perspective some of the traits for the leaders are:

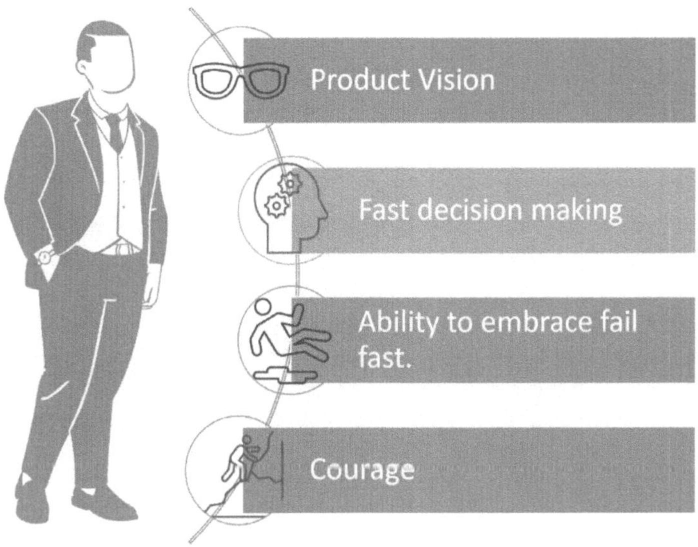

Figure 4.1: Traits of Agile Leader from Market Perspective

- **Product vision:** The leader should be aware of the market dynamics, changing trends in the market i.e., they should have the market pulse. This will help them set a clear vision for their product. It will help them to differentiate their product from the competition. They can prioritize the backlog items such that it delivers maximum value to the end customer.

- **Fast Decision making:** Just as doctors must act fast and save lives in critical situations, leaders must make swift decisions and save their businesses from collapse. Quick decision making can be the difference between thriving and extinction for a company as portrayed by the Kodak example earlier. The leader should not waste time in overthinking and analyzing, but rather act on their intuition and experience. This will allow them to test their ideas in the real world instead of just simulating them on paper or computer. They should have a clear vision and a holistic understanding of the situation.

- **Ability to embrace fail fast:** Leaders should not get stuck with any one strategy. But should be willing to try out multiple options to see if they work out. If the outcome isn't as promising as expected, then they should let go of the strategy and move on to another one.

- **Courage** is the main trait for any leader. They are responsible for an organization, however big or small. Their decisions have an impact on not just themselves, but many people associated with their organization. To let go of fear of failure needs a lot of courage i.e., it is essential for embracing fail-fast outlook. Quick decision making also needs courage.

From Team perspective some of the traits are:

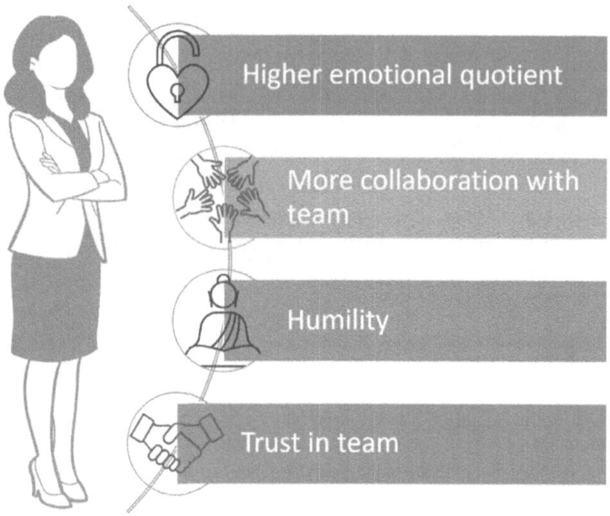

Figure 4.2: Traits of Leader for building high performing teams

- **Higher emotional quotient**
  A leader with higher EQ will be able to not only control their own emotions but also empathize with the team and influence their emotions and actions. This will lead to a more engaged team. More engaged team will be more productive.

- **More collaboration with team:** In today's fast-changing world it is essential that there is frequent productive communication between leaders and their teams. The communication must be bi-directional. This will enable leaders to get ground level feedback from the team and communicate changing priorities to the team. The feedback will help leaders to change strategy as per changing market conditions. The strategy directives can help align the teams quickly to adapt to the dynamic market conditions.

- **Humility:** Humility helps a leader have an open mind. This will make them more approachable. Team members are more likely to provide candid feedback to a humble leader than an egoistic leader.

- **Trust in the team:** Trust in the team demonstrated by a leader goes a long way in increasing the engagement of the team.

We will discuss these topics in **Chapter 5 Unlocking Agile Success: The Crucial Role of Leader's EI.**

> ***Info***: *A value stream consists of things done to add value to the customer.*

Agility in Practice

Currently there is lot of buzz around generative AI. Who will be the market leader in this space will be determined by how quickly the organization can learn this new technology, adapt to this new technology, and leverage it to increase its own efficiency or better serve its clients.

A leader with agile mindset can use following roadmap.

1. **Generate**: One person's ideas are less valuable than those from a diverse group of people. So leaders should leverage their engaged teams to crowd source ideas for generative AI use cases.
2. **Organize**: Next, the ideas should be grouped into value streams that deliver the most value to the customer. This way, each value stream contains related ideas and different teams can focus on different value streams.
3. **Team-Building**: Each team working on a value stream will be self-organizing team with strengths like quick learners, ready to embrace challenge.

4. **Design Thinking**: Each team will do a design thinking session to refine the ideas, find solutions and prioritize them. The team will use design thinking to understand the problem from user's perspective by using tools like Personas, Empathy Maps. They will then use tools like Prototypes, To-Be Scenario mapping to zero in on the appropriate solution.

Designers don't try to search for a solution until they have determined the real problem, and even then, instead of solving that problem, they stop to consider a wide range of potential solutions. Only then will they finally converge upon their proposal.

This process is called Design Thinking.

—Don Norman, author, The Design of Everyday Things

5. **Implement**: The teams will then implement the ideas as per priority to deliver maximum value to the customer.

***Info**: The goal of Design Thinking is to uncover the real business problem, explore wide range of technical or non-technical solutions and then recommend the most optimal solution.*

This section provides a real-life example of agility in practice. It presents a sample roadmap of how a leader can use agile tools and techniques to solve a business problem quickly and efficiently. They can utilize their team to quickly adopt new technology in the market and stay ahead of their competitors.

Conclusion

In this chapter we have discussed about Agility and Strength. Strength and Agility are complimentary and both are needed for successful organizations. A Leader can know about their strengths using various strength assessments available. Knowing one's strength can help build complimentary teams with higher probability of success. We also discussed about the traits required by a leader from market perspective and from building high performing teams' perspective. These concepts of strength and agility are essential for comprehending the tools that enable successful Agile transformations.

In the next chapter, we are going to learn about Emotional Intelligence. The following are key topics to be discussed in the next chapter.

- Difference between emotional intelligence (EI) and emotional quotient (EQ)
- Significance of Agile EI Leadership in agile transformations
- Explore key Emotional Intelligence competencies that contribute to effective Agile transformations.
- Role of EI in each phase of team development and in team dysfunction resolution.
- The significance of people skills in driving Agile success.
- Explore the concept of embodying emotional wisdom and its impact on Agile environments.
- Terminology related to EI
- Tips for improving EI

Test your understanding

Test your knowledge from the chapter by answering the following questions:

Q.1. What is Strength?

Q.2. How can one know about their strengths?

Q.3. What is the importance of strength assessment in agile transformation?

Q.4. What is Agility?

Q.5. What are the qualities of an agile leader from market perspective?

Q.6. What qualities should a leader possess so that they can build high performing teams?

Chapter 5

Unlocking Agile Success: The Crucial Role of Leader's EI

In this chapter we delve into the significance of Emotional Intelligence (EI) in the context of Agile transformations. It explores the concept of Emotional Intelligence, its relevance, and the reasons why it holds a vital role in Agile environments. The chapter also highlights the need for Agile EQ leadership and emphasizes the importance of people skills in facilitating successful Agile transformations. Furthermore, it discusses the impact of Emotional Intelligence on various aspects, such as team development and addressing team dysfunctions.

The process of transformation is intricately tied to the clarity of thought it fosters. Emotions, while a valuable aspect of our being, must be kept in check by the intellect. It is essential to assume mastery over our emotions rather than becoming enslaved by them. By cultivating self-sufficiency, we embark on a journey of self-mastery and personal growth.

This chapter aims to

- To provide an overview of Emotional Intelligence or Emotional Quotient and its underlying facts.
- To explain why Emotional Intelligence matters in the context of Agile transformations.
- To emphasize the importance of Agile EQ leadership in fostering successful Agile implementations.
- To identify key Emotional Intelligence competencies that contribute to effective Agile transformations.
- To highlight the significance of people skills in driving Agile success.
- To explore the concept of embodying emotional wisdom and its impact on Agile environments.
- To analyse how Emotional Intelligence influences different phases of team development.
- To discuss how Emotional Intelligence can address the five dysfunctions commonly observed in teams.

In this chapter we will discuss:

- Emotions and Emotional Intelligence in Agile Transformations
- Key Facts about Emotional Intelligence (EI)
- Emotional Intelligence (EI) – It does matter
- EI importance in Agile Transformations
- Agile EQ Leadership: The Need of the Hour
- Key Emotional Intelligence (EI) Competencies for Successful Agile Transformations
- Agile EQ Leaders
- Know your EQ and Evolve
- Nurturing People Skills and Harnessing the Power of Emotional Wisdom
- Embodying Emotional Wisdom
- Emotional Intelligence (EI) and its Influence on Phases of Team Development
- Emotional Intelligence (EI) and Addressing the Five Dysfunctions of a Team

Emotions and Emotional Intelligence in Agile Transformations

Emotional Intelligence (EI) plays a crucial role in Agile transformations, and to understand its significance, let's first clarify the concept of emotion. Emotion refers to the complex psychological state that arises from various stimuli, impacting our thoughts, behaviours, and physiological responses. It encompasses subjective experiences and is often accompanied by physiological changes.

Figure 5.1: Emotion – Psychological States

Emotional Intelligence, commonly known as EI or EQ (Emotional Quotient), is a term used to describe the ability to understand and manage emotions effectively. While the terms EI and EQ are used interchangeably, they both focus on emotional and social intelligence. EQ serves as a measure of one's EI, like how IQ measures intelligence.

Emotional Intelligence was coined by John Mayer and Peter Salovey in the 1990s. The term has been around for almost three decades.

In the context of Agile transformations, several emotions play a vital role in shaping individuals' experiences and their impact on the Agile process.

Here are some key emotions relevant to Agile transformations:

- **Excitement**: The enthusiasm and positive anticipation that arise when embracing Agile principles and practices, fostering collaborative and innovative work.
- **Frustration**: The feeling of being hindered or blocked by obstacles or challenges in implementing Agile methodologies, processes, or cultural changes.
- **Trust**: The belief in the capabilities and reliability of team members, leaders, and stakeholders, essential for effective collaboration and self-organizing Agile teams.
- **Fear**: The apprehension or concern about the unknown, failure, or potential consequences of Agile transformations, such as resistance to change or uncertainty about new roles and responsibilities.
- **Empowerment**: The sense of autonomy, ownership, and empowerment experienced by team members when given the freedom to make decisions and contribute to the

Agile process.

- **Collaboration**: The feeling of camaraderie and teamwork that arises when individuals work together in Agile teams, fostering cooperation, shared goals, and mutual support.
- **Satisfaction**: The sense of fulfilment and accomplishment when Agile practices lead to successful project outcomes, delivering value to stakeholders and achieving project goals.
- **Stress**: The pressure or strain experienced by individuals in Agile transformations, particularly when dealing with tight deadlines, high expectations, or complex project requirements.
- **Curiosity**: The eagerness to learn, explore, and experiment with new Agile methodologies, tools, or practices, promoting continuous improvement and adaptation.
- **Resilience**: The ability to bounce back from setbacks, embrace change, and maintain a positive attitude amidst challenges and uncertainty in Agile transformations.

These emotions, among others, significantly influence the attitudes, behaviours, and overall dynamics of individuals and teams in Agile transformations. Recognizing the importance of emotional intelligence becomes paramount in effectively navigating and leveraging these emotional experiences for the success of Agile projects.

Key Facts about Emotional Intelligence (EI)

Emotional intelligence is a vital skill for personal and professional success, encompassing self-awareness, self-regulation, empathy, and social skills. Some of the important and key facts about emotional intelligence are as follows:

- High EI is more prevalent among highly productive and successful individuals compared to high IQ alone.
- Emotional intelligence (EQ) is not fixed and can be developed and enhanced through learning and personal growth.
- Developing EI not only improves our own productivity and success but also enables us to support and uplift others in their endeavours.
- EI is a skill that can be taught and cultivated, allowing individuals to strengthen their emotional intelligence over time.
- The development of EI contributes to reduced stress levels for both individuals and organizations by diminishing conflicts, enhancing relationships, and fostering better understanding among team members.

It is crucial for effective leadership, conflict resolution, and communication. Relationships can be strengthened, work performance can increase, and general wellbeing can result from cultivating emotional intelligence.

Emotional Intelligence (EI) – It does matter.

Emotional Intelligence provides a scientifically supported structure that empowers you to present yourself as the optimal rendition of who you are. It encompasses the capacity to: observe and understand both your own and others' emotions, distinguish between various emotions and assign them suitable labels, and utilize emotional insights to influence your thoughts and actions.

In simpler terms, Emotional Intelligence entails employing cognitive abilities to perceive, comprehend, and regulate emotions, thereby guiding our behaviour. This leads to improved self-management and enhanced relationships with others.

EI importance in Agile Transformations

Emotional Intelligence (EI) plays a crucial role in Agile Transformations for several reasons. In the Agile Way of Working (WoW), emphasizing team empowerment and self-organization takes precedence over conventional top-down approaches. In this new paradigm, the success of project delivery relies on the collective efforts and decision-making capabilities of the team itself.

To effectively support Agile teams, it is essential to foster an environment of empowerment and self-organization. This means enabling teams to make autonomous decisions and take ownership of their work. Collaboration is also a key aspect of Agile, both within the team and with the Scrum Master/Servant Leader. These leaders have a vital role in facilitating, mentoring, and coaching the team, and developing a high level of emotional intelligence (EI) is crucial for them. Leaders need to be aware of their own EQ/EI level and be willing to transform themselves to effectively transform the teams. It's important to note that the transformation of leaders and teams can happen simultaneously rather than sequentially, as the awareness of the need for change is pivotal in today's challenging and ever-changing world.

A real-time example of leaders needing to be aware of their own emotional intelligence (EQ/EI) and being willing to transform themselves to effectively transform their teams could be found in a rapidly growing tech startup.

Imagine a tech startup that has experienced tremendous growth over a short period of time. The company's leadership, particularly the CEO, has played a crucial role in this growth. However, as the company expands, the CEO begins to notice increasing tension and conflicts within the teams, decreased employee engagement, and a high turnover rate. This situation prompts the CEO to recognize the importance of emotional intelligence.

1. **Awareness of the Need for Change**: The CEO becomes aware that the company's fast-paced growth has resulted in a stressed and emotionally charged work environment. This awareness is the first step in recognizing the need for change.

2. **Personal Transformation**: The CEO realizes that their leadership style, which was effective in the early stages of the company, is no longer suitable for the current work environment. They understand that they need to develop their own emotional intelligence and leadership skills to effectively lead in this new scenario.

3. **Simultaneous Transformation**: The CEO initiates a process of personal transformation by seeking coaching and training in emotional intelligence. They actively practice self-awareness, self-regulation, and empathy, and they encourage other members of the leadership team to do the same. Simultaneously, they also implement changes at the team level, such as promoting open communication, conflict resolution training, and fostering a more inclusive and supportive work culture.

4. **Positive Impact on Teams**: As the CEO's emotional intelligence grows, they are better equipped to manage conflicts, inspire and motivate their teams, and create a healthier work environment. This has a positive impact on the teams, leading to improved morale, reduced turnover, and enhanced productivity.

5. **Overall Transformation**: Over time, the combination of the CEO's personal transformation and the changes at the team level lead to an overall transformation of the organization. The company becomes better equipped to adapt to the ever-changing tech industry and meet the challenges of a dynamic market.

This example illustrates how the awareness of the need for change in a leader's emotional intelligence can lead to simultaneous transformation at both the individual and team levels, ultimately benefiting the entire organization in a challenging and ever-changing business landscape.

The Agile Manifesto, which outlines the core values of Agile software development, places significant importance on individual interactions and collaboration. These values highlight the significance of strong emotional intelligence skills among Agile leaders and teams. By cultivating emotional intelligence, Agile teams and leaders can navigate individual interactions effectively, communicate with clarity, and foster a collaborative environment.

Emotional intelligence encompasses qualities such as empathy, self-awareness, social awareness, and relationship management. These skills enable individuals to understand and manage their own emotions, recognize, and respond to the emotions of others, and create a positive and productive team environment.

Agile Values: By emphasizing the values of individuals and interactions, working software, customer collaboration, and responding to change, the Agile Manifesto reinforces the need for strong emotional intelligence skills among Agile leaders and teams. Developing and applying these skills is essential for Agile transformations to thrive and deliver successful outcomes.

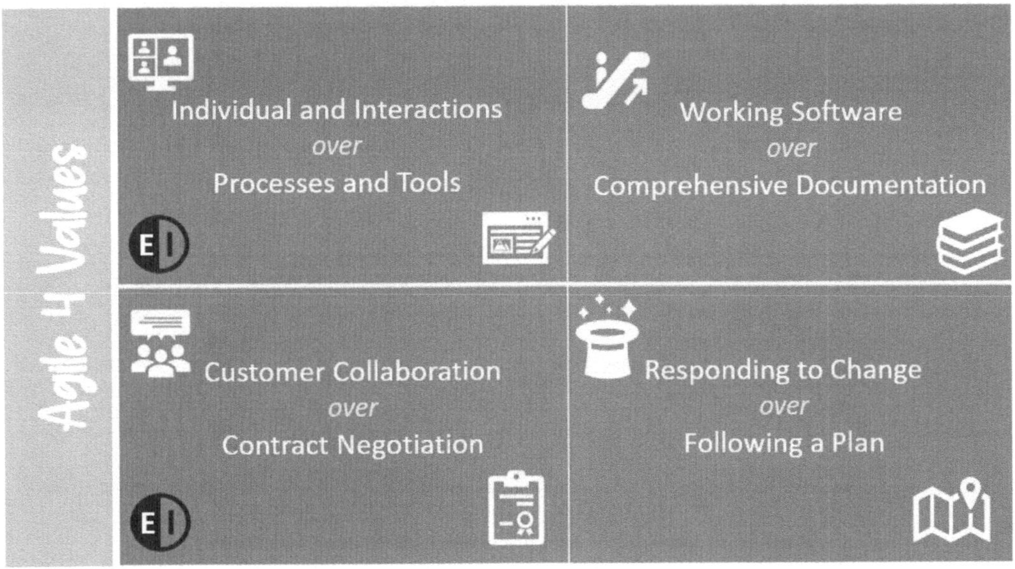

Figure 5.2: Agile Values

Let's delve into these 2 values and illustrate EI importance with examples:

1. **Individuals and Interactions over Processes and Tools**: Agile values the human element over rigid processes and tools. This principle underscores the importance of interpersonal skills and emotional intelligence. For example, a software development team that practices EI would prioritize effective communication and collaboration, fostering a positive environment where team members listen actively and empathize with each other's perspectives.

2. **Customer Collaboration over Contract Negotiation**: Agile emphasizes a close collaboration with customers to deliver valuable products. Emotional intelligence is vital here, as it enables teams to build strong customer relationships. For instance, a product owner with high EI can empathize with the customer's needs, translating feedback into product improvements more effectively.

Agile Principles and Emotional Intelligence (EI): Agile principles are vital in Agile transformations, where organizations adopt and implement Agile methodologies. Out of the 11 principles, six specifically highlight the significance of Emotional Intelligence (EI) skills and capabilities in Agile delivery. This underscores the importance of EI in fostering effective collaboration, communication, and adaptability within Agile teams. EI empowers individuals to understand and manage their emotions, navigate conflicts, build strong relationships, and embrace change, all of which are essential for successful Agile transformations.

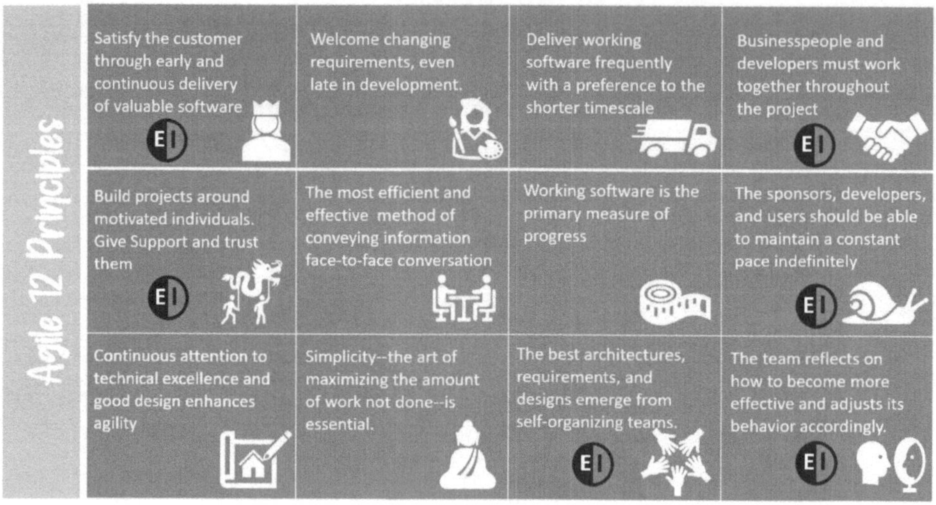

Figure 5.3: 12 Agile principles, 6 of them do have EI impact.

Below, you'll find the Agile principles we've discussed, each accompanied by an Emotional Intelligence (EI) icon in the above picture illustrating the importance of EI skills and providing real-time examples.

1. **"Our highest priority is to satisfy the customer through early and continuous delivery of valuable software."**
    - **Significance of EI**: EI helps build strong customer relationships, enhancing communication and understanding.
    - **Example**: A product owner with strong EI collaborates closely with customers, actively listens to their feedback, and adapts the product accordingly, ensuring customer satisfaction through continuous software delivery.
2. **"Business people and developers must work together daily throughout the project."**
    - **Significance of EI**: EI promotes effective collaboration and empathy, essential for aligning business and development teams.
    - **Example**: A product owner with high EI collaborates daily with developers to clarify backlog user stories. They understand each other's perspectives and work together to ensure the project aligns with business objectives.
3. **"Build projects around motivated individuals. Give them the environment**

and support they need, and trust them to get the job done."

- **Significance of EI**: EI is key to motivating and supporting team members by understanding their emotional needs and fostering a positive work environment.
- **Example**: A Scrum Master with strong EI recognizes team members' stress levels and provides support, encouragement, and a conducive work environment, allowing the team to stay motivated and self-organizing.

4. **"Agile processes promote sustainable development. The sponsors, developers, and users should be able to maintain a constant pace indefinitely."**
   - **Significance of EI**: EI helps in managing workloads, reducing stress, and maintaining a sustainable work pace.
   - **Example**: An Agile team that practices EI effectively distributes workloads, ensuring that developers are not overburdened. This leads to a sustainable pace, reduced stress, and improved well-being.
5. **"The best architectures, requirements, and designs emerge from self-organizing teams."**
   - **Significance of EI**: EI is essential in self-organizing teams as it promotes effective communication, conflict resolution, and decision-making.
   - **Example**: In a self-organizing Agile team, team members with high EI discuss architectural decisions, resolve conflicts, and collectively arrive at optimal design choices, resulting in superior project outcomes.
6. **"At regular intervals, the team reflects on how to become more effective, then tunes and adjusts its behavior accordingly."**
   - **Significance of EI**: EI supports a constructive and empathetic reflection process, making feedback more effective.
   - **Example**: During a retrospective meeting, team members with strong EI provide feedback in a considerate and constructive manner, facilitating the team's adjustment and improvement in performance.

In each of these Agile principles, Emotional Intelligence (EI) plays a vital role in fostering effective communication, enhancing teamwork, and maintaining a positive work environment, ultimately contributing to the success of Agile projects.

Agile EQ Leadership: The Need of the Hour

Leading with Emotional Intelligence (EQ) in Today's Agile World: Unlocking the True Potential of Individuals for Project Success

Current Challenges

In today's complex work environments, characterized by knowledge workers, remote and hybrid work models, increasing project complexity, and comparison-driven teams, navigating the challenges requires a unique approach. However, the ultimate hurdle lies in transforming individuals, as the success of project transformations heavily relies on transforming people.

Agile extends beyond mere practices and principles; it encompasses a mindset and culture. To achieve project success, it becomes imperative to prioritize the transformation of individuals. Agile teams embody essential traits such as self-organization, adaptability to change, high performance, and empowerment through ownership and flexibility.

Emotional Intelligence (EQ) Takes Precedence over Intellectual Intelligence (IQ): To overcome the barriers that hinder progress as a servant leader, it is crucial to prioritize EQ over IQ. EQ empowers leaders to remove obstacles and mentor/coach teams towards high performance. While IQ focuses on knowledge of Agile practices, principles, and values, EQ starts with self-awareness, which fosters a deeper understanding of others.

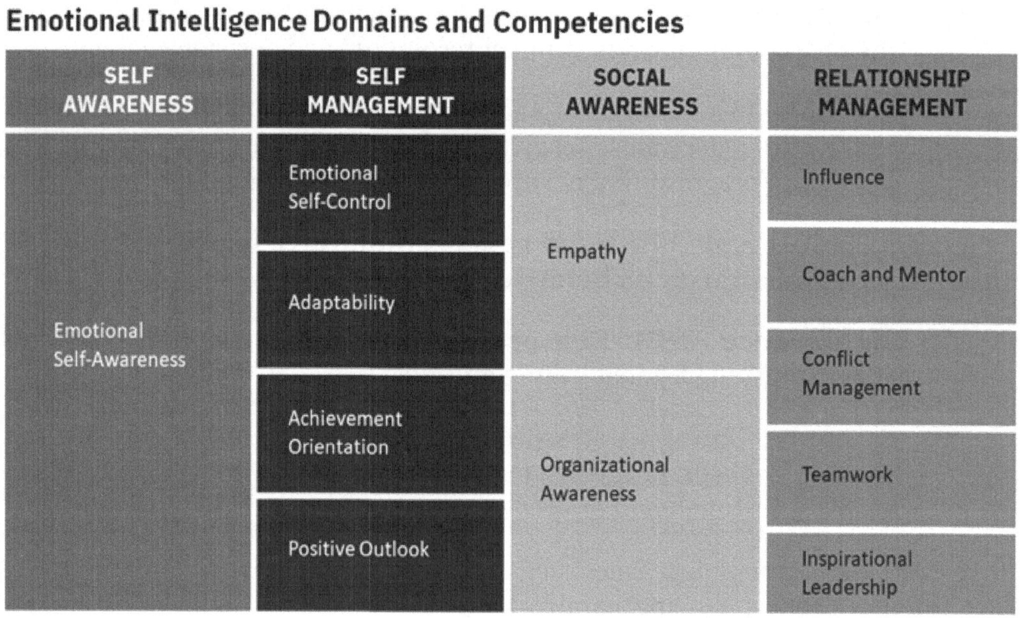

Figure 5.4: Emotional Intelligence Domains and Competencies

Emotional intelligence, also known as EQ (Emotional Quotient), refers to the capacity to effectively navigate and manage emotions.

It encompasses two key components:

1. Self-Awareness and Self-Management: This involves being aware of one's own emotions, controlling them, and expressing them appropriately. It includes recognizing and understanding how emotions impact thoughts, behaviours, and decision-making.

2. Empathetic Interpersonal Relationships: Emotional intelligence also entails the ability to handle interpersonal relationships with empathy. This involves understanding and considering the emotions and perspectives of others, effectively communicating, and resolving conflicts, and building strong connections.

The concept of emotional intelligence gained significant popularity in the 1990s following the publication of Daniel Goleman's book on Emotional Intelligence.

Key Emotional Intelligence (EI) Competencies for Successful Agile Transformations

To achieve successful Agile transformations, it is of utmost importance to prioritize and develop various competencies of Emotional Intelligence (EI). These competencies encompass traits such as adaptability, achievement orientation, positive outlook, organizational awareness, coaching and mentoring, conflict management, teamwork, and inspirational leadership.

Self-Reflection: Leaders, regardless of their hierarchical level, must engage in self-reflection and assess their proficiency in these EI competencies. By focusing on personal growth and development, leaders can enhance their EI and, in turn, facilitate the growth of their teams.

Improving EI and Fostering Leadership Growth: It should be an active pursuit for leaders driving Agile transformations. By embracing self-awareness, actively practicing, and improving their EI skills, and nurturing their teams, leaders can create an environment that is conducive to success.

Nurturing Personal Growth and Embracing Servant Leadership: In the realm of Agile methodologies, the pursuit of personal growth and the embodiment of servant leadership principles play a pivotal role in cultivating high-performing teams. The journey toward excellence requires a relentless commitment to self-improvement while simultaneously uplifting and influencing others positively.

Within this context, several key areas warrant our attention:

Self-Awareness: As Agile Scrum Masters or Agile Coaches, it is crucial to transcend the trappings of titles, years of experience, certifications, and past achievements that may inflate the ego. By dedicating time to self-reflection and introspection, we can cultivate a deep sense of self-awareness, which lays the foundation for true servant leadership. In doing so, we embody the essence of a serene sea, humbly guiding and empowering those around us.

Reflecting on **Tao Leadership Thought** The wisdom encapsulated in the Tao Leadership Thought guides our understanding of true leadership. "All streams flow to the sea because it is lower than they are. Humility gives it its power. If you want to govern the people, you must place yourself below them. If you want to lead the people, you must learn how to follow them." This profound teaching emphasizes the transformative power of humility and the importance of understanding and connecting with those we aim to lead. By adopting a mindset of servitude and empathy, we can create an environment conducive to collaboration, growth, and collective success.

By integrating personal growth and servant leadership principles into our Agile practices, we unlock the immense potential within ourselves and our teams. The ongoing pursuit of self-awareness and the embrace of humble leadership contribute to the cultivation of an environment where collaboration flourishes, innovation thrives, and individuals are empowered to reach their highest potential.

Agile EQ Leaders

To achieve successful Agile transformations, it is crucial for leaders to recognize the significance of emotional intelligence (EI) alongside their technical expertise and intelligence. While leaders may possess excellent engineering skills and high levels of intelligence, it is equally important for them to cultivate and develop their emotional intelligence skills.

Emotional intelligence, often referred to as EQ (Emotional Quotient), encompasses a range of qualities such as self-awareness, empathy, self-regulation, social skills, and motivation. Leaders with strong EI skills can understand and manage their own emotions effectively, while also being attuned to the emotions of others. This awareness and understanding of emotions enable leaders to build strong relationships, communicate effectively, and navigate complex interpersonal dynamics within their teams.

In the context of Agile transformations, where collaboration, teamwork, and effective communication are essential, leaders with well-developed emotional intelligence can greatly contribute to the success of the process. They can foster a positive and supportive team environment, understand the needs and concerns of team members, and provide the necessary guidance and support to facilitate growth and productivity.

Figure 5.5: Transform-To-Transform

While technical expertise and intelligence are valuable, it is the combination of these skills with emotional intelligence that truly sets leaders apart in Agile transformations. Recognizing the importance of EI skills and actively working on developing and improving them allows leaders to better connect with their teams, understand their perspectives, and provide the necessary support and guidance for the successful implementation of Agile methodologies.

In summary, leaders involved in Agile transformations must acknowledge the significance of emotional intelligence alongside their technical expertise. By actively working on developing their EQ, leaders can enhance their ability to understand and manage emotions, build strong relationships, and create a conducive environment for collaboration and teamwork. Ultimately, this will contribute to the success of Agile transformations and the overall achievement of project goals.

Know your EQ and Evolve

Knowing your own emotional intelligence (EQ) is a critical step to personal growth. By recognizing our EQ strengths and weaknesses, we can actively evolve and enhance our emotional intelligence, improving our interactions and relationships.

To assess your EQ (Emotional Quotient), you can follow the steps below:

- Test your EQ: Take an EQ quiz or assessment to gain insights into your emotional intelligence. You can use resources such as the free EQ quiz provided by **https://www.ihhp.com/free-eq-quiz/**. Feel free to explore other available resources as well.
- Identify your strengths and areas for improvement: Analyse the results of your EQ assessment to understand the areas where you excel and the areas where you can enhance your emotional intelligence.
- Reflect on your strengths and strengthen them further: Periodically reflect on the areas where you have a strong EQ and find ways to further develop and reinforce those skills.
- Treat improvement areas as your Self-Product Backlog: Take the areas where you need improvement and treat them as a personal backlog. Plan sprints or focused periods of time to work on these areas, iterate, reflect, and grow. Time boxing, setting specific time limits for your efforts, is crucial in this process.
- Consider engaging with an EI coach if needed: If you feel the need for additional guidance and support, consider working with an Emotional Intelligence coach who can provide personalized insights and strategies to enhance your EQ.
- It is important to note that success does not always guarantee happiness. Many examples in our own network might demonstrate that not all successful individuals are truly happy. In our lifestyles, it is essential to strive for both success and happiness. Let's create a balance between achieving success and cultivating happiness in our lives.

Understanding our own EQ and actively working on its development is a continuous journey towards personal growth and improved relationships. Evolving our emotional intelligence empowers us to navigate life's challenges with greater empathy, resilience, and success.

Nurturing People Skills and Harnessing the Power of Emotional Wisdom

In Agile transformations, people skills (`kindness, empathy, self-awareness, compassionate` and so on) play a more critical role than ever before. Why? Because we expect behavioral changes, shifts in work methodologies, and the development of self-organizing and empowered teams.

While intellectual intelligence (`IQ`) is important for understanding and implementing Agile practices, emotional intelligence (`EQ`) is essential for truly embodying Agile values.

Why EQ is Vital for Agility

EQ provides an evidence-based framework that enables individuals to show up as their best selves. While IQ helps in carrying out Agile processes, EQ is crucial for being Agile. Agile managers, coaches, and Scrum Masters must prioritize and continuously develop their EQ, as well as the EQ of their teams.

Continuous Improvement of EQ

Improving emotional intelligence is a critical skill that Agile managers, coaches, and Scrum Masters need to focus on. By continuously evolving and enhancing their EQ, they can create an environment where individuals and teams thrive in the Agile mindset and achieve greater success.

Let's review given below scenario and reflect on ourselves how we react, if that's not the best behaviour, what needs to be done.... Sounds interesting to know, let's learn.

Figure 5.6: EQ - Improvements

Business Scenario

Let us try to further deep dive into the understanding of how the emotional intelligence can affect our brain and responses.

Consider the following scenario:

- You have a very important agile retrospective meeting with your client, and it is mandatory for your team member to be available for that meeting
- You have reminded your team member about the meeting 3-4 times
- In-spite of multiple reminders, your teammate comes late to this meeting

We can all guess what can be your first reaction, when you see him.

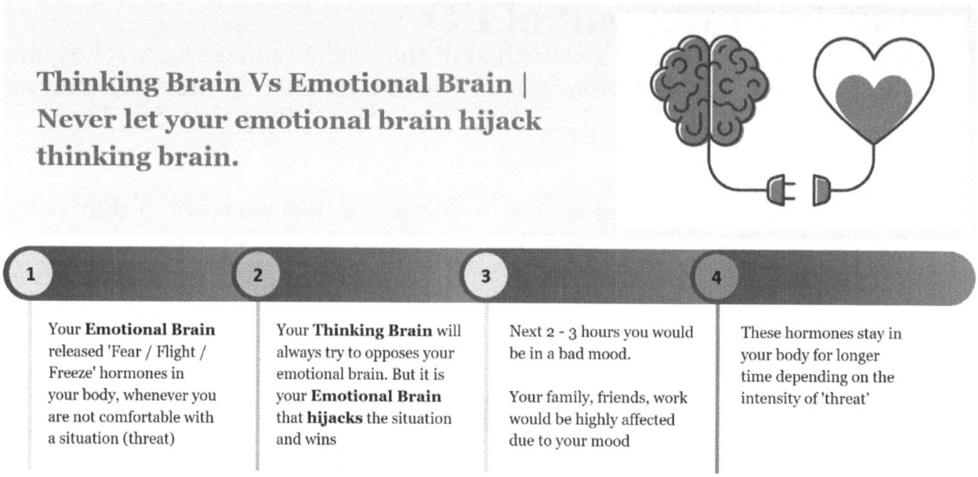

Figure 5.7: Thinking Vs Emotional Brain

In the quest for emotional intelligence, it is essential to understand the interplay between our thinking brain and our emotional brain. One critical aspect is to prevent our emotional brain from hijacking our thinking brain, which can lead to impulsive and irrational reactions.

A simple yet effective strategy is to pause and wait for just six seconds. This short period allows the brain chemicals responsible for amygdala hijacking to diffuse away. By giving ourselves this moment of respite, we prevent these chemicals from lingering in our bodies for an extended period. Otherwise, they may persist for minutes, hours, months, or even years, depending on their intensity.

During this pause, it is helpful to engage in deep breathing or focus on a pleasant image. These practices help counteract the amygdala's control, preventing an overwhelming emotional reaction. By consciously calming ourselves, we create space for the intellect to dominate over our emotions, allowing for a more thoughtful and measured response instead of a knee-jerk reaction.

Shifting from reactions to responses is a fundamental shift in our behaviour, and it is intricately connected to neuroplasticity. Neuroplasticity refers to the brain's ability to modify its structure and function throughout life in response to experience. When we consciously choose to respond rather than react, we are forging new neural pathways and connections. As we engage in this process of learning and growth, our old, negative thought circuits begin to fade, making way for stronger and healthier ones.

Over time, this new behaviour becomes second nature, ingrained in our way of being. Experts affirm that emotional intelligence can be taught and developed, and the example above exemplifies such practices that can be learned and practiced. By continuously honing our emotional intelligence, we can navigate the complexities of human interactions with greater insight, empathy, and composure.

Embodying Emotional Wisdom

Throughout history, numerous leaders have emphasized the significance of emotional wisdom in their messages. Let us contemplate the profound insights conveyed by Aristotle, Swami Vivekananda, and the Bhagavad Gita on this essential aspect of thought and behaviour

Aristotle

Educating the mind without educating the heart is no education at all – Aristotle

Figure 5.8: Mind Vs Heart

To ensure the success of Agile transformations, it is crucial to provide education on Emotional Intelligence (EI) to leaders and teams. Building upon Aristotle's wisdom, we can understand that a comprehensive and effective Agile education goes beyond technical skills and methodologies.

When we talk about educating the mind in the context of Agile transformations, we refer to the traditional aspects of training that focus on imparting knowledge about Agile principles, practices, and frameworks. This includes teaching individuals about Agile methodologies, such as Scrum or Kanban, and equipping them with the necessary skills to implement Agile practices effectively.

However, just educating the mind is insufficient. It is equally important to educate the heart, or in other words, to foster Emotional Intelligence. EI encompasses a range of skills, including self-awareness, empathy, communication, collaboration, and resilience. These skills are vital for creating a positive and supportive Agile environment, where teams can collaborate effectively, manage conflicts, and adapt to change.

By incorporating EI education into Agile transformations, leaders and teams can develop a deeper understanding of their own emotions and the emotions of others. This understanding allows them to build stronger relationships, promote open and honest communication, and effectively manage conflicts and challenges that arise during the Agile journey.

Educating leaders and teams on Emotional Intelligence in the context of Agile transformations ensures that they possess not only the technical knowledge and skills but also the moral and emotional qualities necessary for success. It enables them to navigate the complexities of Agile implementation with empathy, compassion, and ethical decision-making, fostering a culture of trust, collaboration, and continuous improvement.

Swami Vivekananda

Figure 5.9: Swami Vivekananda

This quote by Swami Vivekananda encapsulates a profound message about effective leadership and the qualities that can lead to success. Let's break it down and explore its meaning:

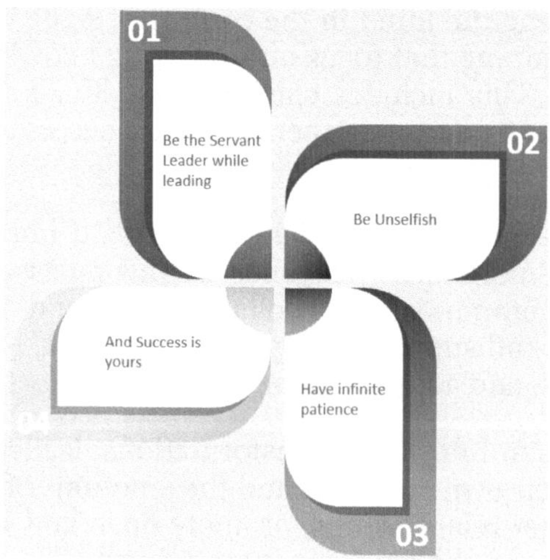

Figure 5.10: Path-To-Success

- **"Be the servant while leading"**: Swami Vivekananda suggests that true leadership involves adopting a servant mindset. Instead of asserting authority or seeking personal gain, a leader should prioritize serving others. This approach emphasizes humility, selflessness, and a genuine concern for the well-being and growth of those being led. By focusing on the needs and interests of others, a leader can inspire trust, build strong relationships, and create a harmonious and productive environment.

- **"Be unselfish"**: In conjunction with being a servant leader, Swami Vivekananda emphasizes the importance of unselfishness. True leadership involves putting the collective interests and welfare of the team or organization above personal ambitions or desires. It requires sacrificing personal gain or recognition for the greater good. By being unselfish, a leader can earn the respect and loyalty of their followers, fostering a culture of collaboration and shared success.

- **"Have infinite patience"**: Patience is a virtue often undervalued in leadership. Swami Vivekananda highlights the significance of possessing infinite patience. Effective leaders understand that progress and growth take time and that setbacks and challenges are part of the journey. By maintaining patience, a leader can navigate through obstacles, remain composed, and provide steady guidance. Patience also allows a leader to foster an environment where individuals can learn, develop, and contribute their best.

- **"And success is yours"**: By embodying the qualities of a servant leader, being unselfish, and practicing infinite patience, Swami Vivekananda suggests that success will naturally follow. Success, in this context, goes beyond individual achievements and encompasses the collective accomplishments of the team or organization. When a leader serves, prioritizes the interests of others, and demonstrates patience, they create an environment that nurtures the growth and potential of everyone involved. This, in turn, leads to the attainment of shared goals and overall success.

In summary, Swami Vivekananda's quote emphasizes the importance of servant leadership, unselfishness, and infinite patience in achieving success. By adopting these qualities, leaders can create a positive and empowering environment, inspire their teams, and foster collective growth and achievement.

Leaders can reflect, analyse, and improve these qualities through various means but surely knowing their EQ levels and focusing on the areas to be improved will help them to be Mindful leaders.

Bhagavad Gita

According to the Bhagavad Gita, a person of emotional stability is one who has complete control of his/her emotions in all situations. It leads to experiencing peace and free from fear. It arises because of controlling senses, desires, anger, and mind.

In the Bhagavad Gita, the term "Sthithapragnya" is used to describe an emotionally intelligent person. This term refers to someone who possesses a stable and composed mind, equanimity, and a deep understanding of oneself and others. In the context of Agile transformations, the importance of Sthithapragnya or emotional intelligence becomes evident in several ways:

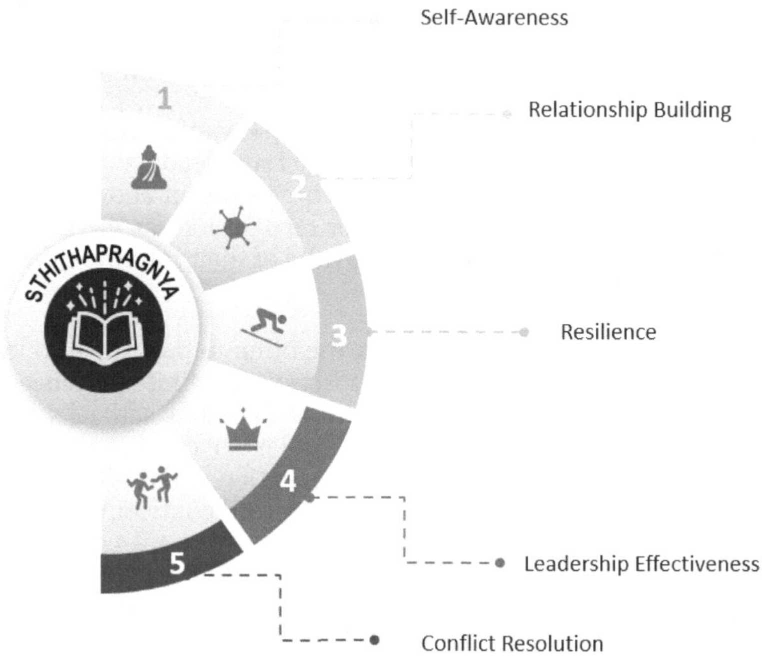

Figure 5.11: Sthithapragnya

1. **Self-awareness**: Emotional intelligence involves a high level of self-awareness, which allows individuals to understand their emotions, strengths, weaknesses, and triggers. In an Agile transformation, self-awareness enables leaders and team members to recognize their own limitations, biases, and areas for growth. This awareness contributes to personal development, adaptability, and a willingness to learn and change. It can also help in choosing complimentary team members building a well-rounded team more likely to succeed.

2. **Relationship building**: Agile transformations thrive on collaboration, teamwork, and effective communication. Emotionally intelligent individuals excel in building and maintaining positive relationships. They are empathetic, able to understand and respond to the emotions of others, and skilled at resolving conflicts. This ability to connect and foster strong relationships within teams and across the organization is crucial for successful Agile transformations.

3. **Resilience**: Emotional intelligence equips individuals with the ability to manage and regulate their emotions effectively. Agile transformations often involve uncertainty, change, and challenges. Emotionally intelligent individuals are better

equipped to handle setbacks, adapt to new circumstances, and maintain a positive outlook. Their resilience helps them navigate through obstacles and continue working towards the goals of the Agile transformation.

4. **Leadership effectiveness**: Leaders play a pivotal role in Agile transformations. Emotionally intelligent leaders inspire and motivate their teams, communicate clearly, and provide support and guidance. They are skilled at understanding the emotions and needs of their team members, fostering a sense of trust and psychological safety. By exhibiting Sthithapragnya qualities, leaders can guide their teams through the Agile transformation process effectively.

5. **Conflict resolution**: Agile transformations can sometimes give rise to conflicts and differences of opinion. Emotionally intelligent individuals possess the skills to manage and resolve conflicts constructively. They can engage in productive discussions, understand multiple perspectives, and find solutions that benefit the team and the organization.

In summary, Sthithapragnya, or emotional intelligence, plays a crucial role in Agile transformations. It enables self-awareness, relationship building, resilience, effective leadership, and conflict resolution. By cultivating emotional intelligence, individuals can contribute to the success of Agile transformations by fostering collaboration, adaptability, and a positive team culture.

Emotional Intelligence (EI) and its Influence on Phases of Team Development

"Tuckman's Team Development Model" was introduced by Bruce Tuckman in 1965. Bruce Tuckman, an American psychologist, proposed a model known as "Tuckman's Stages of Group Development. This model outlines the various stages that teams typically go through as they form, develop, and work together towards their goals. The phases identified by Tuckman are Forming, Storming, Norming, Performing, and Adjourning. This model has been widely recognized and used as a framework for understanding and managing team dynamics and effectiveness.

EI plays a crucial role in shaping and influencing the different phases of team development. In the context of Agile transformation, a leader with high EI can effectively navigate and guide the team through the change process, creating a supportive and adaptive environment that promotes collaboration, learning, and continuous improvement.

Here's how EI impacts each phase:

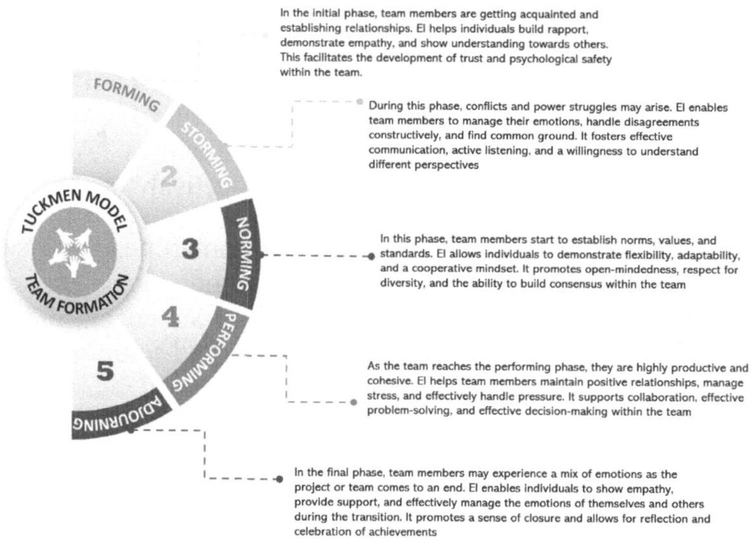

Figure 5.12: Tuckman Model

By developing EI within team members throughout each phase of team development, organizations can enhance team cohesion, collaboration, and overall effectiveness. EI enables individuals to navigate the complexities of team dynamics, manage emotions effectively, and foster positive relationships for successful teamwork.

Emotional Intelligence (EI) and Addressing the Five Dysfunctions of a Team

The concept of the "Five Dysfunctions of a Team" was introduced by Patrick Lencioni in his book titled "The Five Dysfunctions of a Team: A Leadership Fable." Patrick Lencioni is an author, speaker, and management consultant known for his work on team dynamics and organizational health. In his book, Lencioni outlines the five common dysfunctions that hinder team performance and collaboration: absence of trust, fear of conflict, lack of commitment, avoidance of accountability, and inattention to results. By addressing these dysfunctions, teams can become more cohesive, productive, and successful.

EI plays a vital role in addressing the five dysfunctions of a team, as described by Patrick Lencioni. In the context of Agile transformation, a leader with high EI can create a safe and inclusive environment where team members feel empowered to take risks, learn from failures, and embrace change, thereby enabling successful Agile adoption and implementation.

Here's how EI can help mitigate these dysfunctions:

- **Absence of Trust**: Trust is the foundation of a healthy team. EI enables team members to build trust by being authentic, demonstrating vulnerability, and showing empathy towards one another. Individuals with high EI can establish a safe and supportive environment where team members feel comfortable sharing their thoughts, concerns, and ideas.
- **Fear of Conflict**: Conflict avoidance can hinder a team's progress. EI helps team members manage conflicts constructively by fostering open communication, active listening, and understanding different perspectives. Individuals with high EI can navigate disagreements with emotional intelligence, promoting healthy debate and problem-solving.
- **Lack of Commitment**: Commitment arises when team members feel heard, understood, and valued. EI promotes effective communication and collaboration, allowing team members to align their goals, clarify expectations, and make commitments collectively. Individuals with high EI can create a sense of ownership, engagement, and dedication within the team.
- **Avoidance of Accountability**: Accountability is essential for team success. EI enables team members to take responsibility for their actions, deliver on commitments, and hold others accountable in a constructive manner. Individuals with high EI can foster a culture of accountability by providing feedback, setting clear expectations, and encouraging a growth mindset.
- **Inattention to Results**: Teams must prioritize collective goals over individual achievements. EI helps team members focus on shared objectives, set aside personal agendas, and celebrate collective successes. Individuals with high EI can inspire and motivate the team towards achieving outcomes that benefit the entire team or organization.

By cultivating EI within team members, organizations can address the five dysfunctions of a team. EI fosters trust, promotes healthy conflict resolution, encourages commitment, enhances accountability, and ensures a focus on collective results.

EI Terminology Exploration

Let's delve into some frequently employed impactful terms in the field of Emotional Intelligence (EI)

Given below terms quite commonly used by many and often get confused on clarity or it's relationship.

Empathy Vs Sympathy

We often see many get confused between Empathy and Sympathy

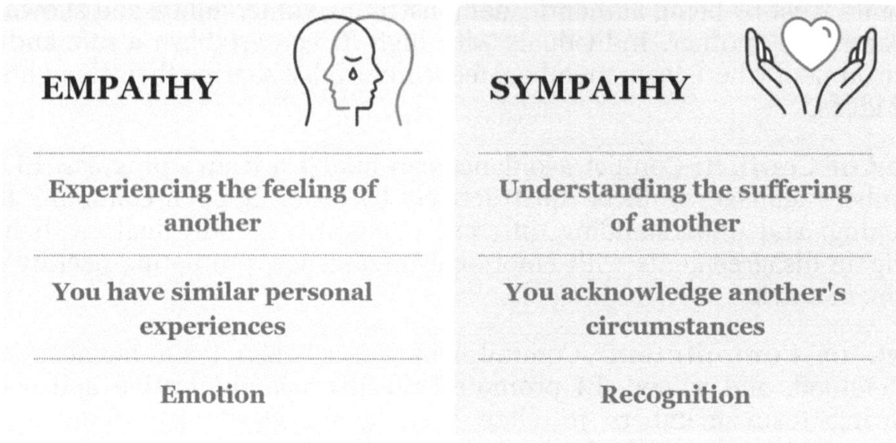

Figure 5.13: Empathy Vs Sympathy

EI and Mindfulness

Emotional Intelligence (EI) refers to the ability to understand and manage one's own emotions, as well as empathize with others. It encompasses self-awareness, self-regulation, social skills, empathy, and motivation.

Mindfulness involves being fully present in the moment, non-judgmentally observing thoughts, feelings, and sensations. It promotes self-awareness, emotional regulation, and the ability to respond thoughtfully rather than react impulsively.

Combining EI and mindfulness practices can enhance emotional awareness, foster empathy, improve decision-making, and cultivate healthier relationships, both personally and professionally

In the context of transformation, practicing mindfulness is a powerful tool for leaders and teams to effectively manage their emotions and enhance their Emotional Intelligence (EI). By cultivating mindfulness, individuals can develop greater self-awareness, regulate their emotions, and make informed decisions, ultimately contributing to a successful transformation journey.

Emotion and Intellect

Having emotions is indeed virtuous, but it would be a grave mistake to let them overpower your intellect, known as "Buddhi ", in Sanskrit. In both the corporate world and our personal lives, we have all witnessed instances where emotions have overridden our ability to exercise sound judgment and make informed decisions.

In the context of Agile transformation challenges, leaders often encounter situations where they are faced with overwhelming emotions. This can lead to a clouding of their judgment and an inability to fulfil their responsibilities effectively. Drawing inspiration from the Bhagavad Gita, we find a parallel in the story of Arjuna, a renowned warrior who experienced a similar struggle.

Arjuna, consumed by his emotions, lost his clarity, and refused to fulfil his duty as a warrior. However, Lord Krishna came to his aid, imparting profound wisdom and guiding him towards the right values in life. This knowledge helped Arjuna overcome his delusion and regain his rational thinking. With his emotions in check, Arjuna rose above his weaker impulses and ultimately fulfilled his obligations as a warrior.

Similarly, leaders in Agile transformations must recognize the potential impact of their emotions on their decision-making and overall leadership effectiveness. They should strive to cultivate self-awareness and seek guidance or mentorship when necessary, allowing them to maintain a balanced perspective and make well-informed choices. By aligning their intellect with their emotions, leaders can navigate challenges more effectively and fulfil their responsibilities towards driving successful Agile transformations.

Conclusion

Emotional Intelligence emerges as a critical factor for unlocking Agile success. The chapter has underscored the importance of Emotional Intelligence in Agile transformations and highlighted its relevance to leadership in an Agile context. By cultivating Emotional Intelligence competencies, leaders can effectively navigate the complexities and challenges of Agile environments, fostering collaboration, empathy, and adaptability. The chapter has also emphasized the significance of people skills in Agile transformations, emphasizing the need for leaders to understand and connect with their team members on an emotional level. Additionally, the exploration of Emotional Intelligence's influence on team development and its potential to address team dysfunctions further solidifies its role in driving Agile success. Ultimately, the chapter serves as a guide for leaders seeking to leverage Emotional Intelligence to create thriving Agile organizations and promote sustainable growth and innovation

Test your understanding

Test your knowledge from the chapter by answering the following questions:

Q.1. How does Emotional Intelligence (EI) contribute to the success of Agile transformations?

Q.2. What are the key competencies of Emotional Intelligence that leaders need to develop for effective Agile leadership?

Q.3. In what ways does Emotional Intelligence influence the different phases of team development in Agile settings?

Q.4. How can Emotional Intelligence help address the five dysfunctions commonly observed in Agile teams and foster a more cohesive and high-performing team dynamic?

Chapter 6

Know Agile, Know Agile Transformation

BookMyShow/Fandango, Uber, and Zomato are examples of broker start-ups recognizing a market need and successfully connecting producers and consumers. They capitalized on this opportunity by offering innovative platforms. Entertainment Ticketing platforms like BookMyShow/ Fandango revolutionized the ticketing experience by making it more convenient and enjoyable. They helped audiences to choose movies/ entertainment shows, movie theaters anytime from the comfort of their homes. Uber created a seamless connection between riders and drivers, transforming the transportation industry. Zomato catered to food lovers by facilitating the delivery of meals to their doorstep, while also helping eateries reach customers who preferred not to dine out. Additionally, Zomato allowed eateries to maximize their kitchen space and staff utilization without expanding physical seating capacity.

These start-ups, alongside numerous others, share several common characteristics. Firstly, they have a smaller headcount compared to traditional companies. This lean approach enables them to maintain focus on a common goal or vision, which the founder or founders typically drive. Furthermore, the smaller team size fosters greater collaboration among team members, leading to increased innovation and efficiency. The reduced hierarchical structure of these start-ups allows for quicker decision-making and implementation, promoting agility. Consequently, they can market their products or services faster, allowing them to capture a larger market share.

However, it is important to note that agility is not exclusive to start-ups. Both large enterprises and small businesses have the potential to be agile. In this chapter, we will explore how organizations of all sizes can embrace agility and adapt to the ever-changing business landscape.

In this chapter, we are going to delve into agile and its transformation. The benefits of agility at different levels of an organization. We will explore how to maximize agile values and build high-performing agile teams.

- To provide an overview of what is an agile mindset, the distinction between agile mindset and agile philosophy.
- To emphasize the importance of agile methodologies in a VUCA (Volatility, Uncertainty, Complexity, Ambiguity) environment.
- To explore levels and types of agility required for successful agile transformations.
- To delve into agile transformation and its myths.
- To highlight a leader's role in agile transformations.
- To accentuate the benefits of embracing product mindset in agile deliveries.
- To convey lean management principles for maximizing business value.
- To offer techniques for building high-performing teams, which are pivotal to the success of any agile transformation.

Agile Mindset

When we envision an agile individual, we may picture a circus acrobat, contortionist, or a skilled yoga practitioner. However, true agility extends beyond physical abilities and resides within the agility of the mind. The way we think influences our actions. Agile mindset is defined by four values, guided by twelve principles and manifested through many practices.

Here are the traits that define a person with an agile mindset:

- **Self-Awareness**: Agile individuals possess a deep understanding of their strengths and weaknesses. They are aware of their limitations and are willing to collaborate with others who complement their areas of weakness. Chapter 4 discussed the benefits of conducting strength assessments and outlined how to perform them.
- **Active Listening**: An agile person does not merely hear what others are saying, they actively listen. Hearing is just taking in the sound vibrations through the ear. Listening involves synthesizing, analyzing, and comprehending the message in one's mind. They refrain from interrupting others and avoid providing solutions without fully grasping the complete problem. Instead, they ask questions to gain a thorough understanding and empathize with the other person's perspective.
- **Empathy**: Empathy entails the ability to understand and share the emotions of others. An empathetic individual can put themselves in someone else's shoes and genuinely connect with their experiences.

- **Non-Judgmental**: Being judgmental is part of our pre-historic toolkit, which enables us to assess threats to our survival. However, our brains have not evolved as rapidly as our environment. In today's normal circumstances, constant life-or-death situations are rare. Foster trust and create a safe environment for everyone by consciously striving to be non-judgmental.
- **Open-Mindedness**: Beliefs are ideas that individuals hold to be true, and they can vary as widely as the stars in the sky or the number of people on our planet. A person with an open mind is willing to question their own beliefs and value systems. This does not mean changing beliefs impulsively but rather acknowledging the existence of different beliefs. They analyze and understand the facts surrounding a belief, and if new evidence contradicts their current beliefs, they are open to revising them.

These traits collectively define an agile mindset, which empowers individuals to adapt, collaborate, and thrive in dynamic environments.

Understanding the Distinction: Agile Mindset vs. Agile Philosophy

The difference between an agile mindset and an agile philosophy lies in their scope and application.

- **Agile Mindset:** An agile mindset refers to an individual's way of thinking and approach towards challenges. It is characterized by flexibility, adaptability, and a focus on continuous learning and improvement. People with an agile mindset embrace change, value collaboration and feedback, and are open to innovative ideas and perspectives. They prioritize delivering customer value, emphasize teamwork, and seek innovative solutions. An agile mindset is applicable at an individual level and can be cultivated by anyone, regardless of their role or the specific methodologies they follow.
- **Agile Philosophy:** The agile philosophy, on the other hand, encompasses a broader set of principles and values that guide the development and management of projects or organizations. It originated from the Agile Manifesto, a foundational document for agile methodologies/frameworks such as Scrum, Kanban, and Extreme Programming. The agile philosophy emphasizes customer collaboration, iterative and incremental development, self-organizing teams, and responding to change. It promotes an empirical and value-driven approach to project management, with a focus on delivering frequent, working increments of software or products. The agile philosophy provides a framework that can be applied at the team, project, or organizational level.

In summary, the agile mindset pertains to an individual's mindset and approach to work, while the agile philosophy encompasses a broader set of principles and values that guide project management and organizational practices. The agile mindset aligns with the agile philosophy, as individuals with an agile mindset are more likely to embrace and implement agile methodologies and principles in their work.

The Agile Advantage: Harnessing Change for Maximum Value Delivery

It is easier to implement requirements and walk on water if both are frozen. But we all know this is hardly ever the case in the real world. Agile methodologies equip us with tools and techniques to manage frequent changes in requirements. Moore's law predicted that the capability of computer chips will double every two years. While there is ongoing debate regarding the validity of Moore's Law, it is undeniable that technology continues to advance at an astonishing rate. This rapid progress is fueled by the vast resources available at fingertips through the internet and smartphones, leading to a constant stream of innovations. These innovations are leading to complete market landscape change and in turn is also shaping changes in customer needs. For example, desktops have become uncommon, whereas laptops and mobile phones have become more common.

Gone are the days when months were spent on gathering requirements, followed by designing for weeks, and then followed by implementation and testing for months. By the time such a traditional project sees the light of the day, the need for the requirement would have changed, and the technology used may have become obsolete. On the other hand, Agile is about frequently delivering maximum possible value to client and constantly building on the base value to enhance it further in each iteration.

In a VUCA (Volatility, Uncertainty, Complexity, and Ambiguity) world, Agile methodologies can be particularly valuable and effective. Here's how Agile can help in navigating the challenges of a VUCA environment:

- **Volatility**: Agile embraces change and is designed to adapt to volatile circumstances. It allows teams to respond quickly and effectively to changes in the market, customer needs, or business priorities. By continuously reassessing and reprioritizing work, Agile teams can manage volatile situations and adjust their plans accordingly.

- **Uncertainty**: Agile thrives in uncertain situations by emphasizing iterative and incremental development. Instead of trying to predict and plan for every possible outcome upfront, Agile promotes learning through experimentation and feedback. It encourages teams to start with a minimum viable product (MVP) and gather feedback early on, allowing them to make informed decisions and course corrections based on real-world data and insights.

- **Complexity**: Agile recognizes the inherent complexity of today's world and provides frameworks and practices to manage it effectively. It promotes collaboration, transparency, and cross-functional teamwork, enabling diverse perspectives to be leveraged for problem-solving. Agile frameworks like Scrum or Kanban provide visual tools and ceremonies to help teams understand and navigate complex workflows, ensuring that work is broken down into manageable units and progress is continuously monitored.

- **Ambiguity**: Agile encourages adaptive planning and embraces ambiguity by focusing on delivering value incrementally. Instead of striving for detailed upfront plans that may become quickly outdated, Agile teams work in short iterations, gathering feedback and adjusting their direction as they learn more about the problem space. This iterative approach allows for greater flexibility and responsiveness to emerging information and changing circumstances.

Overall, Agile methodologies provide a framework that fosters agility, adaptability, and collaboration, enabling teams to thrive in a VUCA world. By embracing change, learning from experience, and continuously delivering value, Agile can help organizations navigate uncertainty and complexity while remaining responsive to evolving circumstances.

Levels of Agility

Agility needs to exist at all levels for an agile transformation to succeed. The levels of agility are as follows.

- **Individual** – This is the lowest level of agility. A person needs to improve his emotional intelligence, embody agile values to have an agile mindset. It helps the individual to adapt to change easily.
- **Team** – If the individuals are agile and are collaborating, then the teams can also become agile. Agile allows individuals and teams to experience autonomy, freedom, creativity, and innovation. Teams need to be empowered and self-organizing. It leads to superior quality outcomes from the team.
- **Portfolio** – The portfolio is a midway step between the organizational level and the team level. Multiple teams form a portfolio. Team level agility can be scaled to portfolio level, providing more benefits as there is more collaboration across teams. It increases efficiency, transparency at portfolio level.
- **Enterprise** – If the enterprise is not agile, it cannot survive for long. It does not help if only the IT department is using agile but not the business team. In enterprise agility, everybody from the top leadership to the lowest ranks of the enterprise are agile. It helps the enterprises to not only face challenges and crises but also seize new opportunities.

Types of Agility

Enterprises need to exhibit diverse types of agility for an agile transformation to succeed. The diverse types of agility are as follows.

- **Business Agility**– The business teams also need to be agile to survive in the fast-changing markets. The business leaders need to be tuned in to the market trends. They should be able to adapt to market and environmental changes in productive and efficient ways. Business Agility leads to quicker time to market. This helps organizations to seize new opportunities or market share.

- **Technical Agility** – Initially, when Agile Manifesto was documented, most of the teams were co-located. The tools (post-its) used at that time were suited to such teams. As adaption of agile has spread across the world, the teams have become increasingly distributed. Especially after the pandemic, distributed teams have become more of a norm than the exception. The tools (e.g., Mural, Trello) used have also evolved to adapt to these situations. These tools are from a governance perspective. From implementation perspective DevOps and CI/CD (Continuous Integration/Continuous Deployment) pipeline play a crucial role in providing technical agility. DevOps is a technique of combining development & operations team for better collaboration, quicker delivery. CI/CD pipeline enables developers to frequently integrate their code changes, run tests, and deploy software quickly and reliably. Techniques like blue-green deployment help to differentiate between release and deployment, thus providing greater flexibility to the development and business teams.

- **Innovation Agility** – Innovation agility can help enterprises to be ahead of the market curve. It can not only help them survive changes in the market but also help them be pioneers in new market segments. Design Thinking workshops can help co-create strategy and also create client-centric solutions for new and existing markets.

Agile transformations and its myths

Agile transformations aim to make the organization nimble in mindset so that it can swiftly respond to any marketplace changes not to only survive the change but to capitalize on it and thrive on it.

Leaders start their journey of agile but end up in either just transitioning to agile or just adopting agile. These are the pitfalls that leaders should look out for and avoid. Help the leaders avoid these pitfalls by understanding these terms in detail.

Transformations vs Transitions

Transformations are like chemical changes. We cannot go back to our original state after we have transformed. For example, once an egg is boiled, it cannot be reversed back to a raw egg. It is transformed into a boiled egg.

Transitions are like physical changes. It is just a temporary state change due to a change in external conditions. For example, if we increase the temperature around a pot of water, it will eventually start boiling, i.e., it will move from liquid to a gaseous state. But as soon as the heat is removed, it will start cooling down, i.e., it will move from a gaseous state to a liquid state.

The aim for any organization or individual should be everlasting transformation instead of temporary transitions. It is better to slowly transform into agile mindset instead of just rapidly transitioning to agile methodology. Transitioning to agile methodology usually just entails using some of the tools and ceremonies of agile methodology. The teams use the tools as per policy directive from top management. But they do not follow agile in spirit. There are following dysfunctions within the teams, which superficially seem to be implementing agile but are not.

- **More communication but less collaboration** – The teams attend standups, use tools but just because the scrum master is insisting. They are not using them as a platform for sharing and removing impediments.
- **Lack of ownership instead of self-organizing teams** – Team members feel that since the team is accountable, no single member is accountable. This may lead to poor productivity in certain team members, which can be hidden due to overload burnt by other team members. Overloading of same team members is not sustainable and can lead to burn outs.
- **No documentation to the point of lacking mutual understanding** – Agile is not against all documentation. It values relevant & useful documentation. Sometimes teams avoid documentation so much that it leads to misunderstanding between all the stakeholders.
- **Flexibility means requirements can change at any time** – Business stakeholders usually think that being agile means changing requirements anytime. Agile allows business to change requirements but not mid-sprint. If requirements are changed mid-sprint, it hampers the momentum of the development team and creates chaos.

When organizations undergo agile transformations, everyone in the organization develops an agile mindset. Starting from leadership to scrum masters, business teams and scrum team members. They embody the scrum values of

- **Openness** – Team members are transparent with each other regarding the work they are doing. Business stakeholders are open about the reasoning behind changes in the priorities. This helps team members to be more aligned with each other and business priorities.
- **Respect** – Team members respect each other and trust that everyone is capable and dedicated to their job. As team members value each other, it increases their trust in each other and overall team morale.
- **Courage** – Team members should have courage to challenge each other as well as business stakeholders. Healthy challenges can increase the quality of the product. Courage is a pre-requisite for openness. The lack of courage leads to less transparent teams.
- **Focus** – Team members should focus on tasks committed for the sprint/iteration. The lack of focus will result in lower productivity.
- **Commitment** – Work is more likely to be done on time if the team member commits to it rather than someone else assigning it.

Transformations vs Adoption

Transformations are organization wide. Everybody from top management to mid managers to individual team members needs to be transformed for any transformations to be successful.

Adoption happens in pockets. Few departments or teams in an organization adopt a particular technology. Adoption can be done as a pilot before rolling out complete transformation. But adoption cannot be a permanent state as that will not work. For example, if only the IT teams adopt agile and the business team is not part of it, then it will fail. There will not be a "One Team." The collaboration between IT and business teams will not be as good as it should be.

The following are the problems faced while adopting agile.

- **Organizational culture at odds with Agile** – As agile adoption happens in pockets, all the departments involved in a delivery may not be aligned to the agile values & principles. This will create hindrances for departments adopting agile, and the true benefits of agile will not be realized.
- **Resistance to change** – Change is the only constant thing in life but still there is always resistance to change. When changing new ways of working, we need to unlearn old ways of working and learn new ways of working. We are forced to work outside of our comfort zone. Those who are selected for the adoption group might wonder about the reason behind their selection. They might perceive it as a penalty if the change is not communicated well.
- **Inadequate management support** – As adoption is limited to a small number of people in the organization, the senior management may not take it sufficiently seriously. This may lead to a lack of resources, governance, and direction available for adoption. For example, adequate training may not be available for the employees' part of the adoption. This will hinder their performance at an optimal level and may also bring down the team's morale.

Before committing to complete transformations, adoptions are still useful for exploring the possibilities and challenges. The leadership should not hope for full benefits of transformations in adoption. They should see it as a sign of what to prepare for.

Agility & transformations

Whether you are a Harry Potter fan or not, everyone would like to have the power of "Alohomora" to open the locked doors of opportunities or have an "Expecto Patronum" save them from the challenges. Fantasy worlds aside in the real world, as well as agile transformations, can help enterprises unlock doors of opportunities and save them from crises.

Agility should be part of vision, so that all teams are aligned to the vision. While undergoing transformations, organizations cannot wait for transformations to be completed at each level sequentially, starting from an individual level. Leaders need to embark on organization-wide transformations to get its full benefits. Leaders can also accelerate transformations by building cross-functional and complementary teams. Such teams can collaborate and help each other to achieve the team's goal. More such aligned teams can help organizations achieve their goals quicker.

Leader's role in Agile transformations

Leaders play a pivotal role in agile transformation. Leaders need to lead by example. They need to adopt an agile mindset first before embarking on organization-wide agile transformation. The traits required by leaders for successful agile transformation are as below.

1. **Growth Mindset** – Agile leaders firmly believe that talent is not fixed with whatever education or skills we acquire at the early stage of our career, but we can keep on learning and developing skills throughout our career. They are more open to new ideas, risk taking and experimentation.

2. **Visionary** – They can tap into market trends and provide a clear direction for agile transformation and organization. The transformation strategy is aligned with the vision.

3. **Servant Leadership** – Servant leaders do not assign tasks to the team or order or command the team. They serve the self-organizing and empowered teams by removing impediments in their path towards the goal. This is already covered in detail in Chapter # 5.

4. **Systems Thinking** – Leaders focus on the whole end-to-end system rather than just the pockets. Systems thinking will help break silos within organization and increase collaboration amongst teams. It can also lead to optimizing processes across the organization, leading to a leaner organization.

5. **Continuous Learning** – One of the critical factors for agile transformations to work is continuous improvement. Continuous improvement can be brought not only by inspection and retrospection but also by continuous learning. Leaders seek continuous feedback, learn from the feedback, and improve upon it.

6. **Lead by example** – It is said that more than half of our communication is non-verbal. The team members will not follow a leader if the leader is not walking the talk. So, it is essential that leaders don't just talk about agile but they also practice being agile.

7. **Entrepreneurial Mindset** – Entrepreneurs are resilient and use critical thinking to get through tough times. Leaders having entrepreneurial mindset can help the team overcome challenges or setbacks.

Embracing a Customer Centric Product Mindset in Agile Delivery

In the industry, there have been many instances where companies initiate a transformation and subsequently plan for another one. Upon closer examination of the reasons behind these multiple transformations, it becomes apparent that most companies initially approach their Agile transformation with a Project Mindset. Consequently, they tend to prioritize Agile transformation over Product Mindset transformations. Therefore, we highly encourage everyone to approach agile transformations with a Product mindset to gain maximum business value.

The Project Mindset and Product Mindset are two distinct approaches to managing and delivering value within an organization. Here are the key differences between these mindsets:

Area	Project Mindset	Product Mindset
Focus On	Delivering specific Projects within timeframe, scope, budget; Output focused	Delivering ongoing value through evolution of product; Outcome focused
Emphasis On	Completing project as per pre-approved requirements	Emphasis on customer satisfaction, continuous improvement, long term business objectives
Timeframe	Defined start and end dates	Entire lifecycle of the product
Customer Orientation	Only considered during initial requirements elicitation phase	Throughout the product lifecycle. Customer centricity is core principle
Value Delivery	Measured by delivery within time and budget	Measured by customer satisfaction, revenue generation, market share, achieving strategic goals
Team Structure	Members come together only for the duration of project	Teams are long-term, stable, and cross-functional, dedicated to the ongoing development and improvement of a specific product

Figure 6.1: Project Mindset Vs Product Mindset

In summary, the Project Mindset focuses on delivering specific projects within defined parameters, while the Product Mindset emphasizes ongoing value creation, customer satisfaction, and long-term product success. Project mindset emphasizes outputs like delivery within budget, whereas Product mindset emphasizes outcomes like business value delivered. The difference between project mindset and product mindset is that the former is about building the product right, and the latter is about building the right product. Adopting a Product mindset enables organizations to prioritize customer needs, deliver continuous value, and adapt to changing market demands.

Consider the following strategies to avoid Agile deliveries with a Project Mindset and instead foster a more product-oriented approach:

1. **Clarity in the product vision and roadmap**: Establish a clear and compelling product vision that outlines the long-term goals and value proposition of the product. Develop a roadmap that outlines the key milestones, features, and iterations to achieve the product vision. This roadmap should guide the Agile delivery and ensure a product-centric focus.

2. **Emphasize customer-centricity**: Encourage a strong customer-centric mindset throughout the implementation. Continuously engage with customers, gather

feedback, and incorporate it into the product development process. Prioritize features and enhancements based on customer needs and market demand to deliver maximum value.

3. **Encourage cross-functional teams**: Form stable, cross-functional teams dedicated to the product's development and success. These teams should include members with diverse skill sets, including product management, development, testing, design, and customer support. By having a cohesive team focused on the product, you can foster collaboration and a shared understanding of the product's goals.

4. **Adopt iterative and incremental development**: Embrace Agile principles and practices, such as Scrum or Kanban, which promote iterative and incremental development. Break down the product development into smaller, manageable increments or sprints, allowing for regular feedback, adaptation, and continuous improvement.

5. **Measure success based on customer and business value**: Move away from measuring success solely based on project milestones and constraints. Instead, establish Objectives and Key Results (OKRs), Key Performance Indicators (KPIs) that reflect customer satisfaction, revenue generation, market share, and other business-oriented outcomes. Regularly assess and review these metrics to ensure the project is delivering value aligned with the product vision.

6. **Foster a learning culture**: Encourage a culture of continuous learning and improvement within the Agile delivery team. Promote experimentation, knowledge sharing, and the application of lessons learned from each iteration to drive innovation and enhance the product's capabilities.

By implementing these strategies, organizations can shift their Agile delivery away from a Project Mindset and foster a more product-oriented approach. This will help ensure a focus on delivering continuous value, meeting customer needs, and achieving long-term business objectives.

Implementing Agile Values

Agile values people over processes. And rightly so. People are the ones delivering the product. Software development requires engaged, creative minds at work. It's a task that demands intelligence and originality, not dull monotony.

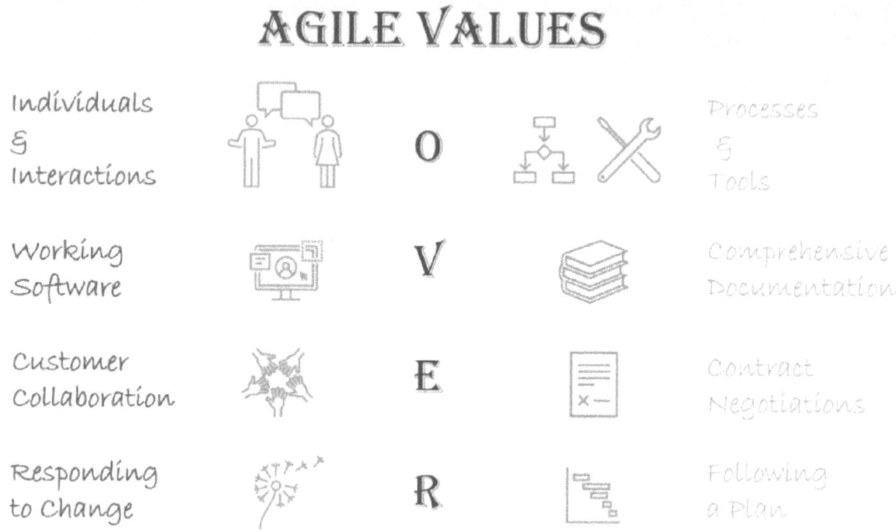

Figure 6.2: Agile Values

In an agile team, the lefthand side is valued more over the righthand side. Let's look at each one in detail.

- Individuals and interactions over processes and tools – If the individuals are engaged and focused on the common goal for the project, then it will increase their productivity. There should be a good rapport with the business team. The business and development team should feel that they are part of one team working towards one goal. This will make the interactions fruitful. Agile also has processes and tools but just doing processes and using tools without the spirit of Agile leads to "Doing Agile" instead of "Being Agile".

- Working software over comprehensive documentation – Agile focuses on frequent feedback from customers through reviews. The reviews also focus on showing the actual working of the system than any presentation about how it should work. A picture can speak a thousand words. Similarly, working software will give more of the customers a better idea than any presentation describing it. Reviews are also helpful in gathering new requirements, as most customers will think more once they see the software. Documentation is required to the extent of having common understanding amongst all the stakeholders, but it shouldn't be overkill and shouldn't delay the actual development.

- Customer collaboration over contract negotiation – The main principle of agile is there are no separate teams. Everybody, including business, is working towards one goal. In the real world, there will be commercial aspects because business and development teams may be from different commercial entities. Businesses are experts in their subject matter and software development is outsourced to experts in technical field. Management on both sides, i.e., business as well as IT, must use ways like staff augmentation, or capacity model so that the commercial aspects don't hamper the working relationship of the team. This will ensure that teams don't waste time on arguing whether a point raised is a change or defect but think of how to get it resolved.

- Responding to change over following a plan – In today's market, there are so many fast-changing variables that it is foolish to plan and stick to it for more than a few months. The business will be tuned into the changing variables of the market. The IT department needs to support business in changing the course of the product based on the changed variables.

Maximizing the business values with agile value implementation will help teams work more efficiently, be more engaged, and deliver high-quality outcomes.

Lean Management for maximizing business value

Lean management originated from Toyota Production system (TPS). TPS was developed by Toyota, a Japanese automobile manufacturer between 1948 and 1975. It mainly focuses on eliminating waste and delivering maximum value to the end customer. Though it originated in the manufacturing sector today, it is widely applied in various industries, including the software industry.

The five principles of lean management are as follows:

1. **Value** – Define what is valuable for the customer. What are the problems that our customers need to solve?
2. **Value stream mapping** – Value stream mapping is a lean management method which visualizes steps taken by an organization to create & deliver products. Visualization helps organizations find bottlenecks, delays, wastage in terms of time and effort in the process and eliminate them. It aims to eliminate steps that don't add value to the end consumer.
3. **Flow** – The value creating steps followed should be flowing smoothly uninterrupted. The outputs from previous steps should be at the same level as the inputs expected by the next steps.
4. **Pull** – The flow is based on pull system rather than push system. Instead of earlier steps pushing outputs to the next steps, the next steps are pulling output from the previous steps.
5. **Perfection** – Find ways to continuously improve the value stream by eliminating waste and delivering efficiency.

Lean management provides us with a structured approach which helps us in maximizing business value. This section covered principles of lean management which will help leaders to implement it in their organizations.

Building high-performing teams

After catching the crabs, they are put into an open box instead of a closed box. It is believed that if a crab is trying to climb up the box, the other crabs will try and pull its leg so that it cannot climb up. This ensures that they will all fail. This belief about crabs may not be true, but it has led to the term crab-mentality.

Conversely, ants cooperate with each other and build nests of huge sizes, which helps them to prosper their species.

While building teams, leaders should aim to build teams like ants instead of crabs.

There is famous quote from Sant Tukaram (Saint Tukaram) which loosely translates to “If we help each other then we will all progress”. Team members should help each other so that the team can achieve its goal.

The festival of Dahihandi (Pot of curd) is celebrated in the state of Maharashtra in India. It takes inspiration from Lord Krishna, who used to love cream, and the maidens used to hang the cream very high in the house to prevent Lord Krishna from eating it. But Lord Krishna used to collaborate with his friends to get to the high-hanging pot. In Dahihandi as well, there is a prize for reaching the pot, which is hung around twenty to fifty feet high. No single person can reach the pot. They build a human pyramid to reach the top. They use complementary skills to arrange the pyramid. The bigger, stronger boys are at the bottom that form the base. The lighter ones form the middle of the pyramid while the lightest and agilest little kid climbs on everyone’s back to reach the pot at the top and shares the spoils of the pot with everyone. This also emphasizes the importance of having people with diverse skills. If there is a team with all the strong and big boys, they will not be able to climb on top of each other to reach the top. On the other hand, if there is a team of only small boys, they also will not be able to support each other’s weight. It is important to have the right mix of skills so that the team can achieve its goal. Trust is of paramount importance in this endeavor. The boys at the top trust the ones below to do everything they can to prevent them from falling. The boys tie a cloth band around their waist, which makes it easier for others to climb onto their shoulders. This emphasizes the usage of tools fit for the purpose. They may not reach the top in the first attempt, but they keep trying to reach the top. This is a classic example of teamwork and high-performing teams.

Awareness about emotional intelligence and efforts taken to improve the emotional intelligence of everyone on the team can help in building and maintaining a high-performing team. This is already covered in detail in the earlier chapter on emotional intelligence.

Traits of high performing teams

From the above examples, we can conclude that performing teams exhibit the following traits.

- **Focus on a common goal** – The Sun's rays, when concentrated through a lens, can light a fire. A team that focuses on a common goal can achieve amazing results, unlike a team that lacks goal alignment, even if everything else is equal. Without a common goal, everybody's efforts will be dispersed and will reduce their impact.
- **Good mix of complementary skills** – Delivering a project requires a myriad of skills and not just technical skills but soft skills as well. Team members can lean on each other depending on each one's strength to get the job done. The team members have T-shaped skills, i.e., they are experts in a specific field but also have a high-level understanding of other fields and can collaborate with experts from those fields.
- **Trust** – Trust within a team is most crucial. Lack of trust will lead to team members holding back information. It will also be detrimental to collaboration amongst the team members.
- **Good collaboration** – Teamwork can move mountains. Even if the team is diverse, focused on a common goal and trust each other, if they don't collaborate to get the work done it is of no use.
- **Usage of tools fit for purpose** – Tools are not exactly deal breakers, but they significantly increase productivity. Tools need not be complicated. They can be simple things like "Post-its" on a board, which provides visibility of the backlog to the whole team.
- **Growth Mindset** – There are bound to be setbacks while executing any project. The team that has growth mindset will learn from the mistakes and continue to progress. It helps to keep the team morale high. Tools like Team Maturity Assessments, Scrum Master Assessments, and Product Owner Assessments can help in monitoring and tracking the progress of the team. Refer to Chapter 7 for more details.

In this section we have seen how the festival of Dahihandi teaches us collaboration, complimentary teams, trust are put in practice to build high performing teams. It also describes the traits displayed by the high performing teams.

Essentials for building high-performing teams

Just as Rome wasn't built in one day, high-performing teams cannot be formed in a single day. They cannot be formed just by bringing together talented individuals. Leaders need to nurture high-performing teams.

Some of the steps which can be taken to build a high-performing team are as follows:

- **Alignment to common goal** – All the individuals on the team need to be aligned to a common goal and they should focus all their efforts towards achieving that goal.

- **Optimum Communication** – There should be adequate (not too much and not too little), clear, timely communication about the progress towards the goal to the team. Communication need not always be good news. Sometimes it may be a call for all hands on the deck to save the project. Other times, it may be the status quo. Whatever it is, the leader should not be afraid to spell it out.

- **Building Trust** – Trust is the bedrock for a high performing team. Leaders need to foster trust. They need to first trust the team members. They need to be vulnerable, honest, supportive, and accountable so that the team also inculcates these values.

- **Conflict Resolution** – If there is more than one human being involved, there are bound to be differences in opinions. Leaders should address conflicts immediately so that they don't fester and create much bigger problems. Leaders should listen actively to all the points of view. Leaders should ensure that all the team members understand each other's perspectives and take decisions which help them get closer to the common goal.

Conclusion

In this chapter, we have learnt about Agile and Agile transformations. Some of the key points learned are as follows.

1. True agility is agility of mind.

2. Agile is about frequently delivering maximum possible value to client and constantly building on the base value to enhance it further in each iteration.

3. Traits of a person with Agile mindset
    a. Self-Awareness
    b. Active Listening
    c. Empathy
    d. Being Non-Judgmental
    e. Open Mindedness

4. The agile mindset pertains to an individual's mindset and approach to work, while the agile philosophy encompasses a broader set of principles and values that guide project management and organizational practices.

5. Transformations are like chemical changes, there is no turning back. While transitions are like physical changes which may revert to original state in the absence of external input.

6. Following are the dysfunctions visible within teams while doing agile transitions.

    a. More communication but less collaboration

    b. Lack of ownership instead of self-organizing teams

    c. No documentation to the point of lacking common understanding

    d. Flexibility means requirements can change at any time.

7. Adoptions can be used for testing waters before undertaking full scale transformations, but they will not give full benefits of transformations.

8. Some of the problems faced while adopting agile are as follows.

    a. Organizational culture at odds with Agile

    b. Resistance to change.

    c. Inadequate management support

9. Traits of a Leader required for an agile transformation are as follows.
    a. Growth Mindset
    b. Visionary
    c. Servant Leadership
    d. Systems Thinking
    e. Continuous Learning
    f. Entrepreneurial Mindset

10. The Project Mindset focuses on delivering specific projects within defined parameters, while the Product Mindset emphasizes ongoing value creation, customer satisfaction, and long-term product success.

11. Strategies to align with product mindset are as follows.
    a. Align with a Product Mindset from the start.
    b. Clarity in the product vision and roadmap
    c. Emphasize customer-centricity.
    d. Encourage cross-functional teams.
    e. Adopt iterative and incremental development.
    f. Measure success based on customer and business value.
    g. Foster a learning culture.

12. Maximizing the agile values will help teams work more efficiently, be more engaged, and deliver high-quality outcomes.

13. Five Principles of lean management that help in maximizing business value are as follows:
    a. Value
    b. Value stream mapping
    c. Flow
    d. Pull
    e. Perfection

14. Traits of high-performing teams are as follows.
    a. Focus on a common goal.
    b. Good mix of complementary skills.
    c. Trust
    d. Good collaboration
    e. Usage of tools fit for purpose.

f. Growth Mindset

15. The steps for building high-performing teams are as follows.

    a. Alignment to common goal

    b. Optimum Communication

    c. Building Trust

    d. Conflict Resolution

Next chapter will help the reader with

- Assessing their strength with respect to agile transformations
- Assessing their agility with respect to agile transformations
- Assessing their emotional intelligence with respect to agile transformations

Test your understanding

Test your knowledge from the chapter by answering the following questions:

Q.1. What is the difference between transformation and transition?

Q.2. What are the pitfalls of agile transitions?

Q.3. What problems are faced while doing agile adoption instead of transformation?

Q.4. What are the traits of an agile transformation leader?

Q.5. How to maximize business value using agile?

Q.6. How to build high-performing teams?

Chapter 7

Agile Maturity Index: Measuring the Success

"`We cannot improve what we cannot measure`" This thought was popularized by Lord Kelvin an Irish mathematician. In 1979, a group of researchers conducted an experiment to test the effects of goal setting and feedback on worker productivity. They divided 23 workers at a sawmill into two groups: one group received specific and challenging goals for their daily output, along with feedback on their performance; the other group received no goals or feedback. The results showed that the goal-setting group increased their productivity by 15%, while the control group decreased their productivity by 10%. So, setting measurable goals and providing feedback can motivate workers to improve their performance.

However, there were unintended consequences of the experiment. The researchers also found that the goal-setting group had more accidents than the control group. They speculated that this was because the workers were so focused on meeting their goals that they ignored safety rules and procedures. They also noticed that the workers tended to cut smaller logs than usual, because they were easier and faster to process. This meant that they wasted more wood and produced lower quality products.

So, measurement can be a powerful tool for improvement, but it can also have negative effects if not used wisely. We need to consider not only what we measure, but also how we measure it, why we measure it, and what we do with the results. We need to balance quantitative and qualitative aspects of our work and goals. And we need to be aware of the potential trade-offs and side effects of measurement. Let's see how measurements can be useful in Agile transformations.

In today's fast-paced business environment, organizations are increasingly turning to Agile methodologies to drive growth and adapt to changing market conditions. However, measuring the success and effectiveness of Agile transformations can be a complex task. This is where the Agile Maturity Index comes into play. The Agile Maturity Index is a powerful tool that allows organizations to assess their progress and maturity in adopting Agile principles and practices. In this article, we will explore the concept of the Agile Maturity Index, understand its importance in measuring organizational transformations, and delve into the difference between OKRs (Objectives and Key Results) and KPIs (Key Performance Indicators) in the context of Agile.

This chapter aims to:

- To introduce the concept of the Agile Transformation Index and its role in measuring the success of organizational transformations.
- To highlight the importance of measuring what truly matters and selecting relevant metrics in Agile transformations.
- To explain the difference between OKRs and KPIs in Agile and their respective roles in goal setting and performance measurement.
- To provide insights into conducting effective Agile assessments for key roles in Agile programs, driving growth and continuous improvement.
- To emphasize the deficiencies in the existing industry processes and propose the appropriate approach

Understanding the Agile Maturity Index

The Agile Maturity Index, also known as the Agile Transformation Index, is a framework designed to evaluate the progress and effectiveness of an organization's Agile transformation efforts. It provides a structured approach to assess the organization's journey towards adopting Agile principles and practices. By measuring various dimensions of Agile maturity, the Agile Maturity Index helps organizations identify gaps, set improvement goals, and make informed decisions to drive continuous improvement.

The specific criteria and assessment framework may vary depending on the organization, industry, and Agile approach being adopted. Agile coaches, consultants, or experts often tailor the assessment framework to fit the specific needs and goals of the organization undergoing the Agile transformation. This customization ensures that the assessment is meaningful and relevant to the organization's context.

To embark on the Agile Transformation Index, it is essential to first explore and grasp several crucial concepts that will contribute to achieving excellence

Importance of Measuring What Matters

When it comes to measuring Agile transformation success, it is crucial to focus on what truly matters. Many organizations make the mistake of incorporating every metric they come across during their learning or training into their set of metrics. However, this approach can lead to confusion and inefficiency. Instead, organizations should carefully select metrics that are relevant to their specific context and aligned with their vision, mission, and objectives.

To determine the relevant metrics, organizations need to consider the stage of their transformation journey and identify the data points that will provide actionable insights. This requires a thoughtful approach and an understanding of the key drivers of success in Agile transformations. By measuring what truly matters, organizations can track their progress effectively and make data-driven decisions to achieve their transformation goals.

Aligning Product and Process Metrics

Product metrics are centred around the achievements of a business, including objectives like gaining new customers, maintaining customer loyalty, increasing cart size, and maximizing product/service usage time etc. The specific metrics can differ based on the industry, the stage of the product life cycle, and the company's overarching vision.

Agile process metrics are used to measure the performance of agile teams and their development process. They can be used to track progress, identify areas for improvement, and make informed decisions about how to allocate resources.

Some of the most common agile process metrics include:

- **Sprint burndown chart:** This chart shows how many story points have been completed during the sprint and how many remain. It can be used to forecast if the sprint scope will be completed on time.
- **Velocity:** This metric measures how many story points were completed by a team, on average, over the past few sprints. It can be used to estimate how much work a team can complete in a future sprint.
- **Lead time:** This metric measures the time it takes to complete a task from start to finish. It can be used to identify bottlenecks in the development process.
- **Cycle time:** This metric measures the time it takes to complete a task from when it is assigned to a developer to when it is completed. It can be used to track the efficiency of the development process.
- **Throughput:** This metric measures the number of tasks completed in a given period of time. It can be used to track the productivity of a team.
- **Work in progress (WIP):** This metric measures the number of tasks that are currently in progress. It can be used to identify if a team is taking on too much work

or if they are not working efficiently.

- **Blocked time:** This metric measures the amount of time that developers spend waiting for resources or approvals. It can be used to identify bottlenecks in the development process.
- **Defects:** This metric measures the number of defects that are found in a product after it is released. It can be used to track the quality of the product and identify areas for improvement.

The specific agile process metrics that a team tracks will depend on their specific goals and objectives.

For agile teams, gaining a deep understanding of their product metrics is crucial. It enables them to assess their competencies and ensure that their processes align with the organization's product metrics. By focusing on these capabilities and process metrics, agile teams can effectively support the achievement of their organization's desired outcomes and these competencies should be part of their assessment index.

Harnessing the Power of Goal setting and Performance Measurement

In any journey you need to know the destination and have relevant milestones on the way to track the progress towards the destination. Goals are the milestones in your Agile transformation journey. They provide direction to the effort. As the saying goes "You cannot improve what you cannot measure." So, we need to measure progress towards our goals. OKRs and KPIs, covered in below sections, are tools which help in goal setting and performance measurement.

OKRs and KPIs in Agile Transformations

In the context of Agile transformations, both Objectives and Key Results (OKRs) and Key Performance Indicators (KPIs) play crucial roles in goal setting and performance measurement. While they share some similarities, there are distinct differences between OKRs and KPIs.

Objectives and Key Results (OKRs):

In the Agile context, OKRs stands for Objectives and Key Results. OKRs are a goal-setting framework that helps teams and organizations align their efforts and focus on achieving measurable outcomes. It focuses on future success.

Objectives: Objectives are the high-level goals that an organization or team aims to accomplish. They provide a clear direction and purpose, answering the question of what needs to be achieved.

Key Results: Key Results are specific, measurable outcomes that indicate progress toward achieving the objectives. They are used to track and measure the success of the objectives. Key

Results are typically quantifiable and time-bound, providing a clear indication of whether the desired outcomes have been achieved.

OKRs are designed to be ambitious yet attainable, encouraging teams to strive for significant results while maintaining a realistic approach. They promote transparency, alignment, and accountability within an Agile organization by setting clear expectations and fostering collaboration across teams.

OKRs are typically set and reviewed in regular cycles, such as quarterly or biannually, allowing teams to adapt their goals based on changing circumstances and priorities. The progress on OKRs is often tracked and discussed in team meetings, ensuring that everyone is aware of the status and can collaborate effectively to achieve the desired outcomes.

Overall, OKRs in Agile provide a framework for setting meaningful goals, measuring progress, and fostering continuous improvement and alignment within an organization or team.

Key Performance Indicators (KPIs)

In Agile, KPIs stands for Key Performance Indicators. KPIs are specific metrics that are used to measure the performance and progress of a team or organization towards its goals. They provide objective data and insights into how well the team is performing and whether it is on track to achieve its desired outcomes. They represent ongoing business performance, often represented as health metrics too.

KPIs in Agile are typically tied to the strategic objectives and business goals of the organization. They focus on the most critical aspects of performance that need to be monitored to ensure success. KPIs can vary depending on the nature of the project, team, or organization, but they are generally designed to be measurable, actionable, and relevant.

Here are a few examples of KPIs commonly used in Agile:

1. **Velocity**: Velocity measures the rate at which an Agile team completes work and delivers value. It is typically measured by the number of user stories or story points completed within a specific time. Velocity helps the team estimate future work and track its capacity and efficiency.

2. **Cycle Time**: Cycle Time is the time it takes for a work item to move through the entire process, from start to completion. It helps identify bottlenecks and inefficiencies in the workflow and enables the team to improve its delivery cycle.

3. **Lead Time**: Lead Time measures the total time taken from when a customer request or user story is submitted to when it is completed and delivered. It provides insights into the overall responsiveness and efficiency of the team.

4. **Customer Satisfaction**: Customer Satisfaction measures the level of satisfaction or happiness of the customers or end-users with the delivered product or service. It can be measured through surveys, feedback ratings, or other customer feedback mechanisms.

5. **Defect Rate**: Defect Rate measures the number of defects or bugs found in the delivered product or software. It helps gauge the quality of the work and the effectiveness of the team's testing and quality assurance processes.

6. **Stakeholder Engagement**: Stakeholder Engagement measures the level of engagement and collaboration between the team and key stakeholders, such as customers, product owners, and other relevant parties. It ensures effective communication and alignment between the team and stakeholders.

KPIs in Agile are typically reviewed and analysed regularly to identify areas for improvement, make data-driven decisions, and take corrective actions to stay on track towards achieving the desired outcomes. They provide valuable insights into the team's performance and help drive continuous improvement and success in Agile projects and organizations.

OKRs Vs KPIs

The key difference between OKRs (Objectives and Key Results) and KPIs (Key Performance Indicators) lies in their purpose and focus within an organization or team.

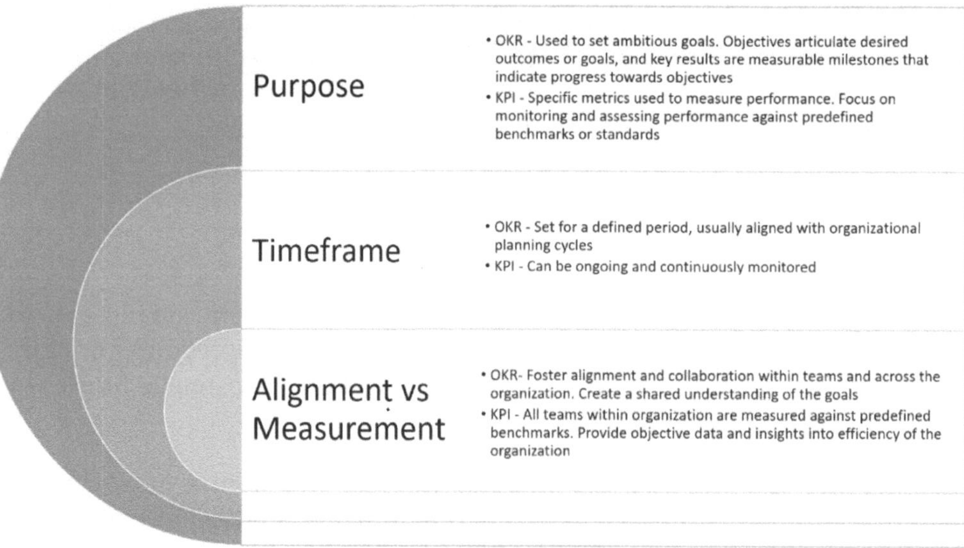

Figure 7.1: OKR's vs KPIs

While there is some overlap between OKRs and KPIs in terms of goal setting and measurement, their primary differences lie in their purpose, focus, and timeframe. OKRs provide a framework for setting and aligning goals, while KPIs provide metrics for measuring and evaluating performance. Both OKRs and KPIs can be used together to create a comprehensive approach to goal setting, measurement, and performance management within an organization or team.

To address the confusion surrounding the subject of OKRs and KPIs in the industry, the following key solutions can be implemented:

- **Clear Communication**: Ensure clear and consistent communication about the purpose, implementation, and use of OKRs and KPIs within the organization. Establish guidelines and documentation that explain how OKRs and KPIs are defined, set, tracked, and measured. Transparent communication will help clarify expectations and reduce misunderstandings.
- **Contextualize and Tailor**: Understand that OKRs and KPIs may differ in their application across different teams, projects, or departments within the organization. Encourage teams to contextualize and tailor these frameworks to their specific needs while aligning with overall organizational objectives. This flexibility will help address specific challenges and enhance understanding.

By implementing these key solutions, organizations can minimize confusion surrounding OKRs and KPIs, ensuring that teams and individuals understand their purpose, how to effectively use them, and how they contribute to achieving organizational goals.

Structuring Missions for Enhanced Agility Assessment

This section emphasizes the significance of structuring missions that align with enterprise agility dimensions, as well as the use of well-defined objectives and key results (OKRs) to assess performance and identify areas of focus. This also emphasizes the importance of clear prioritization and maintaining focus to align with the organization's vision.

To enhance the clarity of assessing the performance of each dimension and identifying areas of focus, the portfolio should be structured into missions that align with the enterprise agility dimensions, including Business Agility, People Agility, and Technical Agility. Each mission should have well-defined objectives and key results (OKRs). This approach enables a comprehensive evaluation of the strengths and weaknesses of each dimension, facilitating strategic decision-making on where to prioritize efforts.

- Business Agility Mission
- People Agility Mission
- Technical Agility Mission

To maintain focus and align with the organization's vision, it is essential to prioritize the key results for each mission objective. Avoid creating an extensive list of objectives and key results, as it can lead to confusion and derailment. Instead, aim for clarity by identifying the most important objectives and their corresponding top two to three results. This approach ensures a concentrated effort on the crucial outcomes that contribute to the organization's vision.

Below is an objective and its corresponding top two to three key results for each mission:

Business Agility: If "Time to Market" is an objective in the context of OKRs (Objectives and Key Results), here are three potential key results that could align with this objective:

Mission	Objective	Key Results
Business Agility	Improve Time to Market	Reduce product development cycle time by 20% in next 2 quarters
		Increase speed of feature delivery by 10% per quarter
		Time to market accuracy to be >85%

Table 7.1: Objectives and Key Results

1. Reduce product development cycle time: Measure the average time it takes to develop and launch new products or features. The key result could be to decrease this cycle time by a certain percentage or to achieve a specific target timeframe.
2. Increase speed of feature delivery: Measure the frequency and efficiency of delivering new features to customers. The key result could be to increase the number of feature releases per quarter or to reduce the average time it takes to deliver a new feature from ideation to deployment.
3. Improve time-to-market accuracy: Measure the ability to accurately predict and meet project deadlines. The key result could be to reduce the variance between estimated and actual delivery dates, ensuring that projects are completed within the projected timelines.

These key results focus on enhancing the organization's ability to bring products or features to market quickly, efficiently, and within the expected timeframes.

People Agility: If "Embed an Agile philosophy across the business functions" is an objective in the context of OKRs, here are three potential key results that could align with this objective:

Mission	Objective	Key Results
People Agility	Embed an Agile philosophy across the business functions	Increase Agile adoption rate by 20% in 70% of the targeted business functions
		Improve cross-functional collaboration by 30% in the first 2 quarters
		Agile training sessions and required badges/ certifications are acquired by 70% of the teams

Table 7.2: People Agility

1. Increase Agile adoption rate: Measure the extent to which Agile practices are being adopted across the business functions. The key result could be to achieve a certain percentage of teams or departments that have fully embraced Agile methodologies and are actively practicing them in their work processes.
2. Improve cross-functional collaboration: Measure the effectiveness of collaboration between different business functions in adopting Agile principles. The key result could be to increase the number of cross-functional initiatives or projects where teams from various departments work together using Agile practices, fostering a culture of collaboration.
3. Enhance Agile training and education: Measure the level of knowledge and understanding of Agile principles among employees. The key result could be to conduct Agile training sessions for a certain percentage of employees, ensuring that they have the necessary skills and knowledge to implement Agile practices in their respective roles.

These key results focus on promoting the adoption and integration of Agile principles throughout the organization. By achieving these key results, the organization can effectively embed an Agile philosophy across its business functions, fostering collaboration, flexibility, and continuous improvement.

Technical Agility: If "DevOps enablement" is an objective in the context of OKRs, here are three potential key results that could align with this objective:

Mission	Objective	Key Results
Technical Agility	DevOps usage across the business functions	Increase deployment frequency by 40% in the first 2 quarters
		MTTR to be improved by 30% in the first quarter
		Collaboration between development and operations teams improved by 50% in the first quarter

Table 7.3: Technical Agility

1. Increase deployment frequency: Measure the frequency of software deployments or releases. The key result could be to achieve a certain number of deployments per day, week, or month, indicating the successful enablement of DevOps practices that support continuous integration and continuous delivery (CI/CD).
2. Reduce mean time to resolution (MTTR): Measure the average time it takes to resolve incidents or issues that arise during the software development and deployment process. The key result could be to decrease the MTTR by a certain percentage, indicating improved efficiency in identifying and resolving problems, leading to faster recovery and reduced downtime.
3. Enhance collaboration between development and operations teams: Measure the level of collaboration and alignment between development and operations teams. The key result could be to implement cross-functional initiatives or practices that foster closer collaboration, such as shared tools, joint planning sessions, or regular communication channels, leading to better integration of development and operations activities.

These key results focus on enabling the principles of DevOps, which include frequent deployments, faster incident resolution, and enhanced collaboration between development and operations teams. By achieving these key results, the organization can effectively enable and leverage DevOps practices to improve software delivery speed, reliability, and overall efficiency.

Effective Self-Assessment Approach

Agile is a people focused approach. A successful agile transformation depends on the quality of team members and collaboration amongst them. Self-Assessments not only help in identifying right new team members but they also help in identifying improvement areas for existing team members

Effective Self-Assessment Approach for Key Roles in Agile Programs: Driving Growth and Continuous Improvement

To drive growth and continuous improvement in Agile programs, it is essential to conduct effective Agile assessments for key roles within the organization. While assessments are commonly conducted at the team level, it is equally important to assess key roles individually to identify areas for improvement and ensure alignment with Agile principles and practices. Therefore, it is crucial for the key roles to undergo self-assessments and collaborate with others to obtain a 360-degree feedback perspective. Engaging with an Agile Coach during this process is of utmost importance to receive the correct guidance, mentoring, and coaching support.

The key roles that should undergo these assessments include the Agile Leader, Scrum Master or Iteration Manager, Product Manager, Product Owner, and Scrum team

Here's an approach to conduct self-assessments for the key roles in an Agile program:

1. **Define Assessment Criteria**: Start by defining clear assessment criteria for each key role. These criteria should align with Agile principles, best practices, and the specific responsibilities of each role. For example, criteria for the Scrum Master could include facilitation skills, team empowerment, and adherence to Scrum processes.
2. **Gather Feedback**: Encourage everyone in the key roles to gather feedback from their peers, team members, stakeholders, and other relevant parties. This can be done through surveys, one-on-one discussions, or group feedback sessions. The feedback should be honest, constructive, and focused on areas of improvement.
3. **Self-Assessment**: Ask each person in the key roles to conduct a self-assessment against the defined criteria. They should evaluate their own performance and compare it with the feedback received. This reflection will help them identify strengths, weaknesses, and areas for growth.
4. **Identify Improvement Areas**: Based on the self-assessment and feedback, identify specific improvement areas for each key role. These areas could be related to skills, knowledge, behaviours, or collaboration with others. It's essential to prioritize the improvement areas to focus on the most critical aspects first.
5. **Engage Agile Coach or Mentor**: The individuals in the key roles should collaborate with an Agile Coach or mentor to discuss their self-assessment results and improvement areas. The Agile Coach can provide guidance, offer insights, and suggest appropriate strategies for development. They can also assist in creating action plans to address the identified improvement areas.
6. **Create Development Plans**: Each person should create a personalized development plan based on the improvement areas identified. The plan should include specific goals, action steps, and timelines for improvement. It's crucial to ensure that the goals are realistic, measurable, and achievable within a reasonable timeframe.
7. **Continuous Learning and Growth**: Encourage continuous learning and growth by providing resources, training opportunities, and support to the individuals in the key roles. Regular check-ins, coaching sessions, and feedback loops can help track progress and adjust the development plans as needed.

For example, the Agile Leader's assessment criteria may include factors such as commitment to Agile principles, empowerment of teams, and the ability to remove organizational barriers. The Scrum Master or Iteration Manager may be assessed on their facilitation skills, team empowerment, and adherence to Scrum processes. The Product Manager and Product Owner may be evaluated on their ability to engage stakeholders, prioritize work, and drive value delivery. The Scrum team's assessment may focus on collaboration, self-organization, and continuous improvement.

By conducting these assessments and collaborating with Agile Coaches or mentors, individuals in key roles can identify their strengths, weaknesses, and areas for development. They can then create personalized development plans, receive guidance and support, and drive continuous improvement within their roles.

The Agile Transformation Index

To operationalize the Agile Maturity Index and measure the progress of an Agile transformation, organizations can structure their assessments around various dimensions. Some common dimensions include Agile Leadership, Agile Mindset and Culture, Agile Practices and Processes, Team Empowerment, Stakeholder Engagement, Continuous Learning and Improvement, Organizational Structure and Support, and Agile metrics and business outcomes.

Within each dimension, organizations can define specific criteria or indicators for evaluation. The Transformation Index typically consists of several dimensions or categories that are assessed.

Here are some common dimensions that organizations may include in their assessment:

1. **Agile Leadership**: Assesses the commitment and support of leaders in embracing agile principles and creating an agile culture throughout the organization. It evaluates their understanding of agile values, their ability to empower teams, and their role in removing organizational barriers.
2. **Agile Mindset and Culture**: Focuses on assessing the organization's mindset and cultural alignment with agile principles. It looks at factors such as trust, collaboration, experimentation, and the willingness to embrace change.
3. **Agile Practices and Processes**: Evaluates the implementation and effectiveness of agile practices and processes, such as Scrum or Kanban, within teams. It assesses the adoption of agile ceremonies, iterative development, continuous integration, and delivery practices.
4. **Team Empowerment**: Assesses the level of autonomy and empowerment given to agile teams. It looks at factors such as team composition, decision-making authority, self-organization, and support for continuous learning and improvement.
5. **Stakeholder Engagement**: Evaluates the organization's ability to engage and involve stakeholders effectively in the agile transformation. It assesses communication channels, feedback loops, and the involvement of stakeholders in planning and prioritization.
6. **Continuous Learning and Improvement**: Focuses on the organization's commitment to learning and adapting. It evaluates practices such as retrospectives, knowledge sharing, and the ability to incorporate feedback into future iterations.
7. **Organizational Structure and Support**: Assesses the alignment of the organizational structure, roles, and support functions with agile principles. It looks at factors such as cross-functional teams, role definitions, and the level of support provided by HR, finance, and other departments.
8. **Agile metrics and business outcomes**: Measuring the impact of Agile transformations is essential. This dimension focuses on assessing the organization's ability to define and track

relevant Agile metrics, such as cycle time, customer satisfaction, and team velocity. It also evaluates the alignment of Agile practices with business outcomes, such as increased innovation, faster time-to-market, and improved customer value.

These dimensions can be further broken down into specific criteria or indicators that provide more granular insights into the organization's agile transformation progress. Each dimension and criteria can be scored on a scale or ranked based on the maturity level achieved.

The Transformation Index assessment can be conducted periodically at different stages of the agile transformation journey to track progress and identify areas for improvement. The results of the assessment can guide the organization in prioritizing actions, allocating resources, and adjusting strategies to ensure a successful agile transformation

Here are a few examples of how the assessment can be conducted for each dimension of the Transformation Index for Agile Transformations:

1. **Agile Leadership**:
   - Assess the level of executive sponsorship and active involvement in agile initiatives.
   - Evaluate the extent to which leaders promote and exhibit agile values and behaviors.
   - Measure leaders' understanding of agile principles and their ability to articulate the benefits of agile.
2. **Agile Mindset and Culture**:
   - Conduct surveys or interviews to gauge employees' perception of the organization's culture and its alignment with agile values.
   - Assess the level of psychological safety within teams and the organization.
   - Evaluate the organization's openness to experimentation and willingness to embrace change.
3. **Agile Practices and Processes**:
   - Review the adoption and consistency of agile frameworks (e.g., Scrum, Kanban) across teams.
   - Evaluate the effectiveness of agile ceremonies (e.g., daily stand-ups, sprint reviews) and the adherence to agile artifacts (e.g., product backlogs, user stories).
   - Assess the organization's use of metrics and feedback loops to drive

continuous improvement.

4. **Team Empowerment**:
    - Evaluate the level of autonomy granted to agile teams in decision-making and problem-solving.
    - Assess the composition of cross-functional teams and their ability to self-organize.
    - Measure the availability of resources and support for teams to learn and acquire new skills.
5. **Stakeholder Engagement**:
    - Assess the frequency and effectiveness of communication channels between teams and stakeholders.
    - Evaluate the involvement of stakeholders in the prioritization of work and the ability to provide timely feedback.
    - Measure the level of collaboration and trust between teams and stakeholders.
6. **Continuous Learning and Improvement**:
    - Review the regularity and effectiveness of retrospective meetings within teams.
    - Assess the organization's mechanisms for sharing knowledge and best practices across teams.
    - Evaluate the organization's ability to incorporate feedback and adjust strategies based on lessons learned.
7. **Organizational Structure and Support**:
    - Evaluate the alignment of roles and responsibilities with agile principles, such as having product owners and Scrum Masters.
    - Assess the availability and effectiveness of support functions, such as HR and finance, in enabling agile teams.
    - Review the level of cross-functional collaboration and the presence of silos within the organization.

In addition to the dimensions mentioned earlier, it is highly advisable to conduct an Emotional Intelligence assessment for all the key roles involved in Agile Transformation. For further information and a more comprehensive understanding, please refer to **`Chapter 5 Unlocking Agile Success: The Crucial Role of Leader’s EI.`**

By conducting assessments periodically at different stages of the Agile transformation journey, organizations can track their progress, identify areas for improvement, and adjust strategies accordingly. The results of these assessments provide valuable insights for prioritizing actions, allocating resources, and ensuring a successful Agile transformation.

Agile Transformation Stages: A Journey Towards Agility

Agile transformations typically progress through various stages, each representing a different level of maturity and adoption of Agile principles and practices. While the specific stages may vary, a common representation includes Emerging, Adapting, Evolving, Accelerating, and Transforming.

1. **Emerging**: The stage where organizations become aware of the need for change and start exploring Agile concepts.
2. **Adapting**: Organizations begin to embrace Agile principles and practices, experimenting with small-scale implementations and learning from the results.
3. **Evolving**: Agile practices become more ingrained within the organization, and teams start to see significant improvements in productivity and collaboration.
4. **Accelerating**: The organization experiences a boost in efficiency and effectiveness as Agile practices are scaled across multiple teams and departments.
5. **Transforming**: Agile becomes the new norm, deeply ingrained in the organization’s culture and processes, leading to continuous improvement and innovation.

These titles aim to capture the progression and evolution that occurs during an Agile transformation journey.

Here are some alternative representations for stages of life connected with Agile Transformation:

1. **Sprouting**: Symbolizing the initial growth and curiosity as organizations explore Agile principles.
2. **Unfolding**: Reflecting the gradual adoption of Agile practices and the discovery of their benefits.
3. **Fostering**: Highlighting the nurturing and development of Agile teams and processes, fostering a culture of collaboration and adaptability.
4. **Galloping**: Signifying the rapid progress and momentum gained as Agile practices are scaled across the organization.
5. **Soaring**: Representing the organization’s ability to achieve high levels of agility, innovation, and continuous improvement.

These alternative representations offer a more imaginative and metaphorical approach to conveying the stages of an Agile transformation, encouraging a fresh perspective on the journey.

Instead of investing excessive time in fretting over the labels assigned to different stages of transformation, it is more productive to shift your attention towards what you are measuring and how you are assessing progress within each category.

Below is an example of how you can incorporate the inputs and tailor them to your Agile transformation or coach's guidance. This will help you establish an assessment index to measure your progress against the planned objectives at each stage of your transformation journey.

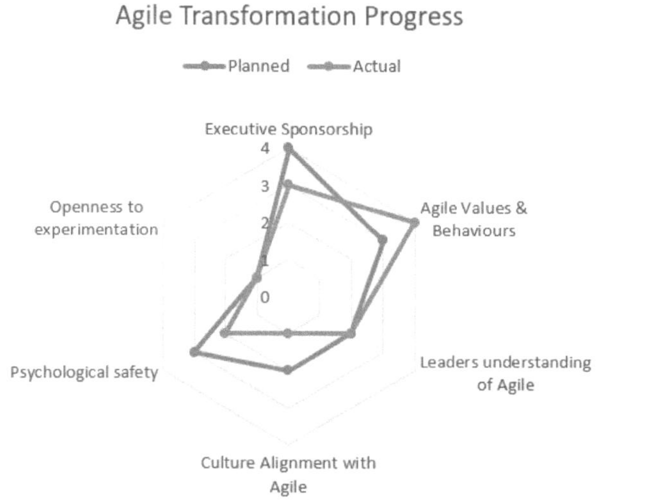

Figure 7.2: Agile Transformation progress tracking

To represent in nice pictorial form, spider graphs it's recommended to give a rating scale for each of stages like `Emerging =1`, `Adapting =2`, `Evolving =3`, `Accelerating =4`, `Transforming =5`

These stages provide a framework for organizations to understand their progress and set expectations during the Agile transformation journey.

Acceptance Criteria for Effective Agile Assessments

To ensure the effectiveness of Agile assessments, organizations should establish clear acceptance criteria. These criteria provide guidelines for conducting assessments and help organizations derive meaningful insights.

Some key acceptance criteria include:

- **Coverage**: The assessment should cover all essential aspects of Agile methodology, including principles, values, practices, and frameworks.

- **Contextual Relevance**: The assessment should be tailored to the specific organization or team, considering industry, size, maturity level, and existing Agile practices.
- **Clear Objectives**: The assessment should have well-defined objectives, such as identifying strengths, weaknesses, and improvement areas, and providing actionable recommendations.
- **Comprehensive Evaluation**: The assessment should evaluate various dimensions of Agile, including team collaboration, customer collaboration, product quality, adaptability to change, continuous improvement, and delivery effectiveness.
- **Quantifiable Metrics**: The assessment should utilize quantifiable metrics whenever possible, enabling objective measurement of Agile practices and progress over time.
- **Inclusive Participation**: The assessment should involve participation from all relevant stakeholders, including Agile team members, product owners, Scrum Masters, and other key roles.
- **Validated Tools and Techniques**: The assessment should employ validated tools, techniques, and questionnaires recognized within the Agile community for accurate insights.
- **Benchmarking Capability**: The assessment should provide benchmarks or comparisons against industry best practices, allowing organizations to gauge their performance relative to peers or established standards.
- **Actionable Recommendations**: The assessment should provide clear and actionable recommendations for improvement, outlining specific steps or initiatives to address identified gaps or challenges.
- **Continuous Improvement**: The assessment process itself should be iterative and adaptive, incorporating feedback from stakeholders and allowing for continuous improvement of the assessment framework and approach.
- **Supportive Documentation**: The assessment should provide comprehensive documentation of the findings, including detailed analysis, visualizations, and summary reports, facilitating effective communication and understanding of the assessment results.
- **Education and Training**: The assessment should be seen as an opportunity for learning and growth, with provisions for providing education and training to address knowledge gaps and build Agile competency within the organization.

By adhering to these acceptance criteria, organizations can ensure that their Agile assessments are meaningful, relevant, and effective in driving continuous improvement and success.

Conclusion

The Agile Maturity Index is a powerful tool that enables organizations to measure their progress and maturity in Agile transformations. By focusing on what truly matters, selecting relevant metrics, and conducting effective assessments, organizations can drive growth, collaboration, and continuous improvement. The Agile Maturity Index, along with the differentiation between OKRs and KPIs, provides a comprehensive framework for setting goals, measuring performance, and achieving success in Agile transformations. As organizations progress through various stages of their Agile journeys, they can leverage the Agile Maturity Index to track their progress, identify improvement areas, and ensure a successful transformation towards agility.

Test your understanding

Test your knowledge from the chapter by answering the following questions:

Q.1. What is Agile Maturity Index and what is its significance in measuring the success of organizational transformations?

Q.2. What is the importance of measuring what truly matters and selecting relevant metrics in Agile transformations?

Q.3. What is the difference between OKRs and KPIs in Agile and their respective roles in goal setting and performance measurement?

Q.4. How do I conduct effective Agile assessments for key roles in Agile programs?

Q.5. How do I engage in self-assessment and collaborate with Agile coaches or mentors to drive growth and continuous improvement?

Q.6. What are the acceptance criteria of effective agile assessment?

Chapter 8

Navigating Industry Level Agile Transformation Challenges & Unlocking Solutions

John McEnroe is considered one of the greatest tennis players of all time. He is the only male player to hold No 1 ranking in both singles and doubles simultaneously. He has the highest men's combined total of singles and doubles titles. He has a career record of 81.7%. He is also notorious for his temper on the court. He always had heated exchanges with umpires, officials, ballboys. He was fined numerous times and even suspended sometimes for these outbursts on the court.

Serena Williams is also considered one of the greatest tennis players of all time. She has 23 Grand slam singles titles and four Olympic gold medals. She has a career record of 84.6%. She has a very aggressive game. She is also known for her Power Serve. When she is in competition mode, her every waking hour is mapped out for training, nutrition and rest.

Even though he is a great player and inspiration to many, McEnroe is often quoted as a classic example for Fixed Mindset. He believed in innate talent only. He thought practicing techniques was a sign of weakness. He blamed others like umpires or officials for his mistakes. He could have achieved greater heights if he had introspected more and worked on his technique rather than blaming others.

Serena on the other hand exhibits Growth mindset behaviours. Initially she was overshadowed by her older sister Venus Williams. But she kept refining her technique and eventually she won more grand slams than her sister. She is ready to learn new things. She definitely has innate talent but also works on her strength building, flexibility, tennis techniques, nutrition so that she can excel at her game while keeping injuries to minimum.

From these examples it is clear that mindset plays a crucial role in the success of an individual. The mindset of the leader will also play a crucial role in the success of any Agile transformation. Having a growth mindset will make the leader open to learn new things, step out of their comfort zone. Since they don't blame others for their failures, they are more likely to mobilize support of others in their initiatives. Growth mindset is necessary for having agile mindset. Agile mindset is one of the critical tools for any successful agile transformation. While both mindsets encourage continuous improvement and learning, the Agile mindset is more closely associated with specific methodologies and practices used in software development. In this chapter we are going to explore more such tools and how they will help us overcome industry level challenges to successful agile transformation.

The objectives of this chapter are to explore important industry level challenges in agile transformations:

- Challenges due to cultural resistance to change and how to overcome them.
- Challenges due to knowledge and skills deficit and how to surmount them.
- Challenges due to hierarchical organization structure and how to overcome them.
- Challenges due to involvement of multiple vendors on varied contract types in delivery of a project or program and agile tools to overcome them.
- Challenges in maintaining legacy systems and how to reduce the technical debt accumulated.

Challenges in Agile transformations at organizational level

General IT industry level challenges as mentioned in the 16th state of agile report - The survey shows that culture, leadership, and consistency are three key challenges to successful Agile adoption in an organization.

Adopting agile at organization level requires complete transformation. Transformation in the way people think (Agile Mindset), transformation in the way people work (Agile ways of working) and transformation in the tools that people use. In this chapter we will have a closer look at major challenges faced by organizations while undergoing agile transformations and how to overcome them.

Cultural resistance to change

Change is the only constant in life but all of us resist change. Why do we resist change? Even though we have made tremendous technological progress in last few centuries our brains have not kept pace with it. Essentially, we have prehistoric brains wired to detect threats in all situations. Our brain also tries to reduce its workload by finding patterns and having a templatized responses to the common situations. If we are changing the way we work or tools we use, then our brain is not able to find an existing pattern to match with these new changes. It has to assess the situation, check if there are any threats to survival, assimilate the new way. This is extra load on the brain, which it tries to resist.

Younger organizations (startups) don't have much set patterns and hence are usually more forthcoming in embracing change. The older the organization, the more it can be set in its patterns and may exhibit more resistance to change. We can say that some organizations have a very rigid culture and exhibit more resistance to change while others are more open to change. How do we tackle the cultural resistance to change challenge?

Embracing Change: Strategies to Overcome resistance

Cultural resistance to change can be tackled by cultural transformation of the organization. A few of the techniques to achieve cultural transformation are as follows:

- **Addressing resistance to change** – To discuss the need for transformation with the team, you can ask them how they think we can achieve business agility, rather than telling them what changes are required. The team will be more willing to embrace change if they come up with the idea that we need to change themselves. We can deal with the opposition to change more easily if we understand what causes it. The root cause of resistance to change is fear. Fear of unknown, Fear of losing power, Fear of losing control. If the root cause is eliminated, then it will be easier to embrace change. We can eliminate fear of unknown by providing a transformation roadmap which highlights the major milestones and the path leading to those. Fear of losing power can be eliminated by empowering teams. Empowering teams does not mean less power for the management. It means daily, tactical decisions are decentralised to the teams so that they can take quick, right actions. Strategic decisions are still in control of the top management. Fear of losing control can be eliminated by monitoring and tracking with metrics that matter. Transforming to agile does not mean that the teams are completely unmonitored. It is about establishing business-oriented metrics like Objectives and Key Results OKRs. These are discussed in detail in Chapter 7.
- **Encouraging Growth mindset and embracing transparency** – To thrive after embracing change is to embrace growth mindset and transparency. Leaders not only need to adopt growth mindset but also need to encourage it within their teams. Leaders & their teams are not afraid to take calculated risks and they aren't afraid of failure. Leaders are transparent. Both these factors help to keep team morale high thus ensuring highly productive teams. Refer to Chapter 6 for more details on Growth mindset.
- **Establishing a culture of continuous learning and improvement** – One of the key aspects of growth mindset is continuous improvement. Continuous improvement can be achieved by taking constructive feedback and learning from the mistakes. If one adopts continuous learning & improvement whole heartedly then retrospectives for process improvement become second nature them and system demos are welcomed by everyone as a means for product improvement.

Knowledge & Skills Deficit

Leaders and the teams may embrace the change of transformations, but knowledge and skills deficit may hinder a successful transformation. Agile adopted with half-baked knowledge becomes fragile and is more dangerous than not following agile completely.

Addressing challenges of knowledge & skill deficit

Following techniques when used in combination can help in reducing the knowledge & skill deficit.

1. **Identifying knowledge gaps and skill deficiencies -** Socrates said, "I am the wisest man alive, for I know one thing, and that is that I know nothing." Awareness of one's own knowledge & skills deficit is the first step in diminishing the shortfall. Leaders can use multiple assessments to identify the gaps. Various assessments are discussed in `Chapter 7` in detail.

2. **Providing comprehensive Agile training programs** – There are three different ways of working (WoW) followed by an individual/team while transforming into Agile champions.

    a. **Labelling Champions** – These follow the traditional waterfall methodology but just give designations/titles like Scrum Master, Product Owner to the team members.

    b. **Process Champions** – These implement agile tools and ceremonies but not in spirit. They are just "Doing Agile" instead of "Being Agile". For example, they conduct retrospective regularly, but it becomes a blaming session instead of process improvement session.

    c. **Empowered Champions** – They are truly transformed into agile mindset. They practice "Being Agile" all the time.

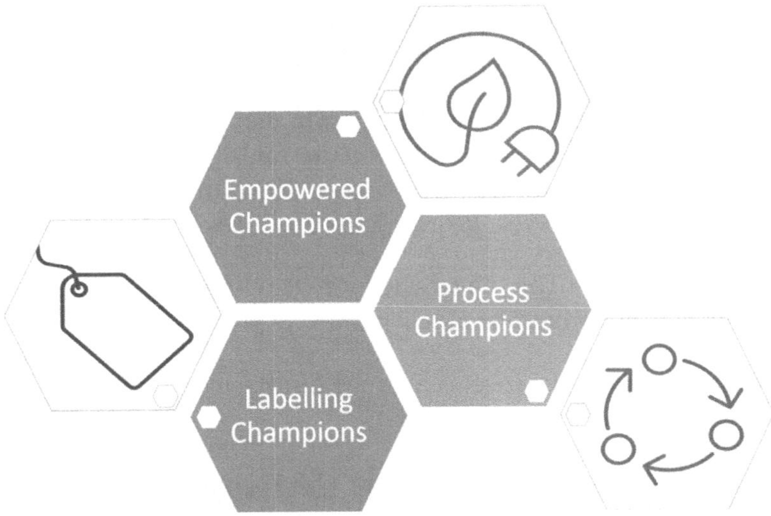

Figure 8.1: Different Ways of Working in Agile transformation for Individuals/teams

Each team/individual may follow a different Way of Working. It is not necessary that all teams have to follow through all the types of Ways of Working. It depends on their leader's and their own maturity with respect to Agile. Leaders must cultivate a culture and implement empowerment initiatives to transform their teams into empowered champions. Throughout this journey, they should consistently monitor and guarantee that their teams are not merely adopting labels or rigid processes, but rather progressing towards becoming agile empowered champions.

3. **Encouraging Agile certifications and continuous learning opportunities** – Einstein said, "Intellectual growth should commence at birth and cease only at death". One should continuously seek opportunities to learn. Certifications provide a structure to the learning as well as validate an individual's knowledge. Leaders should encourage certifications as a learning and growth opportunity. Apart from certifications there can be other learning opportunities like trainings, seminars, hands on shadow/stretch assignments. Self-experience is much better than bookish knowledge. Hands on assignments can help transforming the mindset to agile instead of just doing agile.

Hierarchical Organization Structure

Major challenge of a hierarchical structure is obstacles in communication. The bigger the hierarchy the less clear the communication. Hierarchical structure will create following problems in communication.

Communication Distortion - This is the Chinese whispers challenge. The message given by leadership gets completely distorted by the time it reaches the ground level workforce.

Communication barriers – All the information may not percolate down till the ground level workforce. Hierarchical structures also mean multiple departments working in silos. Separate departments may have separate jargons which may make it hard for them to communicate amongst themselves. Working in silos leads to very little collaboration.

Communication delays – The bigger the hierarchy the longer it takes a message from top management to reach the ground level workforce.

Lack of clear & quick communication is a major hindrance to quick decision making.

Managing Hierarchical Organisation structure challenges

Hierarchical Structure challenges and the communication and decision-making challenges induced by it can be solved by using following techniques:

1. **Dual Operating System –** Dual Operating system was first proposed by John Kotter. It helps bigger & older organizations to maintain stability for existing products while also providing agility for innovations with new products. It consists of functional hierarchy and a development value stream network.

    a. A functional hierarchy is the traditional grouping of people by functions like HR, Marketing etc. It is responsible for day-to-day operations of the business. Hierarchy is predictable and reliable. It reduces variability.

    b. A development value stream network is dynamic structure organised around value streams. Value stream is a sequence of activities that deliver value to the customer. Network is constantly evolving, innovative/experimental. It exploits variability for innovations.

    c. The advantage and disadvantage of using this model are as follows.

        i. **Advantage** - It allows organizations to innovate strategically without compromising on operational excellence. It helps them balance running of current business and creating future business.

        ii. **Disadvantage** - Using this model may lead to tension between the two systems. It will also increase the complexity of managing and coordinating the two systems.

    d. Organizations can choose based on their current situation whether to use dual operating system or not and what will be the proportion of network and hierarchy.

2. **Transitioning to cross-functional teams** – The organizations can be flattened to reduce hierarchy. Also building cross functional teams with representatives from different departments can help break down the silos and increase collaboration.

3. **Empowering self-organizing teams and decentralizing decision-making** – Teams need to pull work from the backlog instead of leaders pushing the work to the team. This makes teams more accountable for the work committed by them. The tactical decisions need to be delegated to the teams so that there no bottlenecks in their day-to-day functioning. An empowered Product owner can guide teams with business context so that they prioritize based on business needs.

4. **Redefining roles and responsibilities to align with Agile principles** – In traditional projects we have roles like

    a. **Project Manager** – Is responsible for managing scope, schedule, budget, risk, and quality along with leading and supporting the team.

    b. **Business Analyst** - Is responsible for eliciting and analysing requirements.

    c. **Designer** – Is responsible for providing optimum solutions for business problems.

    d. **Developer** – Is responsible for implementing solutions provided by the designer.

    e. **Tester** – Is responsible for validating implementation with the help of automation or manual scripts.

    Whereas Agile frameworks like Scrum define only three roles to make team cross-functional and improve on collaboration

    a. **Product Owner** – Is responsible for communicating the product vision and goals, and maximizing the value delivered by the team by prioritising the product backlog.

    b. **Scrum Master** – Is responsible for facilitating ceremonies, coaching the team, removing impediments, ensuring collaboration within the team. They help the team become accountable for their performance and find the way of working that suits their context best. They share this accountability with the team to achieve better outcomes sooner, safer, and with a happier team.

    c. **Developer** – Is responsible for designing, developing, testing, and delivering a potentially shippable product increment at the end of each iteration.

For IT services organisation there may be need for roles like Agile Project Manager, Staffing support team, Finance management team etc. As per the complexity, context the team should choose roles that can add more value to the team and client.

5. **Implementing communication channels** – Covid has paved way for remote working. One can no longer expect the whole team to be co-located. But one positive aspect of covid is, it has given lot of tools for remote collaboration. Leaders can use the appropriate tools like organization wide messenger (Teams, Slack etc) for everybody to have access to others in the organization. They can use tools like MURAL to facilitate sessions like Quarterly Business/Big Room planning, Requirements Workshops where large number of participants need to collaborate in real time. Tools like Trello can be used for daily meetings like standups.

Melting Pot of Vendors & Contract types

IT Outsourcing is a common practice in the modern world, and it is beneficial for companies that are not specialized in IT. They can concentrate on their core competencies, i.e., their business, and let the experts handle the rest. In a typical scenario, a non-IT industry client will have multiple vendors providing different services like build services, testing services, integration services, Project Management services etc. Each vendor may be on different type of contracts like Fixed Price, Time & Material, Capacity model, Staff Aug etc. The teams will be distributed across multiple delivery centers. All these factors are counter-intuitive to agile spirit of “One Team”. They increase the complexity of implementing agile for such projects exponentially. To better comprehend the difficulties, let us examine some of the main types of contracts for service organizations in more detail.

1. **Fixed Price Contract** – In this type of contract, budget, scope and time are fixed. Usually, the vendor organization (IT Services) will agree to deliver a certain scope in certain time at certain price. As depicted in Figure 8.2, the earlier the project is completed the greater will be the profit for the vendor. The longer the project is delayed the lesser will be the profit for the vendor. In this model there is strong governance from the vendor as they need to complete on time and within budget to make profit. It takes longer to initiate projects with this kind of contract, as a lot of time goes into negotiating the terms. Since everything is fixed this type of contract is not very suited for Agile implementation.

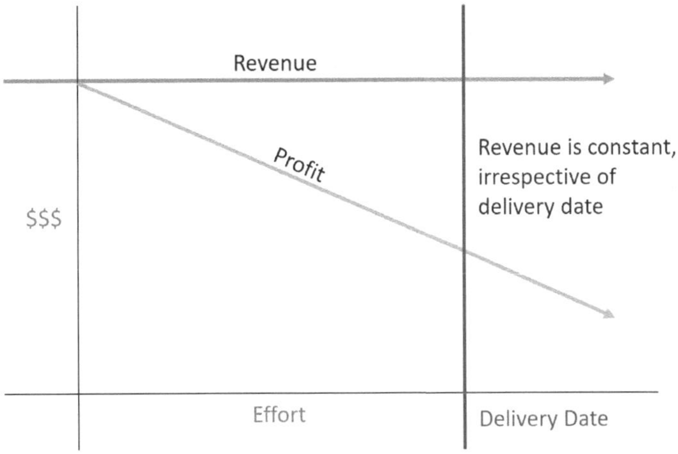

Figure 8.2: Fixed Price Contract

2. **Time & Material (T&M)** – In time & material the scope is controlled by the client. They pay agreed rate for services for a period of time and separately for materials (infrastructure) if required. From vendor organisation perspective as depicted in Figure 8.3, the revenue and profit will increase with the duration of the project. The risk is owned by customer in this type of contract. Strong governance is needed from client side to complete the project within time & budget. This type of contract is usually used for procuring services of multiple people with diverse skills. Since the scope is in control of the client this type of contract is more suited for Agile implementation. It aligns more with principles of Agile. It provides flexibility to the client to change the requirements during the duration of the project.

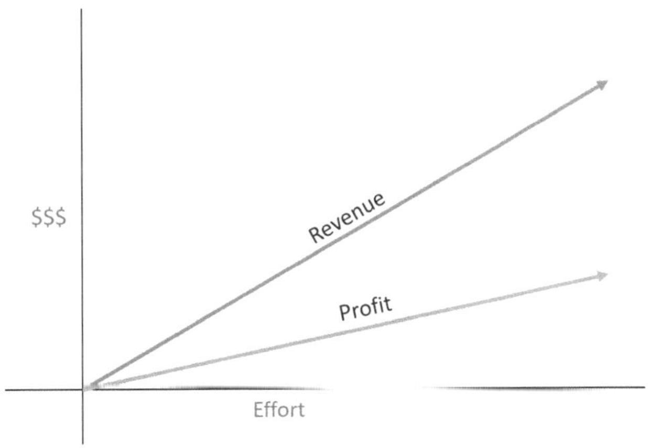

Figure 8.3: Time & Material contract

3. **Capacity Model** – This is also similar to Time & Material. In this model the vendor commits to delivering n number of person hours (capacity) within a fixed duration like six months or one year for a fixed price. The number of resources can vary. The scope is controlled by the client. The budget is capped so it reduces the risk for the client. This is also very suitable for agile implementations.

Some of the challenges based on the contract types are as follows:

1. **Slower Time to Market –**

    a. **Fixed Price -** If the frequency of releases is slower i.e., duration between releases is longer in a fixed price contract, then it increases time to market. The scope fixed at the start of the project may need to be tweaked during the duration of the project. It reduces ability of the client to react to the market dynamics.

    b. **Time & Material -** If T&M is used for implementation with static scope for longer period, then it increases a risk of delivering a product which is no longer required or which is outdated.

2. **Budget overruns** – T&M projects are more prone to project overruns.

3. **Conflicts between vendors** – It is a very likely scenario that to deliver a project the client has different vendors hired based on their areas of expertise. For example, we are undertaking house renovation as a six-month project. In this project the major work will be civil work. But we also require services of plumbers, electricians carpenter etc. The civil contractor & carpenter can be on a Fixed price contract while others can be on T&M contract. Bringing all the teams together whenever required to deliver the project is challenging.

Managing challenges of multiple vendors and contract types

The type of contract needs to be chosen based on client's situation. How volatile is the industry, how many competitors in the industry, how strong is the governance team of the client and so on.

The challenges faced because of having multiple vendors on varied contracts can be tackled using following techniques:

1. **Smaller development cycles**– If your industry requires faster time to market and you want a fixed price contract because of weak governance team then the time to market can be reduced by having contracts of shorter durations like one or three months instead of one year or three- or five-year contracts with smaller scope. If T&M contract

is used, then make sure the scope is validated at frequent intervals. In T&M one can use Agile methodologies and ceremonies like Backlog Grooming, Sprint Planning to adjust priorities according to changing market conditions and change scope for the next iteration/sprint.

2. **Goal/Outcome Focussed development** – T&M projects are more suited to agile ways of working as the client can change the direction of the project i.e., the scope is changed more frequently than a fixed price contract. But if the governance is not strong then the project can overrun the budgets set. This can be mitigated by defining sprint/iteration goals while doing planning. The team needs to meet the sprint goals so that maximum business value is delivered but scope can be reduced if required. For example, in an implementation of payment methods for a retail site the goal is to provide ability for the end consumer to pay for the products purchased. Initial scope is to implement credit cards, online banking methods. During implementation the team notices there are integration challenges with online banking implementation. They consult with the product owner, and he informs that online banking is used only by 1% of the consumers but it would be good to provide option of Cash on Delivery for those not opting for credit card. Teams agree to the change and deliver the credit cards and cash on delivery due to which Sprint goal is met for 99% of the consumers. If the team had focused on scope instead of goal, then may be only credit card would have been delivered thus meeting the goal only for 70% of the consumers. Focusing on the goal helped the team to maximise the business value delivered.

3. **Quarterly Business Planning** – Quarterly business planning tool can help resolve the issues that arise from different vendors having different contracts and ambiguity about their work schedules. Quarterly Business planning is also called as PI Planning in SAFe terminology. It is a tool which allows multiple teams to come together and plan the scope & goals for next 2-3 months. This is higher level planning than sprint/iteration planning. Teams can thrash out dependencies across teams. It helps to optimise the work planned across teams. In our house renovation project of six months, initially the majority of the work will be picked up by the civil team and other support teams can be engaged a little later. During the Quarterly Business Planning the dependencies amongst civil, plumbing & electrical work can be discussed. Each team can be given a tentative date for when their services will be required.

   Example electrical services will be required after four weeks, and plumbing services will be required after 5 weeks whereas full-fledged carpenter services will be required after 3 months but will require them for consultation during designing phase.

   Another way of handling multiple vendors, multiple contracts, is to slice the work in different way. Instead of slicing it as per competencies, it can be sliced by functional area. The end-to-end implementation for a functional area can be handled by a single vendor. So, in our house renovation project a vendor can be given a sub-project of kitchen renovation. They will be responsible for all the civil, carpentry, electrical, plumbing work etc.

Challenges & Solutions for Legacy Systems

IT systems have been around for at least fifty to sixty years. They have matured along the way. But having a legacy also comes with its own baggage. Most clients use different systems for different purposes and are developed at different points in the history. Some systems like chatbots may be 4-5 years old but some systems like core billing or transaction management of a bank can be 50 years old, while an ERP implementation may be 15 years old. There is a generation gap between the system and the technologies used to build these systems. It is difficult for these systems to talk to each other. Some of the key challenges of legacy systems are as follows.

1. **Technical debt -** Years of customisations leads to accumulation of technical debt which makes it harder to maintain, modify or migrate the system. On an average one third of a developer's time is spent in tackling technical debt, Legacy systems may not be able to fulfil current business requirements and may lead to business users using work arounds and offline processes to meet their business needs. This restricts the ability to derive insights from the work as the systems are not completely integrated.

2. **Security Risks** – Legacy systems may have vulnerabilities which may expose them to cyberattacks.

3. **Data Quality** – Legacy systems may have data quality issues like duplicate, incomplete, or inconsistent data. They may not support data formats required for analytics and digital transformation.

Managing challenges of legacy systems

Following are some of the techniques to manage legacy systems.

1. **Application modernisation** – The process of taking legacy systems modernising their platform infrastructure, internal architecture and/or features is known as Application Modernisation. This may involve movement to cloud or re-architecting the applications to take advantage of cloud features like security, reliability, scalability & performance in cost effective manner. Some examples of application modernisation are migration legacy apps to duly managed cloud services, refactoring applications to use microservices architecture, moving applications from legacy systems to virtual machines on cloud.

2. **Curtailing Technical debt** – As any debt technical debt also can be reduced and best practices can be followed. Some of the techniques to reduce and prevent

accumulation of technical debt are as follows.

a. **Refactoring Code** – Refactoring code to improve quality. Refactoring can also be used to address security vulnerabilities.

b. **Redesigning** – Current state of the application can be analysed to find suitable areas for designing. Techniques like Weighted Shortest Job First (WSJF) can be used to find the suitable area. WSJF helps to find most valuable (in terms of Business value) which can be completed in the least effort. Such areas can be redesigned to improve performance, time to market.

c. **Migration** – Migrating to a new platform or architecture that supports modern technologies like Cloud computing, DevOps.

d. **Automating Testing and deployment** – CI/CD pipeline needs to be established so that changes made can be regression tested with minimal effort and frequently released to production.

e. **Standards & Best Practices** – Leaders need to instil discipline for coding standards and best practices in the team, so that it becomes second nature to the team. It can be done by following below steps.

    i. Defining Standards & Guidelines- Work with the team to define appropriate coding standards and guidelines to be followed by the team.

    ii. Monitor compliance - Ensure these standards are implemented using tools like ReSharper, CheckStyle, CAST. Peer Review if done properly can also help maintaining good code quality. It is better than market standard tools because a person in the project has more business context and can apply business checks to the review.

    iii. Lead by Example – Reducing technical debt should be a key priority for the technical leaders right from design to implementation.

Conclusion

In this chapter we have learnt about key industry level challenges in agile transformations and solutions to overcome these. Some of the key points learnt are as follows.

1. Major challenges faced in agile transformations are.

    a. Cultural resistance to change.

    b. Knowledge and Skills Deficit

   c. Hierarchical Organization Structures
   d. Contracts & Pricing Models
   e. Legacy Systems and Technical Debt

2. Cultural resistance to change can be addressed with
   a. Addressing resistance to change
   b. Encouraging Growth mindset and embracing transparency
   c. Establishing a culture of continuous learning and improvement
3. Knowledge & skills deficit can be managed by
   a. Identifying knowledge gaps and skill deficiencies
   b. Providing comprehensive Agile training programs
   c. Encouraging Agile certifications and continuous learning opportunities
4. Challenges arising due to hierarchical organization structure are.
   a. Communication Distortion
   b. Communication barriers
   c. Communication delays
5. These challenges can be solved using following techniques.
   a. Transitioning to cross-functional teams
   b. Empowering self-organizing teams and decentralizing decision-making
   c. Redefining roles and responsibilities to align with Agile principles.
   d. Implementing communication channels
6. Typically, non-IT clients hire multiple IT services companies to deliver their projects. These vendors are on various pricing contracts. All this adds to the complexity of implementing the projects. The challenges resulting from multi-vendor multi contracts are as follows.
   a. Slower Time to Market
   b. Budget overruns
   c. Conflicts between vendors

7. These challenges can be overcome using following agile techniques.
    a. Smaller development cycles
    b. Goal/Outcome Focused development.
    c. Quarterly Business Planning
8. Legacy systems can be very hard to maintain. But at the same time, we cannot get rid of them altogether. Following are the challenges of legacy systems.
    a. Technical Debt
    b. Security Risk
    c. Data Quality
9. These challenges for legacy systems can be surmounted by using following techniques.
    a. Application Modernization
    b. Curtailing Technical Debt
        i. Refactoring Code
        ii. Redesigning
        iii. Migration
        iv. Automating Testing and deployment
        v. Standards & Best Practices

Next chapter will help the reader understanding the technology challenges in agile transformations.

- To understand the complexities associated with Agile Transformation in the context of ERP systems.
- To understand the nuances of Agile Transformation within Cloud Migration Projects
- To understand the challenges entailed in transforming legacy systems into Agile-compatible infrastructures.
- To understand the potential of Artificial Intelligence (AI) in driving transformation
- To understand the importance of empowering Agile and DevOps practices

Test your understanding

Test your knowledge from the chapter by answering the following questions:

Q.1. What are the important industry-wide challenges in agile transformations?

Q.2. How can we surmount cultural resistance to change?

Q.3. How can we address knowledge & skill deficit?

Q.4. What issues arise due to hierarchical organization structure?

Q.5. How to solve the issues faced due to hierarchical organization structure?

Q.6. What problems are faced due to having multiple vendors on varied contracts?

Q.7. How to handle multiple vendors' challenges in agile transformations?

Chapter 9

Navigating the Technology Landscape - Agile Transformation Challenges and Solutions

Businesses that begin on the Agile transformation journey encounter a slew of technological obstacles. These issues originate from a variety of organizational factors, such as legacy systems, automated testing, continuous integration, and cross-functional collaboration tools. With their rigid structures and limited testability, legacy systems frequently struggle to fit with Agile philosophy's iterative and incremental development methodology. Organizations, on the other hand, may struggle with integrating continuous integration and deployment (CI/CD) pipelines to enable frequent and dependable software releases. Furthermore, cross-functional teams may struggle to choose and integrate the correct collaboration technologies that promote seamless communication and cooperation.

Amid these hurdles, enterprises must traverse the technology landscape carefully to successfully implement Agile. This necessitates careful preparation, technical knowledge, and an Agile attitude. Solutions include gradually adopting Agile techniques, investing in automated testing frameworks, fostering collaboration and communication, and solving technical skill gaps through training and upskilling. Adopting DevOps principles can help to expedite continuous integration and deployment processes, while an emphasis on continuous improvement ensures that Agile teams inspect, adapt, and optimize their development processes.

This chapter helps to understand:

- The intricate landscape of technological challenges in Agile Transformation.
- The complexities associated with Agile Transformation in the context of ERP systems.
- The nuances of Agile Transformation within Cloud Migration Projects.
- The challenges entailed in transforming legacy systems into Agile-compatible infrastructures, this chapter explores strategies to modernize outdated technology while incorporating Agile methodologies.
- The potential of Artificial Intelligence (AI) in driving transformation.
- The importance of empowering Agile and DevOps practices in fostering a culture of continuous improvement, and efficient deployment.
- The pragmatic approaches to address the challenges of Agile Transformation, this chapter provides real-world case studies and examples.

Unplugged Agile Transformation: Empowering People, Streamlining Processes, and Leveraging Tools

To stay ahead of the competition in today's fast-paced and ever-changing business dynamics, organizations are continuously looking for methods to improve their agility, adaptability, and efficiency. Agile transformation has emerged as a potent strategy to addressing these issues, enabling firms to build a culture of creativity, collaboration, and continuous improvement. The seamless combination of three important elements: PEOPLE, PROCESS, and TOOLS is at the heart of any successful Agile transformation.

Agile transformation entails more than just a change in methodology; it also entails a fundamental shift in mindset and organizational culture. It takes a people-centric approach, encouraging teams to self-organize, collaborate, and be accountable. Individuals must be equipped with the necessary abilities, a collaborative environment must be fostered, and a growth mindset must be encouraged as part of the transformation path. Hence although this chapter intends to discuss on the technological challenges in agile transformation, let us also have a summary on the important challenges in terms of people and process.

The obstacles inherent in the "People" dimension of organizational transformation are enormous and multifaceted. Cultural resistance remains a significant barrier, as new approaches such as DevOps and Agile can disrupt established norms and habits. This resistance is frequently caused by an unwillingness to embrace change, which leads to pushback against new techniques. Another major difficulty is the occurrence of skill gaps, as the rapid growth of technology necessitates ongoing learning and adaptability. To overcome this barrier, strong training initiatives and a culture of skill development are required. Furthermore, a lack of leadership support might stymie development, as top-level management alignment is critical for successful change. Furthermore, organizational silos, in which departments operate independently, might impede collaboration and communication, contradicting the collaborative spirit of DevOps and Agile. To address these people-centric difficulties, a holistic approach is required that includes change management methods, continual education, leadership advocacy, and attempts to break down silos, all of which contribute to a smoother and more effective transformation path.

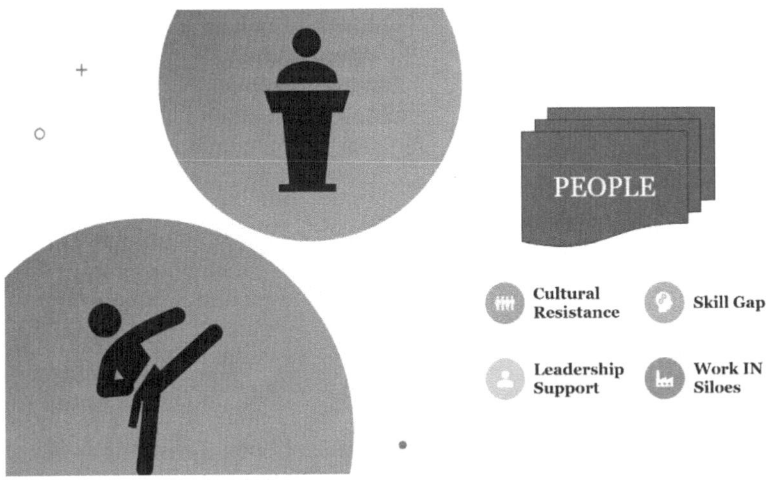

Figure 9.1: Challenges in People

Similarly, there are critical obstacles that organization face in the field of PROCESS transformation. Process rigidity is a substantial barrier to overcome, as existing workflows and procedures might be difficult to change. This tight framework might stymie the flexibility and adaptability that Agile transformation aims to foster. Furthermore, imperfect transformations constitute a critical problem. Adopting Agile concepts necessitates a thorough revamp of processes, from strategy to execution. However, if certain elements of the organization adhere to old techniques while others embrace Agile, it can result in disconnected efforts and a lack of synchronization. To overcome these process-related issues, a holistic approach is required that tackles not just the transformation of individual processes but also the interconnection and coherence of the entire operational framework. This requires cultivating an adaptable culture, extensive training, and an unrelenting commitment to fully embrace Agile principles throughout all aspects of the firm.

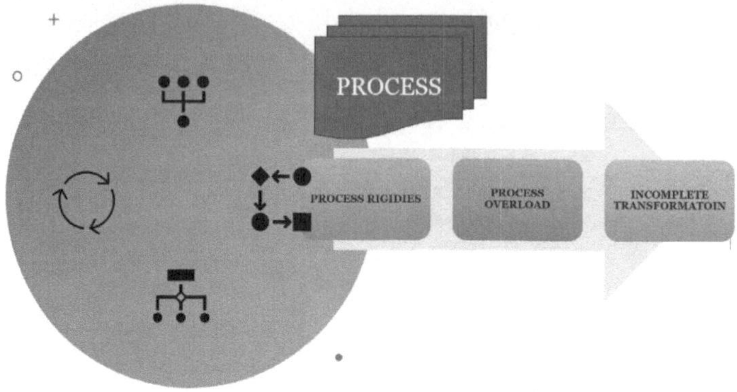

Figure 9.2: Challenges in Process

Just like in the areas of people and process, there are several significant obstacles emerge in the landscape of tool-related problems during Agile transformation. To begin, the version control process can be challenging to pick and install the proper version control system. Inadequate version control can result in code conflicts, lost changes, and hampered team cooperation. Collaboration platforms are also a difficulty since providing seamless communication and information sharing among scattered teams necessitates careful platform selection and implementation. Furthermore, integrating and efficiently utilizing test automation tools can be difficult. While these technologies improve efficiency, their successful use necessitates addressing compatibility concerns and teaching team members on how to utilize them. Furthermore, for Agile success, having a well-structured Continuous Integration/Continuous Deployment (CI/CD) pipeline is critical. Selecting appropriate tools and meticulously building the pipeline to expedite code integration, testing, and deployment is required. To properly support the organization's Agile transformation path, rigorous study, training, clear communication, and a continuing commitment to refining and enhancing the toolset are required.

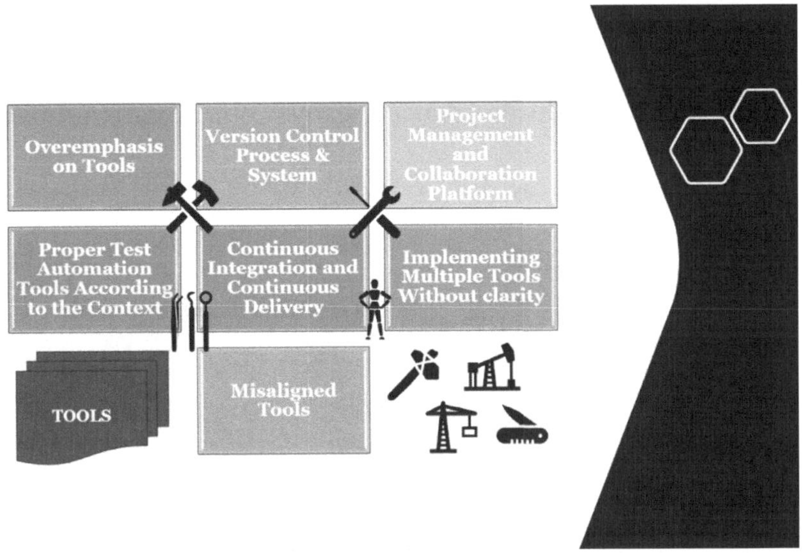

Figure 9.3: Challenges in Tools

Technology Challenges & Solutions in Agile Transformation

We live in a `VUCA` environment, where changes in culture, economy, technology, and entire business models affect us all in faster cycles than ever before. Concisely, learning the "balancing act between stability and agility" is essential. The details about VUCA are already mentioned in Chapter `6`, section "`The Agile Advantage: Harnessing Change for Maximum Value Delivery`".

Agile transformation presents several technological hurdles. These obstacles can impede an organization's capacity to fully reap the benefits of Agile methodology and hamper the smooth transformation to Agile practices. Among the primary technological hurdles in Agile implementation are:

ERP Systems

Although enterprise resource planning (ERP) solutions are an essential component for most large businesses, ERP changes are time-consuming and difficult. Although an agile strategy has the potential to significantly streamline ERP projects, it has long been assumed that agile is incompatible with ERP. However, experience in assisting numerous firms in adopting agile methods across a wide range of contexts has proven the opposite: agile can be successfully applied to ERP programs, with quantifiably better results. The methodology merely needs to be tailored to the specific needs of these complicated solutions.

Despite its importance, three-fourths of ERP transformation projects fail to meet their deadlines or budgets, and two-thirds have a negative return on investment. There are five major causes behind this.

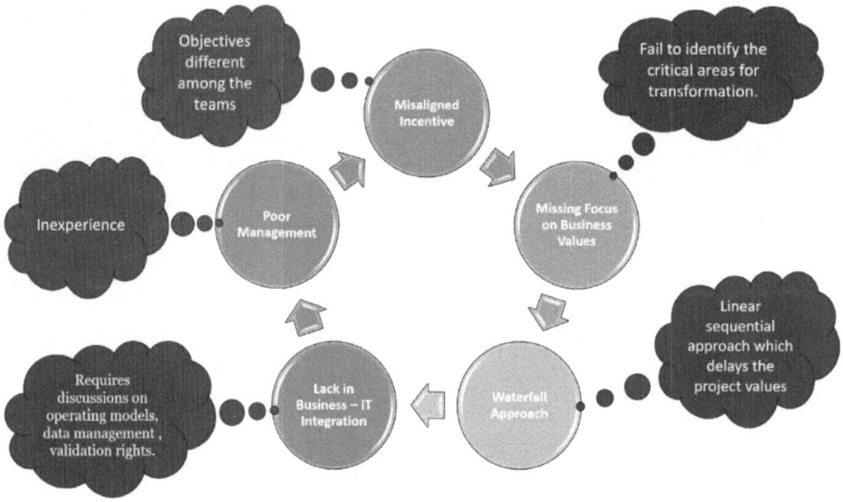

Figure 9.4: ERP Transformation Failures

Myth

The idea that agile methodology cannot be used in implementing ERP solutions is not true. The first thought that comes to our mind is any such implementation is too large and hence unmanageable by small agile teams. The main reason behind this is that we always have a mindset which makes us think that tightly coupled, complex ERP requirements cannot be simplified into user stories which can fit within the sprint timebox.

Agile approaches can significantly reduce the risks and issues that afflict traditional ERP systems in a variety of ways. Agile encourages system integrators and vendors to collaborate as a single team. All the stakeholders, team members, vendors, system integrators agreed on a common set of Key Performance Indicators (KPIs) and objectives.

It entails a faster speed and better openness, making timely, essential decisions easier for management. Contrary to common assumption, agile does not imply "no planning"; rather, agile replaces long, oblique project phases with two- to three-week sprints that allow management to track outcomes, progress, and difficulties.

Furthermore, agile assists in reducing the functional scope of ERP to a smaller set of features that small teams can provide in sprints. This iterative strategy enables projects to swiftly realize business benefit.

In short, agile approaches are exactly what ERP implementations require. It's no surprise that prominent ERP suppliers are supporting a more agile strategy.

Agile ERP Evolution: Merging Flexibility and Efficiency

Some agile practices can be directly applied to ERP implementations without adaptation: forming small, end-to-end, cross-functional agile teams with dedicated product owners from the business and end users; working in short cycles of two to three weeks to produce working software (or configurations, interfaces, etc.) incrementally; adopting scrum-based ceremonies focusing on continuous improvement, with transparency facilitated by the ceremonies and KPIs; and using tools and technologies—such as test automation and continuous integration—that optimize and accelerate the delivery process.

The customer or the product owner must define a whole scope of the project at a higher level for the projects in ERP. On the other hand, Agile promotes the approach of minimum viable product (MVP). But in this case, an overall scope is present, and team adapts and reflects in smaller iterations considering the priority and the detail scope.

Furthermore, to maintain consistent development, team needs to do more work on the business process and define architecture than in a Non-ERP agile implementation, so that the work can be divided among small teams.

Detail plan for shorter iterations needs to be done along with a having a clear whole scope which states the success criteria.

Strong links are required between agile teams supplying functions and "transversal" teams, which are nonfunctional teams that support the functional or feature teams, such as the data-migration team, the integration team, or the change team. All teams should be synced so that they work in the same rhythm and arrive at the same time.

A traditional ERP installation consists of four stages: defining an ERP strategy and road map, establishing the program, implementing, and deploying.

- **ERP Strategy & Roadmap**: Creating an ERP strategy and road map yields a target architecture with high-level principles as well as a business case for implementing the new solution. This stage is mostly unaltered; however, it can be sped up by performing a high-level fit-gap analysis rather than endless blueprinting, and by working iteratively in sprints to avoid a too thorough business case.
- **Setting Up:** Setting up the program changes significantly under an agile method; it is much faster, partly because teams are empowered to swiftly address real-world problems rather than participating in theoretical design. This stage entails rapidly selecting a partner with experience with the solution and agile—rather than engaging in a lengthy request-for-proposal process to find a supplier and negotiate a fixed-priced contract; developing a high-level, macro-feature road map based on a list of identified improvements that is detailed enough to determine the size and form of

the agile organization required to deliver the program; and staffing and training the organization in agile.

- **Implementation:** An agile approach to solution execution differs significantly. Implementation occurs in waves to collect value as quickly as possible. Functional delivery teams leverage most typical scrum procedures. Cross functional team from business and IT, including system integrator complete the design, development and system testing within the sprint timebox. E2E testing and user-acceptance testing (UAT) are performed on a frequent basis, rather than only once at the conclusion of development, resulting in greater code quality and continued test automation.

- **Deployment:** Although deployments are more frequent, and agile approaches can aid in the reduction of bottlenecks, the solution is mostly deployed in the traditional manner. Following the agile philosophy, delivering values quickly to the customer can help in mitigating deployment risks at the earliest possible stage. Analytics helps to optimize the process involving the training of the number of primary users who needs to be trained. Hence the local templates can be established early by onboarding local users. Because of the ongoing emphasis on quality, a shorter hyper care phase can be planned. Because releases in an agile strategy are more frequent, there is more opportunity to industrialize all processes in the deployment.

Planning releases every two weeks may not be realistic or practicable in many ERP projects since system complexity and interdependence are generally greater than in custom applications. However, by modifying the release planning process, Agile principles can still be used to them.

Here are some aspects to think about while planning releases in ERP projects:

Understand the Release Cycle: When incorporating agile practices into the environments, it is critical to understand the release cycle. Most of the ERPs follows a distinct release cycle that includes regular updates, patches, and service packs. To achieve a smooth transformation, Agile release planning must be coordinated with the same release cycle.

Break Down User Stories: Because of the inherent complexity of modules and processes, breaking down user stories is very important in Agile ERP projects. Rather than simply sticking to overall user stories, it is necessary to break them down into individual, doable activities. This method enables accurate estimating, precise planning, and rigorous progress tracking, all within the confines of a set iteration time.

Prioritize Features and Modules: Due to the interdependencies inherent in modules and features, prioritization emerges as a critical aspect inside ERP projects. The collaborative process of aligning with stakeholders is critical since it aids in determining the essential and value-laden items that will be included in each release. This strategic prioritization goes beyond feature value to include dependencies, significant business effect, and a comprehensive project plan.

Coordinate Integration and Testing: The ERP projects' numerous linkages demand rigorous integration and regression testing. An effective plan includes assigning allocated time for these critical operations inside each iteration. This purposeful planning ensures the system's post-release reliability and functionality, mitigating any disruptions. Agile teams that embrace this strategy create a harmonious synergy between integration and testing, matching them with iterative cycles. As a result, the system is resilient and reliable, reflecting the smooth confluence of Agile concepts with the intricate demands of ERP projects.

Release Staging: The concept of staged releases becomes more prominent in the context of Agile ERP projects. This technique advocates for a phased deployment strategy, in which certain modules or features are provided in stages rather than all at once. This methodical process allows for greater control, rigorous testing, and seamless user assimilation.

Continuous Deployment: The concept of continuous deployment is an exciting route in the context of Agile ERP projects. While the release cycle may differ from that of custom apps, there is the possibility of imbuing the process with automation, continuous integration, and continuous deployment approaches. Agile teams can accomplish a streamlined release process that eliminates manual intervention, maximizes efficiency, and adheres to Agile principles by using this approach.

Adapting Agile practices to the ERP projects demands a unique release planning methodology. The structure of the company, the complexities of the project, and the preferences of stakeholders all play a role in determining the strategy. Agile teams build a culture of adaptive refinement by continuously evaluating and improving the release planning methodology through the lens of feedback and experiences, ensuring that the process remains responsive to the project's evolving needs and difficulties.

Cloud Migration Project

Agile transformation in the context of a cloud migration project involves a set of sophisticated technical problems that must be overcome for the transformation to be effective. Disparities in architecture, dependencies, and data formats can make compatibility between legacy systems and cloud settings difficult. Data migration necessitates solutions for maintaining data integrity, minimizing downtime, and streamlining the transfer. To achieve interoperability, integrating traditional applications with cloud-native services necessitates thorough preparation. Scaling and enhancing performance in dynamic cloud systems necessitate extensive testing and tuning. Security and compliance modifications are critical to maintaining a secure cloud posture.

Creating a Target Operating Model (TOM) that incorporates the best practices for cloud migration projects with a focus on Agile transformations is crucial for ensuring that organizations can effectively deliver value through this approach. Here's are guidelines on how few of the best practices can fit into a TOM:

1. **Governance and Leadership:**
    - Define clear governance structures and roles within your TOM. Assign responsibility for overseeing cloud migration and Agile transformation

efforts. Establish an executive sponsor or steering committee to provide direction and support.

2. **Teams and Skillsets:**
   - Define the teams required for the project, including cloud migration teams, Agile development teams, and cross-functional teams. Specify the necessary skillsets and roles within these teams in alignment with your Agile practices.
3. **Processes and Workflows:**
   - Develop and document Agile processes and workflows that integrate with cloud migration activities. These processes should outline how Agile principles are applied to cloud migration tasks, including backlog management, sprint planning, and continuous integration.
4. **Tools and Technology:**
   - Select and implement the necessary tools and technologies to support Agile practices and cloud migration. This includes Agile project management tools, CI/CD pipelines, IaC tools, cloud management platforms, and monitoring solutions.
5. **Communication and Collaboration:**
   - Define communication channels and collaboration tools that facilitate cross-functional teamwork. Ensure that teams can easily share information, updates, and feedback to maintain transparency and alignment.
6. **Metrics and KPIs:**
   - Establish key performance indicators (KPIs) and metrics that measure the success of both the cloud migration and Agile transformation efforts. These metrics should align with your project objectives and overall business goals.
7. **Risk Management and Compliance:**
   - Develop risk management and compliance frameworks that address both cloud security and Agile governance. Specify how risks will be identified, assessed, and mitigated throughout the project lifecycle.
8. **Training and Development:**
   - Include training and skill development plans within your TOM to ensure that team members acquire the necessary knowledge and expertise in Agile and cloud technologies. Consider providing ongoing training opportunities.

9. **Change Management:**

    - Integrate change management practices into your TOM to facilitate a smooth transition to Agile and cloud-centric operations. Develop change management plans that address the cultural shifts and mindset changes required for success.

10. **Resource Management and Cost Control:**

    - Incorporate resource management and cost control practices into your TOM to ensure efficient use of cloud resources. Specify how budgets and resource allocations will be managed, monitored, and optimized.

11. **Documentation and Knowledge Sharing:**

    - Include documentation standards and knowledge sharing processes in your TOM. Define where documentation will be stored, how it will be updated, and how knowledge sharing will be encouraged among team members.

12. **Continuous Improvement:**

    - Ensure that your TOM includes mechanisms for continuous improvement. Implement regular TOM reviews and updates to adapt to changing business needs, emerging technologies, and evolving best practices.

13. **Alignment with Business Strategy:**

    - Make sure that your TOM is closely aligned with your organization's overall business strategy and goals. Ensure that cloud migration and Agile transformation efforts contribute directly to strategic objectives. Business and IT alignment is critical.

14. **Feedback Loops:**

    - Integrate feedback loops within your TOM to gather input from stakeholders, teams, and customers. Use this feedback to make ongoing adjustments and improvements to your cloud and Agile initiatives.

15. **Scalability and Flexibility:**

    - Design your TOM to be scalable and flexible, allowing it to adapt to changing project requirements and organizational growth. Ensure that it can accommodate both smaller and larger initiatives.

By incorporating these elements into your Target Operating Model, you create a structured framework that supports the successful execution of cloud migration projects with Agile transformations. This ensures that your organization can adapt to the changing landscape of technology and business while consistently delivering value to stakeholders.

When working with Cloud settings, data security is a big concern. It is one of the most difficult difficulties in cloud computing since users must accept responsibility for their data, and not all cloud providers can guarantee 100% data privacy

When sensitive data is moved to the cloud, the danger of unwanted access and data breaches grows, especially if security measures are not properly implemented. Cloud providers may store data in a variety of geographic locations, which may contradict with data residency laws and local rules. When you share cloud resources with other users, you run the risk of data leakage or exposure due to insufficient isolation protections. Unauthorized access, data tampering, or loss can all result from poorly designed access restrictions. (IAM (Identity and Access Management)). If suitable backup and recovery measures are not in place, data loss might occur due to inadvertent deletion, hardware failures, or problems during migration. Inadequate encryption and key management policies can expose sensitive data to potential breaches.

Agile principles advocate for a flexible, iterative approach to project management that stresses collaboration, adaptation, and continual improvement. Applying Agile techniques to cloud migration initiatives can assist in addressing typical issues such as adaptability, visibility, communication & collaboration and continuous improvement.

Impact of Technological Challenges on Agile Transformation and Mitigation

Project Delays: Concerns about data security and privacy might cause additional inspection, assessments, and compliance checks.

Implementation Complexity: Putting in place strong data security and privacy safeguards might complicate the transfer process.

Impact on Agility: Agile approaches place a premium on flexibility and quick iterations. However, strict security and privacy requirements may limit the rate at which modifications may be introduced, thus hindering project agility.

Change in Requirements: Addressing security and privacy concerns may necessitate additional security measures, compliance checks, or encryption procedures, affecting the scope and objectives of the project.

Mitigation Strategies

Risk Assessment: Thorough risk assessment is a critical mitigation method for dealing with complexity in cloud migration projects that are undergoing agile transformation. Organizations should proactively identify and prioritize difficulties by undertaking a full examination of potential risks, vulnerabilities, and security concerns relevant to the move.

Data Classification and Control: Data should be classified based on its sensitivity and importance to ensure that suitable security measures are implemented. Implement strong security controls that are in accordance with industry norms and legislation. Audit and evaluate compliance on a regular basis. Using robust encryption methods, encrypt data both in transit and at rest. Implement key management procedures to protect encryption keys. Use robust identity and access management (IAM) techniques to limit access to authorized users and roles. Choose a cloud provider that offers data residency alternatives that are in line with your organization's compliance needs.

Use of Multi Factor Authentication (MFA): Implement multi-factor authentication for user authentication to add an extra degree of security to access controls. Multi-factor authentication works by demanding various kinds of identification from the user during account registration. This ID and user information are saved in the system for future logins.

Leveraging Agile in Cloud Migration Projects:

- Setting Project Goal: Defining Project Goals: One of the most critical activities that leads the entire development process is the definition of project goals. It entails establishing clear and explicit objectives that explain the project's expected outcomes. Agile teams generate a shared knowledge of what needs to be accomplished by creating well-defined goals, facilitating collaboration and alignment among team members.
- Smallest unit of Work: Breaking down the work is a fundamental principle of Agile approach that entails breaking down large projects into smaller, achievable tasks or user stories. This method improves incremental development, transparency, and team member collaboration. Agile teams achieve clarity on project scope by dividing work down into smaller parts, allowing for more precise estimations, continuous progress tracking, and the flexibility to adapt to changing requirements.
- Prioritizing: Prioritizing work is a critical activity in Agile methodology that entails ranking tasks or user stories according to their importance and value to the project's objectives. Popular job prioritization techniques include multiple models. The "MoSCoW" model is one of the popular techniques which divides tasks into four categories: Must Have, Should Have, Could Have, and Won't Have.
    - Must Have: These are crucial requirements that must be met for the project to succeed.
    - Should Have: These needs are crucial, but not as critical as "Must Have." They add value to the project and increase user happiness, although they can be postponed if required.
    - Could Have: These are desired criteria that, if implemented, can bring value, but their absence would not have a substantial impact on the project's success.
    - Won't Have: These are needs that are expressly excluded from the current scope. They may be considered for future phases, but they are not part of the current project.

Agile teams can successfully prioritize work using the MoSCoW technique, ensuring that the most useful and essential features are provided first. This technique aids in scope management, adapting to changing priorities, and efficiently allocating resources while providing incremental value to stakeholders throughout the project.

- Monitoring Progress: A critical practice in Agile methodology, particularly in cloud migration projects, is progress monitoring. It entails tracking the progress of tasks and deliverables to ensure alignment with project objectives. Key metrics are critical in this process, assisting Agile teams in gauging project health and making educated decisions. Relevant important indicators in cloud migration efforts may include:
- Velocity: Velocity is a metric that gauges how quickly Agile teams execute user stories or tasks.
- Lead Time and Cycle Time: Lead time is the time it takes to complete a task, whereas cycle time is the time spent actively working on the activity.
- Burnup and Burndown Charts: These charts show how much work has been performed (burnup) or how much work remains (burndown) over time.
- Downtime: Monitoring downtime during migration shows how seamlessly apps transfer to the cloud without major disruptions.
- Cost Variance: Comparing actual costs to budgeted expenditures provides insight into financial health and ensures optimal resource allocation.

Agile transformation in cloud migration projects entails a range of technological challenges. Addressing legacy system compatibility, ensuring data integrity and security during migration, adapting applications to cloud-native architectures, integrating diverse cloud services, optimizing performance in dynamic cloud environments, and selecting appropriate tools for efficient deployment and monitoring are among these challenges.

Legacy System Transformation:

Integrating legacy systems into an Agile transformation provides unique technological problems due to their complex architecture, old technology stack, and potential data incompatibilities. Agile necessitates a modular and adaptive strategy, which may collide with the rigidity of legacy systems.

The following are the major problems that organizations may confront during this process:

Outdated Technology Stack:

The legacy systems are mostly constructed using out-of-date programming frameworks with outdated capabilities and functionalities. The proprietary components from suppliers that were no longer supported or maintained were included in the technology stack. Integrating with modern technologies, APIs, and third-party services is difficult with the legacy stack. As newer technologies became more popular, it became increasingly difficult to find developers with knowledge in the legacy technology stack. The aging stack struggled to keep up with the increased load and performance expectations of modern applications.

Inadequate documentation and knowledge:

Since the legacy system might have lacked thorough documentation, understanding its design, components, and dependencies is always challenging.

If the employees with knowledge of the legacy system had left the organization over the years, this results in the loss of tribal knowledge. Poorly described code is difficult to understand, resulting in misunderstandings, errors, and trouble implementing modifications.

Undocumented relationships and dependencies between different components made refactoring and integrating new features difficult.

Due to a lack of documentation, new team members were unfamiliar with legacy-specific language and vocabulary.

Compatibility of data and Monolithic Architecture:

The data in the legacy system are saved in formats and structures that might be incompatible with newer database systems. Data quality concerns, inconsistencies, and redundancies accumulated within the legacy data over time. The legacy system had a considerable amount of historical data that needed to be moved without causing any disruptions to operations.

The data must be converted from the legacy format to the new format while maintaining integrity and accuracy. The new tools and technology utilized in the transformation had to integrate seamlessly with current data sources.

The data in the legacy system is stored in formats and structures that might be incompatible with newer database systems. Data quality concerns, inconsistencies, and redundancies had built within the legacy data over the years.

Quality Control and Test Data Management - Automated Testing:

The legacy system lacked adequate test coverage, making it difficult to uncover and correct flaws. Absence of adequate and realistic test data made complete testing and accurate simulation of real-world settings difficult. Manual testing techniques resulted in longer testing cycles, greater errors, and slower feedback loops. The complicated design made testing the integration of historical components with new modules and services difficult. The legacy system's architecture and lack of automation-friendly design make it difficult to conduct automated tests.

Integration of Modern Tools and Technologies:

Integrating current agile tools with the architecture, frameworks, and technology of the historical system proved problematic. To guarantee data integrity, data migration from legacy tools to new tools requires careful planning. Technical challenges rise while integrating modern tools with legacy components and databases. Members of the team had to learn and adjust to the new tools, which hampered their production throughout the transformation phase. Some current tools required to be customized to fit the organization's specific operations and requirements.

Compliance and security:

Addressing compliance and security issues during the agile transformation of a legacy system is a complicated task in the context of technology. Legacy systems frequently have antiquated security methods and may not meet modern regulatory requirements. Integrating agile principles while maintaining compliance and security requires careful consideration of data handling, storage, and access. This includes modifying the design of the legacy system to enable rigorous security measures, implementing encryption methods, and establishing access controls. Overcoming these problems necessitates a systematic approach that protects sensitive data while also ensuring that the legacy system adheres to new security practices and regulatory requirements.

Long Release Cycles:

Dealing with extended-release cycles and sporadic upgrades is a significant technology issue in the agile transformation of a legacy system. Legacy systems frequently have complex structures that make updating them time-consuming. Because these systems are monolithic, testing and validation across several interrelated components may be required, causing delays in the release of new features or bug patches. The purpose of implementing agile principles is to shorten development cycles, but the technical complexities of older systems might make this difficult. To overcome this difficulty, the monolith must be broken down into modular components, automated testing and continuous integration procedures implemented, and deployment processes modernized through containerization and microservices. Such initiatives can aid in shortening release cycle times and enabling more frequent updates, thereby aligning the legacy system with the agile principles of iterative development and value delivery.

Scalability and performance:

Addressing scalability and performance issues during the transformation of a legacy system is critical in the world of technology. Legacy systems frequently lack the natural scalability needed to meet modern expectations. As user loads increase, their monolithic architecture and older technologies might cause bottlenecks and decreased performance. Moving to agile approaches stresses iterative development and continuous delivery, which can exacerbate these issues if the system's underlying architecture is not scalable. To address this, architectural redesign, the use of microservices and containerization, and the implementation of horizontal scalability solutions are required. The legacy system can be better equipped to handle fluctuating workloads by breaking down monolithic components into independently scalable modules and optimizing database and network access patterns. This ensures optimal performance and responsiveness in the face of growing user demands.

Impact on Agile Transformation and Mitigation

Time-To-Market: The impact of Time-To-Market is an essential challenge in the agile transformation of legacy systems, which is heavily influenced by numerous technological obstacles. Outdated technology stacks, inadequate documentation, and monolithic designs impede the rapid agile transformation, causing development cycles to lengthen and new feature releases to be delayed. Data compatibility and data-related difficulties frequently lengthen the time required for data migration and validation, further delaying value delivery. Issues with quality control and a lack of automated testing limit the timely detection and resolution of errors, slowing the release process.

Mitigation: Several technical strategies can be used to alleviate the impact of longer Time-To-Market caused by these problems. Upgrading an old technology stack to a contemporary technology stack can improve development speed and agility. Investing in extensive knowledge sharing results in speedier decision-making and smoother onboarding. Converting monolithic architectures to microservices-based systems allows for incremental development and faster release cycles. Implementing automated testing, quality control, and good test data management reduces the time it takes to identify and resolve defects. To avoid integration delays, modern tool integration necessitates careful planning, adaptation, and training. Ensuring compliance and security from the outset can prevent last-minute hurdles. Time-to-Market is reduced by reducing release cycles through continuous integration and deployment processes. Finally, improving scalability and performance ensures adaptability to shifting demands. Organizations can drastically shorten Time-To-Market by meticulously tackling these obstacles.

Resistance-To-Change: Employee resistance to change is a significant barrier during the agile transformation of legacy systems, which is influenced by many technological hurdles. Employees may be hesitant to adopt new techniques due to perceived complexity caused by outdated technology stacks, limited documentation, and monolithic architectures. Data compatibility difficulties might create questions about data integrity and make staff unwilling to try new ways. Quality control issues and a lack of automated testing may raise doubts about the efficacy of agile approaches.

Mitigation: Employees adapt more confidently when comprehensive training on contemporary technologies, tools, and agile techniques is provided. Improving documentation and knowledge sharing ensures that staff have the resources they need to successfully navigate the transformation. Breaking down monolithic architectures into modular components can help with the shift. Implementing automated testing and quality control increases employees' confidence in the system's stability. Integrating current tools in a way that complements established workflows minimizes disruption and resistance. Demonstrating compliance and security procedures that are in line with industry norms builds trust. Continuous integration and deployment shorten release cycles, demonstrating actual progress and improving morale. Finally, improving scalability and performance answers concerns about the system's ability to react to change. Organizations can reduce resistance to agile methods in the context of legacy system change by addressing these obstacles with technical solutions.

Hidden Dependencies: Legacy system dependencies have a significant impact on agile transformation efforts, echoing across numerous technology problems. Undocumented dependencies in outdated technology stacks might impede the easy incorporation of new technologies. Inadequate documentation and knowledge gaps might mask critical interconnections, making it difficult to discover relationships influencing decision-making and development processes. Data compatibility concerns might worsen hidden dependencies since data interactions are not always fully understood. Monolithic designs can lead to complicated interdependencies that limit agile practices, slowing development and innovation.

Mitigation: Organizations should apply technical strategies that address the core causes of hidden dependencies to lessen their impact. Thorough architecture analysis and documentation projects aid in the discovery and documenting of hidden dependencies. Employee knowledge exchange, particularly among those familiar with the legacy system, ensures that critical information about dependencies is transmitted. The complexity of hidden interdependencies is reduced by adapting monolithic architecture into more modular solutions. To identify and address hidden dependencies that may affect quality control and test data management, rigorous testing and validation processes are required. To achieve seamless integration, modern tools should be integrated after a thorough examination of existing dependencies. Compliance and security measures must be improved with an awareness of potentially ignored hidden dependencies. Organizations can assure a smoother agile transformation and avoid disruptions caused by these covert difficulties by actively identifying and eliminating hidden dependencies through technical methods.

Inefficient Development: The impact of inefficient development because of spending too much time reading old code and understanding complicated interactions is a common issue that exacerbates a variety of technological issues during the agile transformation of legacy systems. Outdated technology stacks, limited documentation, and monolithic designs add to developers' workload, resulting in longer development cycles as they struggle to grasp ancient technologies and sophisticated code structures. Data compatibility concerns compound inefficiencies and stymie progress as developers seek to harmonize data formats and structures.

Mitigation: Organizations should implement targeted technological methods to offset the impact of inefficient development caused by these difficulties. Implementing a robust documentation effort aid in the deciphering of legacy code and makes it more understandable for developers. Knowledge sharing across the team bridges comprehension gaps, allowing developers to cooperate efficiently. Refactoring legacy code to conform to new coding techniques and architectural patterns reduces its complexity. By providing constant input, the introduction of automated testing and quality control accelerates the validation process. Adopting current development tools and methods shortens the learning curve for developers, increasing their productivity. Continuous integration and deployment strategies shorten release cycles, while code reduction and modularization aid in scalability and performance optimization. Organizations can accelerate the transformation process by addressing wasteful development with technological strategies, resulting in more efficient development cycles, and aligning with the goals of agile methodologies.

Data Structure Variation: The influence of data structure variation, which is defined by legacy data stored in formats that are incompatible with modern database systems, has a substantial impact on different technological aspects during the agile transformation of legacy systems. This dilemma exacerbates the issues of data interoperability and monolithic design. Due to conflicting data formats, incompatibility stymies the integration of new technologies and components. Monolithic designs make it difficult to update data structures to meet new demands without creating significant disturbance.

Mitigation: Organizations should use focused technical strategies to limit the impact of data structure variance. The use of data transformation and migration scripts aids in the conversion of legacy data into formats compatible with newer database systems. Modularizing monolithic architectures allows for isolated data structure changes without affecting the overall system. During the transformation, rigorous testing, and validation of changed data ensures data correctness and integrity. Integrating contemporary tools and technologies needs careful consideration of data compatibility, which necessitates essential changes throughout integration. The issues provided by data structure variation are addressed by prioritizing efficient data access patterns in scalability and performance enhancements. By tackling this issue with technical solutions, businesses can ensure a smooth data flow, allowing for the successful integration of new technologies, enhanced quality control processes, and optimized system scalability and performance in the context of agile transformation.

Agile Unleashed: Harnessing AI's Power for Transformational Success

Agile transformation can be complicated and difficult, but AI technology can assist in making them more efficient and productive. The potential of AI to automate repetitive operations, freeing up time and resources for more strategic work, is one of the key benefits of Agile transformations. Furthermore, AI can learn from data and generate intelligent predictions, assisting teams in identifying and addressing possible concerns before they become major difficulties. This contributes to the success of Agile transformations and the ability of teams to fulfill their objectives in a timely and effective manner. Advanced analytics and data visualization tools are another significant way AI is being used to assist Agile transformations. These technologies help teams better analyze their data and find trends and patterns that might help them make better decisions. Overall, the application of AI in Agile transformations is a promising trend that is assisting teams in more effectively and efficiently achieving their goals. As technology advances, we should expect to see even more creative use of AI in the Agile space.

Risk Assessment and Predictive Analysis

Using AI-powered tools has become increasingly vital in today's fast-paced world. These systems can analyze massive volumes of data and provide useful insights to project managers, allowing them to make more educated decisions. Using Machine Learning algorithms, these technologies may recognize patterns and trends in previous initiatives, allowing them to accurately forecast the outcomes of future ones. This can be quite beneficial for project managers who want to ensure that their projects are completed on time and on budget. One of the most significant benefits of employing AI-powered products is their ability to predict potential dangers and hazards before they materialize. These technologies can identify trouble areas and make recommendations on how to prevent them by evaluating data from previous projects.

This can assist project managers in making better judgments and avoiding costly errors that could jeopardize the success of their projects.

Another advantage of utilizing AI-powered technologies is that they can assist project managers in more effectively allocating resources. These tools can provide advice on optimizing resource allocation and ensuring that the proper resources are available when needed by analyzing resource usage and availability data. This can assist guarantee that projects are finished on schedule and within budget, while reducing waste and increasing efficiency. Overall, employing AI-powered tools is critical for every team who wants to ensure project success. These tools can assist project managers in making educated decisions and avoiding typical errors that might affect project timelines and costs by giving valuable insights and advice. Whether you are working in a small project or a large-scale endeavor, AI-powered solutions can assist you in meeting your objectives and completing your tasks successfully.

Automated Testing:

Agile has long been a popular software development style due to its emphasis on continual iteration and improvement. One of the most difficult difficulties that agile development teams encounter is the continuous code changes that make it tough to automate testing. Fortunately, artificial intelligence has evolved as a solution to this problem. It is now possible to automate the entire process of test creation, execution, and analysis using AI. This saves time while also ensuring that the tests are always current and relevant. By managing the time-consuming and laborious work of testing, development teams may focus on activities that provide value to the project, such as building new features or upgrading current ones.

AI-powered testing has the potential to improve software quality by enabling for more extensive testing. Traditional testing methods may overlook some edge cases or scenarios, but AI can detect and address these flaws before the product is published. Overall, AI-powered testing is a game changer for agile development teams. It enables them to operate more effectively, increase the quality of their software, and ultimately provide better products to their customers.

Effective Collaboration

AI-powered testing has the potential to improve software quality by enabling for more extensive testing. Traditional testing methods may overlook some edge cases or scenarios, but AI can detect and address these flaws before the product is published. Overall, AI-powered testing is a game changer for agile development teams. It enables them to operate more effectively, increase the quality of their software, and ultimately provide better products to their customers. AI-powered testing has the potential to improve software quality by enabling for more extensive testing. Traditional testing methods may overlook some edge cases or scenarios, but AI can detect and address these flaws before the product is published. Overall, AI-powered testing is a game changer for agile development teams. It enables them to operate more effectively, increase the quality of their software, and ultimately provide better products to their customers.

Backlog Refinement

When it comes to Agile transformation, task management and prioritization are critical to success. This is where AI-powered algorithms come in handy, as they can help determine the time and effort required for certain jobs. As a result, teams may better prioritize their task and minimize the backlog, resulting in a more effective Agile transformation process. This enables teams to focus on the most vital work at the appropriate moment, freeing up resources and increasing production. Agile teams can use AI algorithms to streamline their operations and achieve their goals more quickly and efficiently.

Integrating AI and Agile is a game changer for firms trying to increase the predictability, efficiency, and adaptability of their Agile transformations. This exciting collaboration is just getting started, and as AI technologies evolve, we should expect to see even more growth and improvement in the future. AI has enormous potential for use in Agile transformations, and it will become more sophisticated and integrated into the process over time.

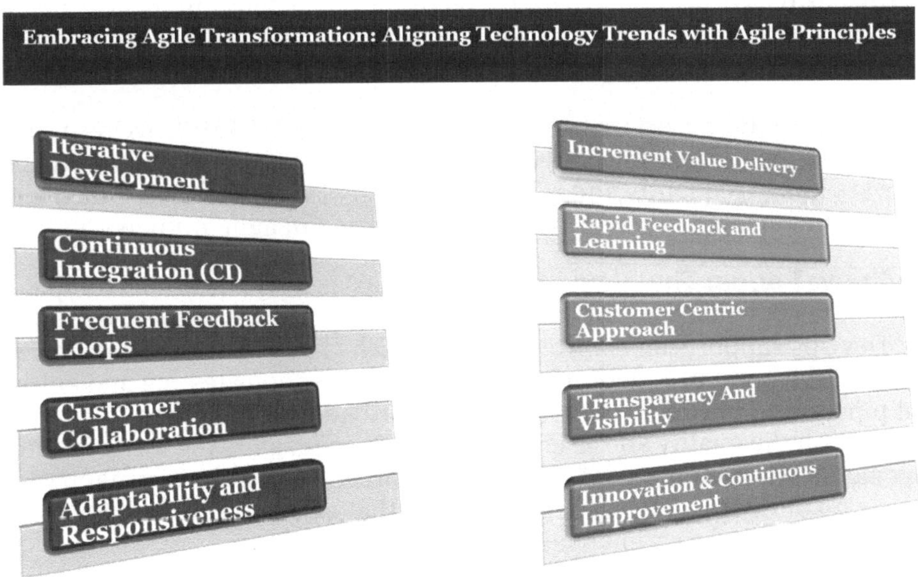

Figure 9.5: Aligning Technological Trends

Accelerating Agility: Empowering Agile and DevOps

DevOps is critical to the success of Agile transformations because it bridges the gap between development and operations teams and fosters a culture of cooperation, automation, and continuous improvement.

Product development and IT operations are linked through a set of practices known as "DevOps" to enable faster and more consistent product delivery. To expedite the software development process, DevOps encourages collaboration and communication between development and operations teams to speed up the software development process. DevOps is based on a set of fundamental concepts, which include:

- Communication and collaboration between the development and operational teams.
- Making as much of the software delivery process as automated as feasible.
- Continuous testing and monitoring are emphasized to swiftly discover and resolve issues.
- Promoting a culture of constant improvement.
- Ensuring that security and compliance are incorporated into the software delivery process.
- DevOps is often seen as a natural extension of Agile, focusing on delivering software rapidly and efficiently while maintaining high levels of quality and reliability.

The following are the primary ways in which DevOps aids Agile transformations:

Collaboration and Communication: Collaboration and communication are important aspects of DevOps because they stress cross-functional collaboration and communication between development, operations, and other stakeholders.

Continuous Integration and Continuous Delivery (CI/CD): DevOps processes automate the development, testing, and deployment of code updates. Agile teams can provide software more frequently and reliably by using CI/CD pipelines, which aligns with the iterative and incremental delivery approach suggested in agile frameworks.

Rapid Feedback Loops: The "Rapid Feedback Loop" is a significant technique in driving Agile transformations, with a special emphasis on automating testing and deployment procedures. DevOps supports an environment in which changes may be quickly assessed, validated, and pushed into production by integrating continuous testing and automated deployment pipelines. This iterative feedback loop provides development teams with immediate input on the quality and usefulness of their code, allowing for quick adjustments and enhancements. The automated nature of these processes minimizes manual errors even further, speeds up development cycles, and assures that each iteration adheres to Agile principles of flexibility and customer value.

Time-to-Market: DevOps approaches, such as automated deployment and continuous delivery, are critical in shortening the time it takes for features to go from development to production. These approaches are perfectly aligned with Agile principles, which emphasize providing valuable products to clients in a timely and efficient manner. Development teams may quickly move new features and updates through various phases of testing and integration by automating the deployment process and developing a continuous delivery pipeline, reducing manual intervention and associated delays.

Infrastructure as Code ("IaC"): Infrastructure as Code (IaC), a key principle that fundamentally improves the productivity and dependability of development operations, is at the heart of DevOps. DevOps promotes the use of IaC, which allows teams to architect, deploy, and maintain infrastructure using code-based configurations. This technique provides Agile teams with an effective means for quickly provisioning and maintaining environments while ensuring consistency throughout multiple stages of development and deployment. Manual errors are reduced, and repeatability is accomplished by treating infrastructure as code, which aligns perfectly with Agile mindset's emphasis on consistent, predictable, and iterative processes.

Fail-Fast Culture: DevOps fosters a fail-fast culture that is firmly aligned with Agile principles of continuous improvement. This culture encourages teams to try new things and see failure as a great learning opportunity. Teams may iterate and improve their processes, products, and services by quickly detecting and addressing concerns. This approach is consistent with Agile's emphasis on inspecting, adapting, and cultivating a mindset of continuous growth and refinement. The fostering of a fail-fast culture by DevOps not only reduces the fear of failure but also stimulates creativity by empowering teams to take calculated risks and explore creative solutions.

Lean Thinking: A strategic alignment exists at the intersection of DevOps and Lean thinking, emphasizing the push for efficiency and value in the software development process. By focusing on waste reduction, avoiding needless handoffs, and optimizing workflow, DevOps principles mimic the key pillars of Lean thinking. This convergence is especially significant in Agile techniques, which emphasize the timely and efficient delivery of value to clients. Teams improve their capacity to respond to changing client needs, iterate quickly, and consistently provide high-quality solutions by decreasing inefficiencies, bottlenecks, and delays using DevOps methods. This seamless combination of DevOps and Lean thinking expands on Agile's way of thinking, enabling organizations to maximize productivity, responsiveness, and, ultimately, the value they deliver to their clients.

Continuous Monitoring and Feedback: DevOps approaches involve continuous monitoring of in-production applications and infrastructure. This feedback loop enables Agile teams to gain insights from real-world usage and make data-driven decisions.

Organizations may lay a solid basis for DevOps practices that support and enhance the Agile transformation by addressing these essential issues. A well-integrated DevOps approach enables Agile teams to produce software more quickly, with higher quality, and with more customer satisfaction, eventually boosting the overall success of the Agile transformation process.

Empowering Transformation with Cutting-Edge Tools and Technologies

To support Agile principles and enable efficient collaboration and delivery, Agile transformations necessitate a variety of tools, software, and technology.

These tools address a wide range of Agile development topics, including as project management, version control, continuous integration and delivery, automated testing, and collaboration. Let's take a closer look at several crucial tools, Agile-specific software, and technology that help in Agile transformations:

Project Management and Issue Tracking Tools: The tracking tools provide a single platform for tracking tasks, user stories, problems, and project progress in general. They are critical in fostering collaboration, managing work items, and guaranteeing transparency across Agile teams. Here's a quick rundown of these tools and their importance in Agile and Agile transformation:

Jira:

- Jira is one of the most popular tools used for Agile projects for tracking applications. It supports several Agile techniques, including Scrum and Kanban.
- Jira is used by agile teams to develop and manage user stories, organize tasks, for relative estimations and prioritization of work items. The progress of the sprint or iterations can be tracked.
- Jira includes boards (Scrum and Kanban), backlogs, and reports that enable real-time visibility into work status and aid with backlog prioritizing and sprint planning.

Azure DevOps (formerly Visual Studio Team Services or VSTS):

- Azure DevOps is a comprehensive DevOps platform with project management, version control, build automation, testing, and release management capabilities.
- It smoothly interfaces with common version control systems like as Git and TFVC, making it ideal for Agile development and Continuous Integration (CI)/Continuous Delivery (CD).

Digital.ai (Formerly VersionOne):

- Digital.ai is a dedicated Agile project management and ALM (Application Lifecycle Management) application for Agile development.
- It includes Agile-specific capabilities such as backlog management, sprint planning, release tracking, and reporting.
- Digital.ai provides an in-depth view of team progress, sprint burndown, velocity, and other Agile metrics, allowing for data-driven decision-making.

Trello:

- Trello is a popular visual project management solution that organizes tasks and projects using boards, lists, and cards.

- Trello allows Agile teams to construct boards for various projects or initiatives, with cards representing user stories, tasks, or features.
- It has a simple drag-and-drop interface that allows teams to easily edit and manage their work items in a visually pleasing manner.

Version Control Systems – Assisting Agile or Agile Transformation: VCSs (Version Control Systems) are essential tools in Agile and Agile transformation processes. They let teams to manage and track source code changes, collaborate efficiently, and ensure code integrity throughout the development lifecycle. VCS is important in supporting Agile ideals such as collaboration, transparency, and gradual development. Here are some of the most widely used Version Control Systems in Agile and Agile transformation:

Git:

- In Agile, Git is one of the most extensively used distributed version control systems. It enables teams to collaborate without disagreement on the same codebase, complementing Agile's emphasis on cooperation and teamwork.
- With Git, teams can build branches for features or fixes and then merge them back into the main branch (sometimes known as the "master" or "main" branch) when they are finished. This is consistent with Agile's iterative and incremental development methodology.
- Because Git is distributed, each team member has a complete copy of the repository, allowing work to continue even when the computer is turned off. This demonstrates Agile's agility and willingness to welcome change.

Mercurial:

- Mercurial, like Git, is a distributed version control system. It is less popular than Git, but for special reasons or as an alternative to Git, some teams may use it.
- Mercurial, like Git, enables teams to collaborate and manage code changes efficiently.

Continuous Integration and Continuous Delivery (CI/CD) Tools – Embracing Agile and Agile Transformation: Continuous Integration (CI) and Continuous Delivery (CD) are critical practices in Agile and Agile transformation, allowing teams to release software fast, reliably, and to a high standard. CI/CD systems automate the development, testing, and deployment processes, allowing for more frequent releases and lowering the chance of errors. A full description of the CI/CD tools used in Agile and Agile transformation follows:

Jenkins:

- Jenkins is a prominent open-source CI/CD technology that is frequently used in Agile development. It offers a versatile and expandable framework for automating the complete software delivery pipeline.
- Jenkins integrates with version control systems like as Git, Subversion, and Mercurial, allow-

ing teams to automatically trigger builds when code changes are pushed.
- It has many plugins for building, testing, and deploying applications, making it very configurable for various project needs.
- Jenkins supports parallel and distributed builds over numerous agents, reducing build times and maximizing resource use.

GitLab CI/CD:

- GitLab CI/CD is a CI/CD solution that is embedded within the GitLab version control system. It delivers a consistent and unified experience for teams that use GitLab for version control and project management.
- GitLab CI/CD defines the CI/CD pipeline steps and stages in a YAML-based configuration file called "gitlab-ci.yml", making it simple to maintain and manage the pipeline configuration alongside the codebase.
- It supports a variety of phases, such as build, test, deploy, and even custom stages, allowing teams to customize the pipeline to their individual requirements.
- GitLab CI/CD supports Docker containers, allowing teams to build and test apps in consistent and isolated environments.

Bamboo:

- Atlassian's Bamboo is an enterprise-grade CI/CD technology that is ideal for Agile transformations requiring larger teams and complex projects.
- Bamboo integrates well with other Atlassian tools such as Jira and Bitbucket, resulting in a holistic DevOps environment.
- It enables the automation of builds, tests, and deployments, allowing teams to produce software more quickly and confidently.
- Bamboo is excellent for large-scale Agile transformations due to its easy scalability and support for distributed builds.

Azure DevOps:

- Azure DevOps, originally Visual Studio Team Services (VSTS), is a Microsoft DevOps platform that incorporates version control, project management, build automation, testing, and release management.
- Azure DevOps' CI/CD capabilities enable teams to develop and manage pipelines for continuous integration, testing, and deployment.
- It interfaces effortlessly with common version control systems like as Git and TFVC, making it ideal for Agile development and continuous integration and delivery.

It is essential to note that while there are some interesting parallels, philosophy and Agile are distinct domains. Agile methodologies are practical frameworks designed for project management and software development, whereas non-dualistic philosophy is a broader and more metaphysical concept. However, exploring the connections between these perspectives can offer valuable insights into how we approach work, collaboration, and the ever-changing nature of reality.

Real Life Case Studies – Transformations Overcoming Technological Challenges

`Case Study #1`: An online streaming service that requires a subscription. This book does not reveal the original name. We can refer to it as XYZ for convenience.

Challenge: XYZ, a popular streaming provider, had technological issues throughout their Agile transformation. The company's global footprint was rapidly increasing, and they needed to increase the speed and efficiency of their development procedures.

Solution: To address these technological problems as part of their Agile transformation, XYZ used the following strategy:

Cloud-Native Architecture: XYZ took a cloud-native approach, developing their apps from the ground up to fully utilize the capabilities of cloud services. As a result, they were able to achieve high availability, fault tolerance, and scalability.

Microservices and Polyglot Architecture: They adopted microservices and employed several programming languages and technologies for various services. This strategy enabled XYZ to select the optimal tools for each assignment, encouraging creativity and adaptability.

Chaos Engineering: XYZ created a Chaos Engineering culture in which they purposefully introduced failures into their systems to test resilience and identify weaknesses. This method assisted them in developing more robust and dependable services.

Automated Testing and Deployment: XYZ has made significant investments in automated testing and deployment pipelines. This allowed them to add new features and improvements to their streaming service several times per day.

Data-Driven Decision Making: XYZ took a data-driven strategy, relying on analytics and user input to make educated product development and feature prioritization decisions.

The following are the outcomes of XYZ's technology-driven Agile transformation:

- The usage of cloud-native architecture and microservices enabled XYZ to accommodate an ever-growing user base while providing a flawless streaming experience to millions of viewers globally.
- Because of their automated testing and deployment methods, they were able to provide new features and upgrades on a regular basis.
- Chaos Engineering assisted XYZ in identifying and fixing vulnerabilities before they impacted the user experience, hence improving service reliability.
- XYZ's data-driven approach enabled them to constantly enhance their content recommendations and user interfaces, resulting in increased user engagement and customer happiness.

`Case Study #2`: While pursuing an Agile transformation, a multinational conglomerate faced technological hurdles. Their complicated technology landscape, which included numerous legacy systems, posed challenges to seamless integration and effective team collaboration. Let's call it by the name AE.

Solution: AE employed the following solutions to solve these technological issues throughout their Agile transformation:

Rationalization and standardization: AE tried to rationalize their technological environment by retiring obsolete systems and standardizing their technology stack. This expedited and simplified their development process.

Microservices Architecture: They used a microservices architecture to divide their monolithic apps into smaller, self-contained services. This gave them more flexibility and adaptability in their software development.

API-First Strategy: AE adopted an API-first strategy, allowing for better integration among multiple systems and teams. APIs served as the foundation for internal communication and data exchange.

Automation and DevOps: They invested in DevOps principles and tools to improve communication between development and operations teams. As a result, deployments were faster and more dependable.

Cloud Migration: To take advantage of cloud benefits like as scalability, cost-efficiency, and rapid provisioning, AE transferred some of their applications to cloud platforms such as AWS and Azure.

The results of AE's technology-driven Agile transformation were significant:

- The use of microservices and an API-first strategy increased the versatility and scalability of their systems, allowing for continuous delivery and deployment.
- AE generated cost savings and boosted operational efficiency by streamlining their technological environment and utilizing cloud services.
- DevOps principles and automation were implemented, which increased the speed and dependability of their software development operations.
- The technological transformation also enabled AE to develop more quickly, respond to market changes, and provide more value to their customers.

Both are real-world examples of firms that overcame technological obstacles while undergoing Agile transformations. Their dedication to updating their technological infrastructure, adopting DevOps techniques, and implementing scalable and flexible solutions enabled them to accelerate business growth, improve customer experiences, and remain competitive in their respective industries.

As technology evolves, it has a huge impact on Agile transformations. The right technology choices can significantly enhance an organization's ability to embrace Agile methodologies effectively.

Conclusion

The goal of this chapter we learnt a thorough grasp of the varied landscape of technology obstacles that organizations face on their path to Agile Transformation. The chapter delves into the fundamental ideas of Empowering People, Streamlining Processes, and Leveraging Tools as critical components in addressing these obstacles. It investigates how equipping personnel with the necessary skills and mindset, streamlining procedures to increase efficiency, and strategically deploying cutting-edge tools may all contribute to the success of Agile Transformation.

The chapter digs into specific issues that arise in the field of Enterprise Resource Planning (ERP) systems, cloud migration projects and legacy systems.

Furthermore, the chapter summarizes the transformational potential of utilizing Artificial Intelligence (AI). It explains how AI can be a catalyst for dramatic change by optimizing procedures, anticipating problems, and improving decision-making.

In next chapter we will cover the unique challenges and opportunities that arise with people at the center of Agile transformations. We will explore various aspects related to the human element in Agile, including personal growth, leadership development, communication strategies, and addressing people challenges with agility.

Test your understanding

Test your knowledge from the chapter by answering the following questions:

Q.1. What are the important challenges in terms of PEOPLE with respect to agile transformations?

Q.2. What are the important challenges in terms of TOOLs with respect to agile transformations?

Q.3. What is the full form of VUCA?

Q.4. What are the major challenges in agile transformations of ERP projects?

Q.5. In Cloud migration projects summarize the strategy for agile transformations?

Q.6. What are the major technological challenges in agile transformations of Legacy systems?

Q.7. Summarize how AI can assist in Agile Transformation.

Chapter 10

The Human Element: Navigating People Challenges and Unlocking Solutions

In this chapter we delve into the critical role that individuals play in Agile environments. While Agile methodologies have revolutionized the way we work, it is essential to recognize the unique challenges and opportunities that arise with people at the center of Agile transformations. This chapter explores various aspects related to the human element in Agile, including personal growth, leadership development, communication strategies, and addressing people challenges with agility and insight.

This chapter aims to:

- To compare traditional ways of working with Agile methodologies, highlighting the power shift that occurs in Agile environments.
- To emphasize the importance of embracing Agile thinking for personal growth, fostering a harmonious balance between the mind and intellect.
- To explore the significance of the human element in Agile and its potential to unlock individual and team success.
- To understand the impact of process, tools, and people in nurturing a culture of agility during Agile transformations.
- To highlight the role of Agile leaders as people managers and the skills required to effectively navigate people challenges in an Agile context.

- To uncover personal, team, and leadership development practices that can enhance Agile performance and promote continuous improvement.
- To provide insights and strategies for navigating the ambiguities of hybrid work, tailoring solutions to meet unique needs in an Agile environment.
- To explore the power of informal communication channels, such as the grapevine, in fostering effective Agile transformations.
- To showcase the value of Agile games as a means of boosting collaboration and facilitating learning within Agile teams.
- To introduce the concept of Gen AI and how it empowers Agile leaders to address people challenges with agility and insight.
- To highlight the importance of storytelling as a powerful tool for inspiring teams and creating a shared vision in Agile environments.
- To encourage the adoption of the values of saburi (patience) and shraddha (faith) as essential qualities for individuals undergoing Agile transformations.

Traditional vs. Agile Ways of Working: Unveiling the Power Shift

In Agile ways of working, a transformative "Power Shift" occurs, driven by self-organized and empowered teams. Although Agile trainings emphasize and expect this shift as a fundamental part of the Agile Manifesto and Principles, the reality often falls short. Traditional work methods persist, creating a disconnect that gives rise to fictional scenarios and significant challenges for individuals involved. Let's see what traditional ways of working (Wow) is and how it is different to Agile ways of working (Wow)

Traditional Wow	Agile Wow
Hierarchical structure	Value network
Top-Down Decision Making	Collaborative Decision Making
Authoritarian Leadership	Servant Leadership
Micromanagement	Adaptive and flexible leadership
Physical presence in the office	Hybrid working model
Focus on Productivity > Output	Results-oriented focus > Outcome

Figure 10.1: Traditional Vs Agile WOW

Traditional leader ways of working (Wow)

- Hierarchical structure: Clear chain of command and authority.
- Top-down decision-making: Leaders making decisions and cascading them down to subordi-

nates.

- Authoritarian leadership: Leaders exercising strict control and enforcing compliance. It's also called as Command-and-control leadership - Leaders exerting control and directing the work of their team members.
- Micromanagement: Leaders closely monitoring and controlling every aspect of their team's work.
- Physical presence in the office: Leaders being present at the workplace to oversee operations.
- Focus on efficiency and productivity: Emphasizing productivity metrics and output.

Agile Leader ways of working (Wow)

- Leaders value network i.e., Cross-functional teams: Encouraging diverse skills and expertise within teams. They often come from various hierarchical leaders.
- Collaborative decision-making: Involving team members in the decision-making process.
- Servant leadership: Leaders focus on serving and supporting their team members. Empowering teams by motivating to take decisions and take ownership of their work.
- Adaptive and flexible leadership: Adjusting leadership style based on the needs of the team and project. They are with Agile mindset embracing the values and principles of agile methodologies.
- Hybrid working model with Adaptive planning: Adjusting plans based on changing priorities and feedback. Embracing change, welcoming, and adapting to changes in requirements or circumstances.
- Results-oriented focus: Emphasizing delivering value and achieving outcomes over rigid processes or documentation.

Let's deep dive into the reasons why the shift, transformation of people into new ways of working not happening as expected.

Harmonizing Mind and Intellect: Embracing Agile Thinking for Personal Growth

Human beings possess a composite personality consisting of a physical body, mind, and intellect. The physical body enables us to perceive the world through our senses and act, while the mind serves as an emotional barometer. However, it is the interplay between the intellect and the mind that warrants our attention. Often, we allow our emotions to dominate our decision-making, neglecting the potential of our intellect. Even when we do engage our intellect, we frequently rely on established patterns and fail to adapt to the changing demands of a dynamic world. In this section, we explore the importance of balancing the mind and intellect and advocate for embracing agile thinking to foster personal growth.

Balancing the Mind and Intellect: The mind plays a crucial role in our daily lives, acting as a conduit for our emotions. It helps us experience and navigate the complex tapestry of feelings that arise within us. However, it is important to recognize that our emotions, while essential, should not govern our every decision. By developing an awareness of our emotional states, we can avoid being swayed solely by our feelings and instead make decisions that align with our long-term goals and aspirations.

Simultaneously, we must cultivate the intellect, which provides us with the ability to think critically, reason, and analyse. The intellect allows us to evaluate situations objectively, consider multiple perspectives, and make informed choices. However, relying solely on past patterns and preconceived notions limits our growth and inhibits our ability to adapt to new circumstances. Instead, we must strive for intellectual agility, constantly challenging our assumptions and embracing new ways of thinking.

Embracing Agile Thinking: Agile thinking involves adopting a flexible and adaptive mindset, ready to pivot and adjust as needed. It encourages us to question established norms and explore innovative approaches. By integrating agile thinking into our decision-making processes, we open ourselves up to fresh perspectives, ideas, and solutions. This approach enables us to break free from the constraints of old habits and adapt to the ever-changing world around us.

In the realm of personal growth, agile thinking allows us to shed the limitations imposed by our emotions and expand the horizons of our intellect. It empowers us to embrace new challenges, seek continuous learning opportunities, and remain open to diverse perspectives. Agile thinking encourages experimentation and iteration, recognizing that failure is not a setback but a steppingstone towards progress.

In our composite personality, the mind and intellect form an intricate relationship. By achieving a harmonious balance between the two, we can make decisions that are grounded in both emotional intelligence and intellectual agility. Embracing agile thinking enables us to break free from the confines of past patterns and embrace new ways of working and living. As we embark on this journey of personal growth, let us strive to nurture both our minds and intellects, forging a path that is adaptable, innovative, and fulfilling.

Now, let's reflect on our ways of working formed over period.

It's important to note that while Scientific Management principles were influential in shaping management practices, they have also been criticized for their emphasis on task specialization and the potential for dehumanizing workers. Time to reflect if we are still stuck with these principles when the situations and world got changed so much and power is shifting to knowledge people.

Scientific Management, with its focus on standardization, division of labour, and top-down control, may not align perfectly with the principles and values of Agile transformations. Agile methodologies, such as Scrum or Kanban, emphasize flexibility, collaboration, and self-organizing teams. However, certain aspects of Scientific Management can still be relevant and applicable in an Agile context. Here are a few suggestions:

1. **Time and Motion Studies**: While Agile promotes flexibility and adaptability, it's still essential to understand how work is being done and identify opportunities for

improvement. Teams can benefit from analysing their workflows and identifying bottlenecks or inefficiencies. However, rather than imposing top-down changes, Agile encourages teams to self-organize and continuously improve their processes.

2. **Scientific Selection and Training**: Agile teams should be composed of individuals with the necessary skills and abilities to deliver value. When forming Agile teams, it's crucial to consider individuals' strengths and align them with the team's objectives. Training and development should also be an ongoing process to support the growth and learning of team members.

3. **Elimination of Waste**: Agile methodologies, like Lean Agile, aim to reduce waste by focusing on delivering value and eliminating unnecessary activities or processes. The principles of Scientific Management can inform the identification and elimination of waste, but the approach should be collaborative and involve the entire Agile team.

4. **Cooperation between Workers and Managers**: Agile transformations emphasize the importance of collaboration and shared decision-making between team members and stakeholders. Managers should act as servant leaders, supporting the team and removing obstacles rather than exerting top-down control. The principles of Scientific Management can be adapted to foster cooperation and create an environment of trust and collaboration.

It is crucial to bear in mind that Agile transformations aim to foster a culture of agility, continuous learning, and adaptability. While considering the Scientific management theory, which focuses on analysing workflows to enhance economic efficiency, particularly labour productivity, it is important to note that this theory was popularized by Frederick Winslow Taylor in the 1880s and 1890s within U.S. manufacturing industries. The nature of work has evolved significantly since then, especially in today's software development practices. However, some organizations culture still adhere strictly to those principles.

While certain aspects of Scientific Management may have value, they should be applied in a manner that aligns with the Agile values and principles, rather than enforcing rigid control and standardization. It is crucial to customize each organization's Agile transformation to suit its specific context and requirements.

Lord Buddha has cautioned humanity over 2,500 years ago on the important role of reason in human life:

- Do not believe what you have heard.
- Do not believe in tradition because it is handed down many generations.
- Do not believe in anything that has been spoken of many times.
- Do not believe because the written statements come from some old age.
- Do not believe in authority or teachers or elders.

But after careful observation and analysis, when it agrees with reason and it will benefit one and all, then accept it and live by it. We discussed about Intellect, and it's plays critical role to agree with right reason that helps in right thinking and actions.

We discussed about harmonizing mind and intellect, influence of scientific management principles designed ages back and Lord Buddha's message to humanity, so let's apply reason to the needs of current ways of working that helps our Agile transformations.

The Human Element in Agile: Unlocking Potential and Fostering Success

Human element: As we strive for personal growth, it is crucial to reflect on the established ways of working and patterns that have developed over time, which often lead us to overlook the human element. Agile methodologies provide a solution by reintroducing the human element and preventing leaders and teams from becoming trapped in outdated patterns and ways of working.

The human element refers to the recognition and prioritization of the needs, emotions, and interactions of individuals within a team or organization. It emphasizes the importance of considering the unique perspectives, strengths, and limitations of people involved in any work or project.

In the context of Agile methodologies, the human element is about fostering effective communication, collaboration, and empathy among team members. It involves creating an environment where individuals feel valued, heard, and supported, allowing them to contribute their best efforts and talents.

The Human Element in Agile: Unlocking Potential and Fostering Success

By focusing on the human element, Agile approaches encourage leaders and teams to:

1. **Emphasize open and transparent communication**: Agile methodologies promote frequent and honest communication among team members, enabling them to express their ideas, concerns, and challenges. This fosters a sense of trust, collaboration, and mutual understanding.

2. **Empower individuals**: Agile encourages empowering individuals to take ownership of their work, make decisions, and contribute their unique skills and expertise. It recognizes that individuals are more motivated and engaged when they have autonomy and the opportunity to make meaningful contributions.

3. **Adapt and respond to change**: Agile methodologies prioritize flexibility and adaptability. They recognize that humans are not machines, and that unforeseen

challenges and opportunities will arise during a project. By valuing the human element, Agile teams can effectively respond to change, adjust plans, and accommodate evolving needs.

4. **Encourage continuous learning and growth**: Agile promotes a culture of learning and improvement. It encourages individuals to reflect on their experiences, seek feedback, and embrace a growth mindset. By prioritizing the human element, leaders and teams can create an environment that supports personal and professional development.

Overall, the human element in Agile methodologies acknowledges that success in any endeavour ultimately depends on the individuals involved. By valuing and integrating the unique contributions and needs of team members, Agile approaches strive to create a more fulfilling and effective work environment.

One minute praising : Most managers will wait for the annual or quarterly performance review to give feedback, there will be too many target tasks to come up with details and solve at this point. Managers will set a part of the goals for employees to continuously manage performance and provide regular feedback. This is not to micromanage staff members, but so he or she can appreciate them when they're doing something right and recognize them for it. After praising the staff, take a slight pause to let the compliment sink in and give the person pat on the back or give them a hand to congratulate them on doing such a great job

One-minute reprimands (One-minute redirect): On the opposite end of praise, organizations also have reprimands(redirect). Just as organizations are taking a few moments to praise, but the reprimands (redirect) happen at about the same time instead of longer. This is important because the staff may begin to think they have more shortcomings than strengths, and that will never end well. During the 'one-minute redirect,' we want to catch unproductive or negative behaviour immediately and explain to the employee the consequences and to emphasize the issue with the work, not the person.

Note: A problem always has a solution. If organizations can't identify the solution, then don't waste time talking about the "problems". Don't tell someone what they're doing wrong until organizations can tell them what they should be doing right.

In the given paragraphs, the emphasis on human element factors can be summarized as follows:

1. **Regular Feedback and Recognition**: The importance of continuous performance management is highlighted, where managers should provide regular feedback to their employees. Instead of waiting for annual or quarterly performance reviews, managers should catch their employees doing something right and recognize them for their efforts. This approach focuses on acknowledging and praising employees for their accomplishments, which helps build motivation and morale.

2. **Balanced Approach**: While praise is important, the paragraphs also emphasize the need for reprimands or redirects when necessary. By addressing unproductive or negative behaviour immediately, organizations can prevent issues from escalating. It is crucial to approach reprimands with a focus on the work issue rather than criticizing the person. This helps maintain a balanced approach and ensures that employees do not feel overwhelmed with criticisms.

3. **Solution-Oriented Mindset**: The paragraphs highlight the significance of focusing on solutions rather than dwelling on problems. Managers are encouraged not to waste time discussing problems unless they can identify a solution. It is important to provide constructive feedback by explaining to employees the consequences of their actions and emphasizing what they should be doing right. This approach promotes a positive and forward-thinking environment.

In summary, the human element factors of continuous feedback, recognition, adaptability, empowerment, trust, and solution-focused mindset are essential for Agile leaders. These factors contribute to creating a collaborative, engaged, and high-performing Agile team that embraces change, learns from experiences, and delivers value effectively.

Let's focus on two corporate scenarios that often highlight the importance of the human element, which can be overlooked by Agile leaders:

1. **Employee Burnout and Well-being**: In Agile environments, there is a strong emphasis on productivity, delivery, and meeting deadlines. While these aspects are important, Agile leaders sometimes overlook the well-being of their team members, which can lead to employee burnout. Burnout occurs when employees experience chronic stress, exhaustion, and a lack of work-life balance.

Scenario: An Agile team is working on a high-pressure project with tight deadlines. The team consistently puts in long hours, works weekends, and faces constant pressure to meet sprint goals. The Agile leader solely focuses on task completion and may not notice the signs of burnout among team members. As a result, team morale decreases, productivity declines, and the risk of attrition increases.

The Human Element: Agile leaders need to prioritize the well-being of their team members. This includes promoting work-life balance, encouraging breaks, and providing support and resources for managing stress. Regular check-ins, open communication channels, and fostering a supportive team culture can help Agile leaders identify signs of burnout and take proactive measures to address them.

2. **Team Collaboration and Engagement**: Agile methodologies emphasize cross-functional collaboration and self-organizing teams. However, Agile leaders may overlook the human dynamics within the team, leading to disengagement and reduced collaboration.

Scenario: An Agile team consists of individuals with diverse skills and backgrounds. However, due to lack of effective communication and understanding, team members struggle to collaborate and align their efforts. The Agile leader focuses primarily on task allocation and progress, without addressing the underlying human dynamics. This results in decreased engagement, siloed work, and a lack of shared ownership and accountability.

The Human Element: Agile leaders need to foster a collaborative and engaging team environment by promoting effective communication, trust, and psychological safety. They should encourage team members to share knowledge, support each other, and work collectively toward shared goals. Facilitating team-building activities, creating opportunities for feedback and reflection, and addressing conflicts proactively are essential for maintaining a healthy team dynamic.

By recognizing and addressing these human element factors, Agile leaders can cultivate a positive work environment, enhance team morale, and ultimately improve the overall effectiveness and success of Agile projects.

Nurturing a Culture of Agility: The Impact of Process, Tools, and People in Agile Transformations

While process, tools, and people play important roles in an Agile transformation, the primary driver of change in culture is the mindset and behaviours of the individuals involved.

In Agile transformations, the focus is on fostering a culture of collaboration, adaptability, and continuous improvement. This cultural shift requires a change in the mindset of the people involved, including leaders, teams, and stakeholders.

Process: The Agile approach emphasizes iterative and incremental development, with a strong focus on delivering value to customers early and frequently. Adopting Agile processes, such as Scrum or Kanban, can help create a foundation for a more collaborative and adaptive culture. However, simply implementing Agile processes alone does not guarantee a change in culture.

Tools: Agile transformations often involve the adoption of specific tools and technologies that support Agile practices, such as project management software, collaboration platforms, and communication tools. While these tools can facilitate Agile practices and enhance collaboration, they are not the sole determinants of cultural change.

People: The most crucial aspect of an Agile transformation is the people involved. Agile encourages self-organizing teams, empowers individuals to make decisions, and promotes a culture of trust and accountability. Creating an environment where people feel safe to voice their opinions, experiment, learn from failures, and collaborate with others is essential. This involves leadership support, fostering a growth mindset, providing training, and coaching, and encouraging cross-functional collaboration.

Ultimately, the success of an Agile transformation depends on individuals embracing the Agile values and principles, adapting their behaviours and mindset, and actively participating in the process. Process and tools can support and enable this cultural shift, but the primary focus should be on empowering and engaging the people involved in the transformation. Of course, the process and tools are designed by people and used by people only.

Agile Leaders as People Managers

Leaders have a vital role in driving Agile transformations as they possess the authority to shape and influence the organizational culture. It is essential to recognize the importance of individuals in achieving success, leading to the clear realization that every leader must adopt the traits of a people manager. Being a people manager goes beyond a designated role; it reflects the Agile leader's approach to working with their team, fostering collaboration, empowerment, and servant leadership.

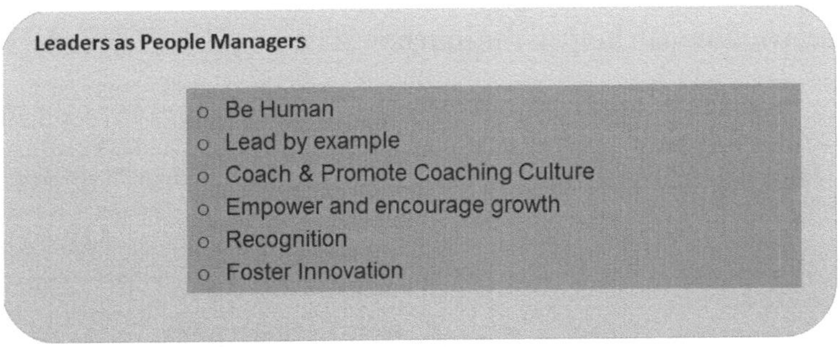

Figure 10.2: People Manager

Every leader needs to be a people manager in Agile transformations as it inspires and motivates team in right direction and helps to give right solutions for people challenges:

1. **Being Human**: By showing empathy, understanding, and respect towards team members, leaders create a positive work environment that fosters collaboration and productivity.

2. **Leading by Example**: Leaders should embody the Agile values and principles themselves, demonstrating transparency, accountability, and adaptability, inspiring others to do the same.

3. **Coach & Promote Coaching Culture**: Leaders should act as coaches, guiding and supporting their team members, while also encouraging a culture of coaching where individuals can learn from and empower each other.

4. **Empower and Encourage Growth**: Leaders should empower their team members

by providing them with autonomy, trust, and opportunities for growth, enabling them to take ownership and develop their skills.

5. **Recognition**: Leaders should recognize and appreciate the efforts and achievements of their team members, fostering a sense of value and motivation within the Agile transformation journey.

6. **Foster Innovation**: Leaders should create an environment that encourages innovation, where individuals feel safe to experiment, share ideas, and collaborate, driving continuous improvement and adaptation.

Unveiling Personal, Team, Leadership Development Practices

Teams can practice these techniques and tools that are relevant to their context to continuously reflect and evolve to their next version of the personality. It's a journey.

Let's see how Johari window can help in the journey of personal, team, leadership development:

The Johari Window is a psychological model that provides a framework for understanding and improving communication and interpersonal relationships. It was developed by psychologists Joseph Luft and Harry Ingham in 1955, hence the name "Johari" derived from their first names.

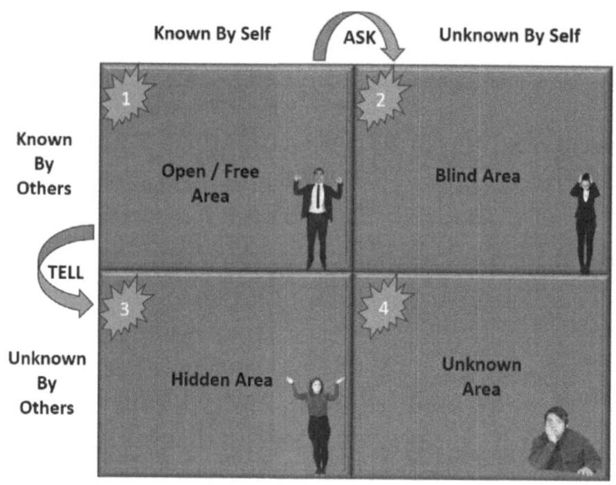

Figure 10.3: Johari Window

The Johari Window consists of a grid divided into four quadrants, each representing different aspects of information known to oneself and others:

- **Open Area (Arena)**: This quadrant represents information about oneself that is known to both the individual and others. It includes characteristics, behaviours, feelings, and thoughts that are openly shared and understood.
- **Blind Spot**: This quadrant represents information about oneself that others are aware of, but the individual is not. These may be blind spots or unconscious biases that others observe but are not recognized by the individual. Feedback from others can help expand self-awareness in this area.
- **Hidden Area (Facade)**: This quadrant represents information about oneself that is known to the individual but kept hidden from others. It includes personal secrets, fears, insecurities, or private thoughts that the individual chooses not to disclose to others.
- **Unknown Area (Unknown)**: This quadrant represents information that is unknown to both the individual and others. It consists of potential talents, abilities, or unconscious aspects of personality that have not yet been discovered or recognized.

The Johari Window encourages individuals to expand their self-awareness, improve communication, and build trust by increasing the size of the open area. This is achieved through self-disclosure, actively seeking feedback, and providing honest and constructive feedback to others.

As individuals and groups work together to reduce blind spots and hidden areas, the Johari Window can help foster better understanding, collaboration, and personal growth. It is often used in various contexts, including therapy, team building, leadership development, and interpersonal skills training.

The Johari Window is a psychological tool that is often used in the context of personal development, team building, and communication. While it is not specifically designed for Agile transformations, it can be a valuable tool in facilitating transformational processes for leaders and teams in Agile contexts. Here's why:

- **Self-awareness**: The Johari Window helps individuals and teams increase self-awareness by providing a framework for understanding their own behaviours, strengths, weaknesses, and blind spots. In Agile transformations, self-awareness is crucial as leaders and team members need to recognize their current capabilities, mindset, and areas for improvement. This awareness allows them to identify their strengths to leverage and any personal barriers that may hinder Agile adoption.
- **Building trust and collaboration**: The Johari Window promotes trust and collaboration by emphasizing open and transparent communication. As teams embark on Agile transformations, trust becomes essential to foster a culture of collaboration, experimentation, and continuous improvement. The tool encourages individuals to share their thoughts, perspectives, and feedback, reducing hidden information and increasing the open/shared information quadrant. This transparency promotes better understanding, empathy, and teamwork.
- **Feedback culture**: Agile transformations require a culture of feedback and continuous learning. The Johari Window can facilitate the development of such a culture by encouraging

individuals and teams to provide and receive feedback openly and constructively. By expanding the open quadrant through giving and receiving feedback, leaders and teams can uncover blind spots, recognize the impact of their behaviour on others, and adjust accordingly.

- **Facilitating personal growth**: Agile transformations often necessitate personal growth and development. The Johari Window can serve as a tool for self-reflection and self-assessment, enabling leaders and team members to identify areas for growth and take ownership of their learning journey. By exploring the hidden quadrant, individuals can become aware of aspects of their personality, beliefs, or skills that they may have previously overlooked or not fully utilized.
- **Enhancing communication**: Effective communication is a cornerstone of successful Agile transformations. The Johari Window helps individuals and teams understand different communication styles, preferences, and barriers. By increasing the open quadrant and sharing relevant information, leaders and team members can enhance communication, align expectations, and ensure that everyone is on the same page.

It's important to note that while the Johari Window can be a valuable tool, it is not a standalone solution for Agile transformations. It should be used in conjunction with other Agile practices, frameworks, and methodologies to achieve the desired transformation outcomes. Additionally, the support and guidance of experienced Agile coaches or facilitators can greatly enhance the effectiveness of utilizing the Johari Window in Agile transformations. Yes, there are several other tools and frameworks commonly used in the context of personal development, team building, and communication. While the Johari Window is a popular tool, here are a few alternatives:

- **DISC Assessment**: The DISC model is widely used to assess and understand individual behavioural styles. It categorizes individuals into four main behavioural styles: Dominance, Influence, Steadiness, and Conscientiousness. DISC assessments can help teams understand their members' communication preferences, work styles, and potential areas of conflict.
- **Myers-Briggs Type Indicator (MBTI)**: MBTI is a widely recognized personality assessment tool that categorizes individuals into 16 different personality types based on four key dimensions: extraversion/introversion, sensing/intuition, thinking/feeling, and judging/perceiving. MBTI can provide insights into individual preferences, decision-making styles, and communication patterns.
- **StrengthsFinder**: The Clifton Strengths assessment, commonly known as StrengthsFinder, helps individuals identify their top strengths out of a list of 34 themes. This tool focuses on uncovering and leveraging individuals' natural talents and strengths to enhance team performance and collaboration.
- **Emotional Intelligence (EQ) assessments**: EQ assessments measure an individual's emotional intelligence, which includes self-awareness, self-regulation, empathy, and relationship management. These assessments can provide insights into emotional strengths and areas for improvement, helping individuals and teams enhance their emotional intelligence and interpersonal relationships.
- **Nonviolent Communication (NVC)**: NVC is a communication framework developed by Marshall Rosenberg. It emphasizes empathetic listening, expressing oneself authentically, and resolving conflicts peacefully. NVC provides a structured approach to communicate with clarity, empathy, and understanding, promoting effective collaboration and conflict resolution.

- **Team Canvas**: The Team Canvas is a visual tool that helps teams clarify their purpose, roles, goals, and values. It facilitates discussions and alignment among team members, enhances collaboration, and provides a shared understanding of team dynamics.

These tools can complement the Johari Window or be used independently, depending on the specific goals and needs of personal development, team building, and communication within an Agile transformation context. It's essential to choose the most appropriate tool based on the desired outcomes, the team's characteristics, and the facilitator's expertise.

Navigating the Ambiguities of Hybrid Work: Tailoring Solutions for Your Unique Needs

In the pre-covid era most work happened at offices. But Covid forced us all to work from home for a few years. Though work from home is good for avoiding commute times, nothing beats face to face interactions. Most companies have now settled into hybrid working rhythm. Hybrid working has become a norm in the post-covid era.

Several research reports indicate that approximately half of the workforce prefers either exclusively on-site or exclusively remote work. The remaining individuals seek a middle ground between the two options. However, when it comes to employees who desire a hybrid work arrangement, there is a lack of consensus on what "hybrid" entails. Some interpret it as primarily working from the office, while others perceive it as rarely being physically present.

Consequently, it is crucial to avoid adopting generic "best practices" or a standardized hybrid model currently. Crafting a successful hybrid work strategy requires leaders to recognize that there is no one-size-fits-all solution. Even the most forward-thinking and innovative companies have not fully determined what approach works best. Ultimately, the effectiveness of a hybrid work model is highly influenced by various factors unique to each organization & teams within the organization, such as industry dynamics, demographics, talent pool, company culture, and customer expectations.

Therefore, it is important for leaders to carefully consider and tailor their hybrid work arrangements to suit the specific needs and characteristics of their organization. A customized approach that considers the individual circumstances and requirements of the company will likely lead to greater success in implementing and managing a hybrid work environment.

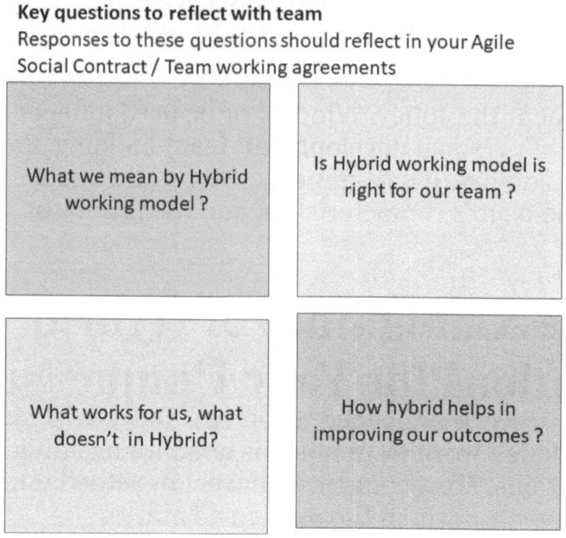

Figure 10.4: Reflection Questions

Remember, these questions should serve as a starting point for a comprehensive discussion with your team, allowing everyone to share their thoughts and concerns, and collectively develop a successful hybrid working model strategy and ensure below points are covered in your discussion:

- Hybrid working models can have a significant impact on employee well-being and work-life balance. It's essential to address these concerns to maintain a healthy and engaged team. By asking this question, you encourage the team to suggest initiatives such as flexible working hours, time management techniques, mental health support, and policies that foster a healthy work-life integration.
- With team members working in different locations, it becomes crucial to preserve a sense of team culture and identity. This question prompts the team to brainstorm ideas on fostering team spirit, promoting shared values, and organizing team-building activities that transcend physical boundaries. It could lead to discussions on virtual social events, recognition programs, or regular check-ins to ensure everyone feels connected and engaged.

The term "Agile Social Contract / Team working Agreement / Social Alliance" refers to the set of agreements, principles, and values that guide the interactions and expectations between individuals and teams in an Agile organization. It defines the working relationship, collaboration, and responsibilities of team members, stakeholders, and management within the Agile framework. Please ensure your hybrid working model plans are part of the social contract so that team are aligned and in complete agreement to the hybrid ways of working too.

In this extraordinary era, exceptional leaders will recognize the immense potential it holds and seize this unique opportunity to revitalize and reshape their organizational culture. Their aim is to cultivate a workplace environment where employees not only experience increased happiness but also exhibit heightened engagement and productivity.

Leveraging the Power of Informal Communications and Grapevine in Agile Transformations

Informal communication or the grapevine is frequently overlooked, and only a few effective leaders prioritize leveraging it to support teams in their transformation journeys. However, in team dynamics, it plays a crucial role, and leaders should place more emphasis on it along with their formal communications.

Informal communication and grapevine networks can play a significant role in Agile transformations by facilitating information flow, building relationships, and promoting a culture of collaboration.

Here are some effective ways to leverage informal communications and grapevine in Agile transformations:

- **Encourage open and transparent communication:** Create an environment where team members feel comfortable sharing information and ideas. Encourage open discussions, feedback sessions, and informal interactions to foster collaboration and knowledge sharing.
- **Establish communication channels**: Identify and establish communication channels that facilitate informal interactions. This can include team chat platforms, social media groups, online forums, or even informal gatherings like lunchtime or coffee breaks. Encourage team members to use these channels for sharing updates, asking questions, and exchanging ideas.
- **Promote cross-team collaboration**: Agile transformations often involve multiple teams working together. Encourage informal communication and collaboration across teams by providing opportunities for cross-team interactions. This can be through joint meetings, workshops, or social events that allow team members to build relationships and share experiences.
- **Embrace storytelling and narratives**: Informal communications often rely on storytelling and narratives to convey information. Encourage team members to share stories, anecdotes, and examples that illustrate Agile principles, success stories, and lessons learned. This helps in spreading knowledge and creating a shared understanding of Agile practices.
- **Emphasize the role of influencers:** Grapevine networks typically have influential individuals who act as information hubs within the organization. Identify these influencers and engage them as advocates for the Agile transformation. They can help disseminate information, address concerns, and promote the benefits of Agile methodologies.
- **Foster a culture of trust**: Trust is essential for effective informal communication. Foster a culture of trust by encouraging transparency, respecting diverse opinions, and promoting psychological safety within the organization. When team members trust each other, they are more likely to engage in informal communication and share valuable insights.
- **Leverage Agile ceremonies:** Agile ceremonies, such as daily stand-ups, sprint reviews, and retrospectives, provide structured opportunities for formal and informal communication. Encourage team members to use these ceremonies not only for discussing work-related matters but also for sharing updates, challenges, and ideas in a more relaxed and informal manner.
- **Lead by example**: Agile leaders should demonstrate the value of informal communication by actively participating in informal discussions, being approachable, and showing genuine

interest in hearing others' perspectives. When leaders lead by example, it encourages others to follow suit and embrace informal communication channels.

- **Monitor and address rumours**: Grapevine networks can sometimes amplify rumours and misinformation. It's crucial to monitor the grapevine and address any false or misleading information promptly. Provide regular updates, clarify any misconceptions, and ensure that accurate information is available through formal channels as well.
- **Encourage continuous improvement**: Agile transformations are iterative and continuously evolving. Encourage team members to provide feedback, suggest improvements, and participate in continuous improvement initiatives. Informal communication channels can be valuable in collecting insights and ideas for refining Agile practices.

By leveraging informal communications and grapevine networks effectively, organizations can enhance collaboration, foster a culture of continuous learning, and accelerate the adoption of Agile methodologies during transformations.

Agile Games: Boosting Collaboration and Learning in Teams

Agile games are interactive activities or exercises that are designed to promote learning and understanding of agile principles, values, and practices. These games are often used in agile teams and organizations to enhance collaboration, communication, problem-solving, and decision-making skills. It's highly recommended to include Agile games as part of your trainings, enablement and team building activities.

Here are a few popular agile games that you can explore:

- **The Ball Point Game**: This game focuses on improving collaboration and self-organization within a team. Participants stand in a circle and pass a ball around while following specific rules. The objective is to complete as many passes as possible within a given time, and the team tries to improve their performance through iterations.
- **Paper Airplane Game**: This game emphasizes the importance of feedback and adaptation. Participants work in teams to build paper airplanes and test them by throwing them towards a target. The teams then receive feedback and can make improvements to their design, applying agile principles like continuous improvement and iteration.
- **Lego Scrum Simulation**: In this game, participants use Lego blocks to simulate the Scrum framework. They create a product backlog, plan and execute sprints, hold daily stand-up meetings, and review and adapt their progress. This game helps teams understand and practice the Scrum methodology in a hands-on and engaging way.
- **The Marshmallow Challenge**: This classic game encourages teams to collaborate, experiment, and iterate. The objective is to build the tallest freestanding structure using spaghetti sticks, tape, string, and a marshmallow. Teams have a limited time to plan, build, and test their structures, and they learn the importance of prototyping, quick feedback, and adapting their approach.
- **Kanban Pizza Game**: This game is inspired by the Kanban method and focuses on visualizing workflow and optimizing the delivery process. Participants simulate a pizza delivery system using cards representing customer orders, and they learn to balance workload, identify

bottlenecks, and optimize the flow of work.

These are just a few examples of agile games, and there are many more available. Agile games provide a hands-on and engaging way to learn and reinforce agile concepts, and they can be adapted to suit the specific needs and context of different teams and organizations.

Gen AI: Empowering Agile Leaders to Address People Challenges with Agility and Insight

Agile transformation is a journey that organizations undertake to adopt agile methodologies and principles in their operations. As with any significant organizational change, there are various challenges that arise, especially in relation to people and their ability to adapt to new ways of working. In recent years, the emergence of Generation AI (Gen AI) has provided new opportunities to address these challenges and empower Agile Transformation Leaders.

Gen AI refers to the generation of artificial intelligence systems and technologies that can interact with humans in more sophisticated and intelligent ways. These systems can analyse vast amounts of data, identify patterns, and generate valuable insights. When it comes to agile transformation, harnessing Gen AI can help address people challenges in the following ways:

- **Data-driven decision-making**: Agile Transformation Leaders can leverage Gen AI to collect and analyse data related to team performance, individual capabilities, and organizational dynamics. By using AI-powered tools, they can gain insights into bottlenecks, areas of improvement, and potential roadblocks. These data-driven insights enable leaders to make informed decisions and take appropriate actions to address people challenges effectively.
- **Predictive analytics**: Gen AI can be employed to forecast and predict potential people challenges in the agile transformation process. By analysing historical data, AI systems can identify patterns and trends, allowing leaders to anticipate issues before they arise. This proactive approach enables Agile Transformation Leaders to devise mitigation strategies and implement preventive measures to ensure a smoother transition.
- **Personalized coaching and support**: Agile Transformation Leaders can utilize AI-powered coaching tools to provide personalized guidance and support to individuals and teams. These tools can leverage Gen AI capabilities to understand the unique needs, strengths, and weaknesses of team members. By tailoring coaching and support based on individual requirements, leaders can facilitate skill development, address resistance to change, and enhance overall team performance.
- **Collaboration and communication**: Gen AI technologies offer opportunities to improve collaboration and communication within agile teams. Virtual assistants and chatbots can be used to facilitate real-time communication, provide instant feedback, and foster knowledge sharing among team members. Additionally, AI-driven collaboration platforms can streamline project management, task allocation, and progress tracking, thereby enhancing team productivity and alignment.
- **Continuous learning and improvement**: Agile Transformation Leaders can leverage Gen AI to facilitate continuous learning and improvement within their organizations. AI-powered learning platforms can deliver personalized training programs, suggest relevant resources, and track individual progress. This enables team members to acquire new skills, stay up to

date with agile practices, and adapt to evolving demands effectively.

While harnessing Gen AI can be beneficial for addressing people challenges in agile transformation, it is essential to consider the ethical implications and ensure responsible use of AI technologies. Leaders must prioritize transparency, fairness, and accountability to maintain trust and avoid unintended consequences.

In summary, by harnessing Gen AI, Agile Transformation Leaders can leverage data-driven insights, predictive analytics, personalized coaching, enhanced collaboration, and continuous learning to effectively address people challenges and drive successful agile transformations in their organizations.

Storytelling: Inspiring Teams

Storytelling plays a crucial role in Agile transformation by fostering effective communication, creating a shared understanding, and inspiring teams. It allows leaders to provide an opportunity for individuals to share their experiences and successes related to Agile transformation. By encouraging storytelling, leaders can create a platform for team members to connect with one another and gain valuable insights.

One important aspect of storytelling is that it humanizes the transformation process. Agile transformation can be challenging, and team members may encounter obstacles along the way. By sharing stories of people who have successfully navigated these challenges and achieved positive outcomes, leaders can provide inspiration and motivation to their teams. These stories serve as real-life examples of how Agile principles and practices can be applied in various situations, making them relatable and applicable.

Furthermore, storytelling helps in creating a sense of community within the team. When team members hear stories from their colleagues, it helps build trust and empathy among team members. They can relate to the challenges faced by their peers and learn from their experiences. This shared understanding enhances collaboration and cooperation within the team, as individuals can draw upon the collective wisdom gained through storytelling.

In addition to sharing stories from external sources, leaders should also encourage team members to share their own stories. Each team member has unique experiences and perspectives, and by providing a platform for them to speak, leaders can tap into the diverse knowledge and insights within the team. This not only empowers team members but also enables them to contribute to the overall Agile transformation process. It gives them a voice and allows them to share their successes, challenges, and lessons learned.

Overall, storytelling in Agile transformation serves as a powerful tool for leaders to inspire, connect, and educate their teams. By creating an environment where stories are shared and valued, leaders can reinforce the principles and values of Agile, promote a culture of learning, and facilitate continuous improvement. It helps teams build a collective narrative that guides their Agile journey, while also fostering a sense of belonging and shared purpose.

Embracing Saburi and Shraddha: For People in Agile Transformations

"Saburi" and "Shraddha" are two important concepts in Sai Baba's teachings that are relevant for people in Agile transformations:

- **Saburi**: Saburi means patience and perseverance. In the context of Agile transformations, patience is essential as it takes time for individuals and teams to adapt to new ways of working. Agile transformation involves a shift in mindset, processes, and behaviours, which may require individuals to learn new skills and change their habits. Practicing Saburi encourages individuals to stay committed to the Agile transformation process, even during challenging times. It reminds people that change takes time and requires patience and resilience.
- **Shraddha**: Shraddha refers to faith and trust. In the Agile context, Shradda emphasizes the importance of trust within teams and between individuals and the organization. Agile methodologies rely on self-organizing teams and trust in the abilities and expertise of team members. It encourages individuals to have faith in the Agile principles and practices and trust in the process of iterative and incremental development. Practicing Shradda helps build a collaborative and transparent culture, where individuals have confidence in each other's capabilities and believe in the value of Agile approaches.

In Agile transformations for people, incorporating the principles of Saburi and Shradda can contribute to a more successful and sustainable transformation. Patience and perseverance foster an environment where individuals are open to learning, adapting, and embracing Agile practices. Trust and faith build strong relationships, promote collaboration, and enable individuals to take ownership and make decisions in self-organizing teams. These two words remind us of the importance of these qualities in Agile transformations, supporting individuals and teams in their Agile journey.

Conclusion

The human element is a crucial factor in Agile transformations, and this chapter has explored its various dimensions. By embracing Agile thinking, individuals can unlock their potential for personal growth and contribute to the success of Agile teams. Agile leaders play a critical role in managing people challenges and fostering a culture of agility. By implementing effective personal, team, and leadership development practices, organizations can continuously improve their Agile performance. Navigating the ambiguities of hybrid work requires tailored solutions that align with the unique needs of individuals and teams. Informal communication channels and Agile games can enhance collaboration and facilitate learning. The emerging concept of Gen AI equips Agile leaders with the tools and insights to address people challenges with agility. Additionally, storytelling serves as a powerful means of inspiring teams and fostering a shared vision. Finally, embracing qualities like saburi and shraddha enables individuals to navigate Agile transformations with patience and faith. By considering and addressing the human element in Agile, organizations can unlock the full potential of their Agile initiatives and achieve long-term success.

Test your understanding

Test your knowledge from the chapter by answering the following questions:

Q.1. How can I embrace Agile thinking for personal growth and enhance my contribution to Agile teams?

Q.2. What are the key skills and qualities required for Agile leaders to effectively navigate people challenges in an Agile context?

Q.3. How can I nurture a culture of agility within my organization by considering the impact of process, tools, and people during Agile transformations?

Q.4. What are some effective personal, team, and leadership development practices that I can implement to improve Agile performance and promote continuous improvement?

Q.5. How can I leverage informal communication channels and Agile games to enhance collaboration and facilitate learning within my Agile team?

Appendix-A

Answers - Test your understanding

CHAPTER 1

Answers to test your understanding, Chapter 1

Ans.1. Accepting and embracing transformations can be challenging due to numerous factors, particularly when it comes to shifting mindsets. The most important ones are Uncertainty, Attachment, Beliefs, Fixed Mindset, Loss of Control, Lack of Awareness, etc.

Ans.2. Leaders play a vital role in driving and ensuring the success of a transformation. They should exemplify their commitment by actively participating in and embracing the changes themselves. Once leaders have a clear understanding of the transformation, they can provide teams with clear direction. This necessitates effective communication of the vision and the provision of necessary resources and guidance throughout the transformation process. It is important to differentiate between change, transition, and transformation. Leaders need to recognize that the seeds of agility exist in nature and were present long before the evolution of humans. By understanding this, leaders can gain a deeper insight into the essence of agility and its relevance to organizational transformations. With this understanding, leaders can effectively nurture the seeds of agility within their teams and organizations, allowing them to flourish and drive successful transformations.

Ans.3. Transition is a process of movement from one state, condition, or phase to another. During a transition, there is often a change in focus or priority.

Ans.4. Transformation is a more profound and comprehensive form of change. It involves a fundamental and often radical shift in the underlying nature, structure, or essence of something. Transformation typically involves a rethinking and reconfiguration of the entire system, resulting in a new paradigm or state.

Ans.5. For organizational transformations to be successful, it is essential to comprehend the differences between change, transition, and transformation. Transition is the internal psychological and emotional adjustments that people and teams must make to adapt to those changes, whereas change refers to the external modifications made to structures, procedures, or technologies. Transformation, on the other hand, goes deeper; it signifies a profound and lasting shift in the organization's core values, culture, and strategic direction. Recognizing these differences is pivotal because it enables leaders to approach transformations holistically. Organizations may build a more flexible and resilient workforce by addressing not only the structural changes but also concentrating on assisting people through the emotional and psychological shifts. The success of the transformation effort is ultimately attributed to the organization's willingness to embrace transformation as an ongoing cultural shift that guarantees the changes are ingrained in the organization's DNA, making them endure and in line with the long-term strategy.

CHAPTER 2

Answers to test your understanding, Chapter 2

Ans.1. The four Mahavakyas are as follows:

- "Prajnanam Brahma" (Consciousness is Brahman)
- "Ayam Atma Brahma" (The Self is Brahman)
- "Tat Tvam Asi" (That Thou Art)
- "Aham Brahmasmi" (I am Brahman)

Ans.2. The sources of Mahavakyas are as follows:

- "Prajnanam Brahma" (Consciousness is Brahman): This Mahavakya is from the Aitareya Upanishad in the Rig Veda.
- "Ayam Atma Brahma" (The Self is Brahman): This Mahavakya is from the Mandukya Upanishad in the Atharvana Veda
- "Tat Tvam Asi" (That Thou Art): This Mahavakya is from the Chandogya Upanishad in the Sama Veda.
- "Aham Brahmasmi" (I am Brahman): This Mahavakya is from the Brihadaranyaka Upanishad in Yajur Veda.

Ans.3. Yes. The Mahavakyas remind leaders to cultivate awareness, foster collaboration, recognize the intrinsic value of individuals, and create a shared understanding of purpose.

Ans.4. Yes. If we understand and practice the concept of universal consciousness, then we will automatically be more collaborative and will work towards collective success.

Ans.5. Following are the ways in which the Mahavakyas help us address some of the agile transformation challenges:

Challenge	Inspiration from Mahavakyas
Resistance to Change	focus on creating consciousness and awareness among individuals and teams about the reasons behind Agile transformation and its benefits.
Fostering Collaboration and Self-Organization	emphasize the interconnectedness of individuals and the recognition that the self (individual) is inherently valuable and capable.
Creating a Shared Understanding of Purpose and Belonging	signify the underlying unity between the individual and the universal consciousness.
Individual Empowerment and Self-Actualization	signify the recognition of the divinity and limitless potential within everyone.

CHAPTER 3

Answers to test your understanding, Chapter 3

Ans.1. An Agile mindset is a set of attitudes, values, and beliefs that underpin the Agile approach to work and problem-solving. It emphasizes flexibility, collaboration, and a focus on delivering value to customers. An Agile mindset goes beyond specific Agile methodologies and can be applied in various fields, encouraging a more responsive and customer-driven approach to work. It's a fundamental cultural shift that drives innovation and problem-solving in a rapidly changing world.

Ans.2. Factors contributing to the evolution of agile mindset are Increasing Complexity, Accelerated Pace of Change, Customer-Centric Approach, Continuous Improvement, Flexibility and Adaptability etc.

Ans.3. The essential values and guiding principles of agile software development are outlined in the Agile Manifesto which is produced by a group of seventeen software professionals in February 2001 with the goal of advancing a more adaptable and flexible method of software development. The manifesto places a strong emphasis on people and relationships, functional software, client participation, and adapting to change.

Ans.4. Agile manifesto was created in February 2001.

Ans.5. Agile manifesto has four agile values and twelve agile principles.

Ans.6. A self-organizing team refers to a group of individuals capable of independently managing and organizing their own work. Unlike traditional hierarchical structures, self-organizing teams operate cooperatively and autonomously, without direct supervision or control from a manager or external authority.

Ans.7. 'Doing Agile' involves implementing popular Agile frameworks like Scrum or Kanban and adhering to their prescribed rituals, roles, and artifacts. However, this approach can be superficial, lacking a genuine embrace of Agile's core values. Embracing Ideals and Mindset 'Being Agile' goes beyond merely following Agile principles. It involves embracing Agile ideals and adopting an Agile mindset, as well as understanding the fundamental concepts that drive Agile approaches.

Ans.8. Swami Vivekananda believed that youth is a critical period in life where the foundation is laid, and challenges are inevitable. According to Swami Ji, struggle is essential for growth, and stagnation leads to demise.

He placed his trust and respect in the strength of ordinary people, considering them the true pillars of a nation, and envisioned a great India built on their capabilities. These values resonate with the principles we follow in Agile.

Swami Ji's advice to focus on one task entirely, giving it your whole soul, aligns with the concept of "Limit Your Work in Progress" in Kanban, which emphasizes completing the existing tasks before starting new ones.

Swami Ji's insistence on taking risks and seeing both success and failure as opportunities to gain experience and grow reflects the agile notion of failing fast, adapting, and retrospectively improving. Just as we conduct regular retrospectives in Agile to learn from both successes and failures, Vivekananda's emphasis on introspection and talking to oneself mirrors the idea of self-retrospection and the importance of motivated individuals in Agile.

CHAPTER 4

Answers to test your understanding, Chapter 4

Ans.1. Strength is defined as the quality of being physically strong. Strength for organizations can mean strong brand loyalty, high efficiency/productivity, Quick time to market, high adaptability.

Ans.2. One can know about their strengths by using strengths assessments.

Ans.3. Strength assessments can help in Agile transformations by

1. Identifying Individual Strengths
2. Building complementary teams
3. Empowering Self-Organizing Teams
4. Encouraging Growth and Learning
5. Enhancing Team Collaboration and Communication
6. Supporting Agile Leadership Development.

Ans.4. Agility means being able to shift quickly and smoothly in a position or direction.

Ans.5. Traits that demonstrate leader's agility from market perspective are

1. Product Vision
2. Fast decision making
3. Ability to embrace fail fast.
4. Courage

Ans.6. The leadership traits that can help build high performing teams are as follows

1. Higher emotional quotient
2. More collaboration with team
3. Humility
4. Trust in team.

CHAPTER 5

Answers to test your understanding, Chapter 5

Ans.1. Emotional Intelligence (EI) plays a crucial role in Agile transformations. Emotion refers to the complex psychological state that arises from various stimuli, impacting our thoughts, behaviors, and physiological responses.

The values and the principles in the Agile manifesto, highlight the significance of strong emotional intelligence skills among Agile leaders and teams. By cultivating emotional intelligence, Agile teams and leaders can navigate individual interactions effectively, communicate with clarity, and foster a collaborative environment.

The values and principles mentioned in the Agile Manifesto reinforces the need for strong emotional intelligence skills among Agile leaders and teams. The two of the agile values and six of the agile principles are directly connected with EI.
These are vital in Agile transformations, where organizations adopt and implement Agile methodologies.

EI empowers individuals to understand and manage their emotions, navigate conflicts, build strong relationships, and embrace change, all of which are essential for successful Agile transformations.
We know the popular saying "Charity begins at home". Similarly, the transformation starts with us, the people, the mindset of the people. Hence EI is significant in effective collaboration, communication, and adaptability within Agile teams and has critical role for fostering agile transformation.

Ans.2. The key competencies of Emotional Intelligence that leaders need to develop for effective Agile leadership are as follows:

- Self-Reflection
- Improving EI and Fostering Leadership Growth
- Nurturing Personal Growth and Embracing Servant Leadership
- Self-Awareness

Ans.3. EI plays a crucial role in shaping and influencing the different phases of team development. In the context of Agile transformation, a leader with high EI can effectively navigate and guide the team through the change process, creating a supportive and adaptive environment that promotes collaboration, learning, and continuous improvement.

Here's how EI impacts each phase:

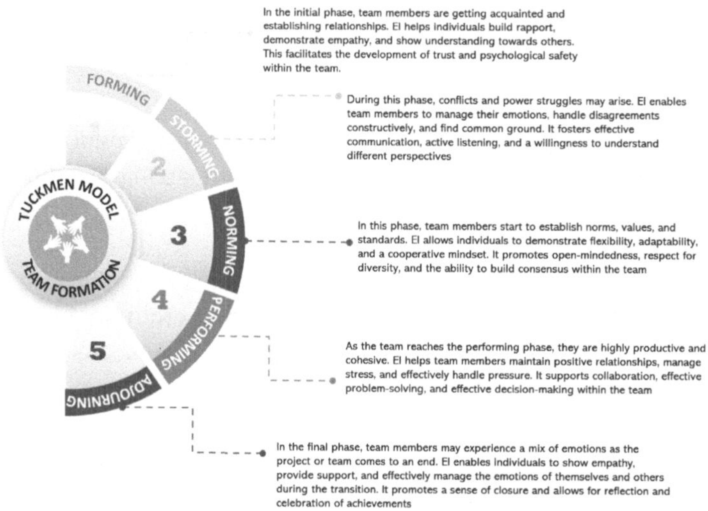

Ans.4. EI plays a vital role in addressing the five dysfunctions of a team, as described by Patrick Lencioni. In the context of Agile transformation, a leader with high EI can create a safe and inclusive environment where team members feel empowered to take risks, learn from failures, and embrace change, thereby enabling successful Agile adoption and implementation.

Here's how EI can help mitigate these dysfunctions:

- **Absence of Trust**: Trust is the foundation of a healthy team. EI enables team members to build trust by being authentic, demonstrating vulnerability, and showing empathy towards one another. Individuals with high EI can establish a safe and supportive environment where team members feel comfortable sharing their thoughts, concerns, and ideas.
- **Fear of Conflict**: Conflict avoidance can hinder a team's progress. EI helps team members manage conflicts constructively by fostering open communication, active listening, and understanding different perspectives. Individuals with high EI can navigate disagreements with emotional intelligence, promoting healthy debate and problem-solving.
- **Lack of Commitment**: Commitment arises when team members feel heard, understood, and valued. EI promotes effective communication and collaboration, allowing team members to align their goals, clarify expectations, and make commitments collectively. Individuals with high EI can create a sense of ownership, engagement, and dedication within the team.
- **Avoidance of Accountability**: Accountability is essential for team success. EI enables team members to take responsibility for their actions, deliver on commitments, and hold others accountable in a constructive manner. Individuals with high EI can foster a culture of accountability by providing feedback, setting clear expectations, and encouraging a

growth mindset.

- **Inattention to Results**: Teams must prioritize collective goals over individual achievements. EI helps team members focus on shared objectives, set aside personal agendas, and celebrate collective successes. Individuals with high EI can inspire and motivate the team towards achieving outcomes that benefit the entire team or organization.

By cultivating EI within team members, organizations can address the five dysfunctions of a team. EI fosters trust, promotes healthy conflict resolution, encourages commitment, enhances accountability, and ensures a focus on collective results.

CHAPTER 6

Answers to test your understanding, Chapter 6

Ans.1. Transformations are like chemical changes, there is no turning back. While transitions are like physical changes which may revert to original state in the absence of external input.

Ans.2. Following are the pitfalls while doing agile transitions.

- More communication but less collaboration
- Lack of ownership instead of self-organizing teams
- No documentation to the point of lacking common understanding
- Flexibility means requirements can change at any time

Ans.3. Some of the problems faced while adopting agile are as follows.

- Organizational culture at odds with Agile
- Resistance to change.
- Inadequate management support

Ans.4. Traits of a Leader required for an agile transformation are as follows.

- Growth Mindset
- Visionary
- Servant Leadership
- Systems Thinking
- Continuous Learning
- Entrepreneurial Mindset.

Ans.5. Lean management can help us in maximizing business values. Five Principles of lean management are as follows:

- Value
- Value stream mapping
- Flow
- Pull
- Perfection.

Ans.6. The steps for building high-performing teams are as follows.

- Alignment to common goal
- Optimum Communication
- Building Trust
- Conflict Resolution:

CHAPTER 7

Answers to test your understanding, Chapter 7

Ans.1. The Agile Maturity Index, also known as the Agile Transformation Index, is a framework designed to evaluate the progress and effectiveness of an organization's Agile transformation efforts. It helps organizations identify gaps, set improvement goals, and make informed decisions to drive continuous improvement.

Ans.2. Focusing on all possible metrics can lead to confusion and inefficiency. Instead, organizations should carefully select metrics that are relevant to their specific context and aligned with their vision, mission, and objectives. To determine the relevant metrics, organizations need to consider the stage of their transformation journey and identify the data points that will provide actionable insights. By measuring what truly matters, organizations can track their progress effectively and make data-driven decisions to achieve their transformation goals.

Ans.3. OKRs stands for Objectives and Key Results. OKRs are a goal-setting framework that helps teams and organizations align their efforts and focus on achieving measurable outcomes. It focuses on future success. KPIs stands for Key Performance Indicators. KPIs are specific metrics that are used to measure the performance and progress of a team or organization towards its goals. OKR's foster alignment and collaboration within teams and across the organization. They create a shared understanding of the goals. KPIs are benchmarks against which all teams within organization are measured. They provide objective data and insights into efficiency of the organization.

Ans.4. Organizations may include following dimensions in their assessments:

- Agile Leadership
- Agile Mindset and Culture
- Agile Practices and Processes
- Team Empowerment
- Stakeholder Engagement
- Continuous Learning and Improvement
- Organizational Structure and Support
- Agile metrics and business outcomes

Ans.5. The Transformation Index assessment can be conducted periodically at different stages of the agile transformation journey to track progress and identify areas for improvement. The results of the assessment can guide the organization in prioritizing actions, allocating resources, and adjusting strategies to ensure a successful agile transformation.

Ans.6. Some key acceptance criteria for effective agile assessments are:

- Coverage
- Contextual Relevance
- Clear Objectives
- Comprehensive Evaluation
- Quantifiable Metrics
- Inclusive Participation
- Validated Tools and Techniques
- Benchmarking Capability
- Actionable Recommendations
- Continuous Improvement
- Supportive Documentation
- Education and Training

CHAPTER 8

Answers to test your understanding, Chapter 8

Ans.1. Major challenges faced in agile transformations are.

- Cultural resistance to change.
- Knowledge and Skills Deficit
- Hierarchical Organization Structures
- Contracts & Pricing Models
- Legacy Systems and Technical Debt.

Ans.2. Cultural resistance to change can be addressed with

- Addressing resistance to change
- Encouraging Growth mindset and embracing transparency
- Establishing a culture of continuous learning and improvement

Ans.3. Knowledge & skills deficit can be managed by

- Identifying knowledge gaps and skill deficiencies
- Providing comprehensive Agile training programs
- Encouraging Agile certifications and continuous learning opportunities

Ans.4. Challenges arising due to hierarchical organization structure are.

- Communication Distortion
- Communication barriers
- Communication delays

Ans.5. Hierarchical structure challenges can be solved using following techniques.

- Transitioning to cross-functional teams
- Empowering self-organizing teams and decentralizing decision-making
- Redefining roles and responsibilities to align with Agile principles.
- Implementing communication channels

Ans.6. The challenges resulting from multi-vendor multi contracts are as follows:

- Slower Time to Market
- Budget overruns
- Conflicts between vendors

Ans.7. Multi-vendor, multi contract challenges can be overcome using following agile techniques:

- Smaller development cycles
- Goal/Outcome Focused development.
- Quarterly Business Planning

CHAPTER 9

Answers to test your understanding, Chapter 9

Ans.1. The important challenges in terms of PEOPLE with respect to agile transformations are Cultural Resistance, Skill Gap, Leadership Support, Working in Silos.

Ans.2. The important challenges in terms of TOOLs with respect to agile transformations are Overemphasis on Tools, Version Control Process & System, Tool-Centric Behavior, Learning Curve Distraction, Complexity of Maintenance, Implementing Multiple Tools without clarity.

Ans.3. The full form of VUCA is Volatility, Uncertainty, Complexity, Ambiguity.

Ans.4. Some agile practices can be directly applied to ERP implementations without adaptation: forming small, end-to-end, cross-functional agile teams with dedicated product owners from the business and end users; working in short cycles of two to three weeks to produce working software (or configurations, interfaces, etc.) incrementally; adopting scrum-based ceremonies focusing on continuous improvement, with transparency facilitated by the ceremonies and KPIs; and using tools and technologies—such as test automation and continuous integration—that optimize and accelerate the delivery process.

The customer or the product owner must define a whole scope of the project at a higher level for the projects in ERP. On the other hand, Agile promotes the approach of minimum viable product (MVP). But in this case, an overall scope is present, and team adapts and reflects in smaller iterations considering the priority and the detail scope.

Furthermore, to maintain consistent development, team needs to do more work on the business process and define architecture than in a *Non-ERP* agile implementation, so that the work can be divided among small teams.

Detail plan for shorter iterations needs to be done along with a having a clear whole scope which states the success criteria.

Strong links are required between agile teams supplying functions and "transversal" teams, which are nonfunctional teams that support the functional or feature teams, such as the data-migration team, the integration team, or the change team. All teams should be synced so that they work in the same rhythm and arrive at the same time.

Team cannot deliver a product version which is "production ready" as frequently as in traditional agile software development. To aggregate the increments produced by various teams and to test complicated interfaces with legacy systems, an end-to-end (E2E) testing and cut-over phase is required; this sometimes takes longer than one sprint to accomplish. In many ERP projects, the working of product backlog items in one sprint corresponds with the activities of making production readiness of the items from the previous sprint.

Ans.5. Here's are guidelines on how few of the best practices for Agile Transformations in Cloud Migration project are as follows:

- Governance and Leadership:
- Teams and Skillsets:
- Processes and Workflows:
- Tools and Technology:
- Communication and Collaboration:
- Metrics and KPIs:
- Risk Management and Compliance:
- Training and Development:
- Change Management:
- Resource Management and Cost Control:
- Documentation and Knowledge Sharing:
- Continuous Improvement:
- Alignment with Business Strategy

Ans.6. The major technological challenges in agile transformation of Legacy systems are Outdated Technology Stack, Inadequate documentation and knowledge, Compatibility of data and Monolithic Architecture, Quality Control and Test Data Management - Automated Testing, Integration of Modern Tools and Technologies, Compliance and security, Long Release Cycles, Scalability, and performance etc.

Ans.7. The potential of AI to automate repetitive operations, freeing up time and resources for more strategic work, is one of the key benefits of Agile transformations. Furthermore, AI can learn from data and generate intelligent predictions, assisting teams in identifying and addressing possible concerns before they become major difficulties. This contributes to the success of Agile transformations and the ability of teams to fulfill their objectives in a timely and effective manner. Advanced analytics and data visualization tools are another significant way AI is being used to assist Agile transformations. These technologies help teams better analyze their data and find trends and patterns that might help them make better decisions. Overall, the application of AI in Agile transformations is a promising trend that is assisting teams in more effectively and efficiently achieving their goals. As technology advances, we should expect to see even more creative use of AI in the Agile space.

CHAPTER 10

Answers to test your understanding, Chapter 10

Ans.1. Agile thinking involves adopting a flexible and adaptive mindset, ready to pivot and adjust as needed. It encourages us to question established norms and explore innovative approaches. In the realm of personal growth, agile thinking allows us to shed the limitations imposed by our emotions and expand the horizons of our intellect. It empowers us to embrace new challenges, seek continuous learning opportunities, and remain open to diverse perspectives. In our composite personality, the mind and intellect form an intricate relationship. By achieving a harmonious balance between the two, we can make decisions that are grounded in both emotional intelligence and intellectual agility.

Ans.2. The key and qualities required for Agile leaders to effectively navigate people challenges in an Agile context are as follows:

- Being Human: By showing empathy, understanding, and respect towards team members, leaders create a positive work environment that fosters collaboration and productivity.
- Leading by Example: Leaders should embody the Agile values and principles themselves, demonstrating transparency, accountability, and adaptability, inspiring others to do the same.
- Coach & Promote Coaching Culture: Leaders should act as coaches, guiding and supporting their team members, while also encouraging a culture of coaching where individuals can learn from and empower each other.
- Empower and Encourage Growth: Leaders should empower their team members by providing them with autonomy, trust, and opportunities for growth, enabling them to take ownership and develop their skills.
- Recognition: Leaders should recognize and appreciate the efforts and achievements of their team members, fostering a sense of value and motivation within the Agile transformation journey.
- Foster Innovation: Leaders should create an environment that encourages innovation, where individuals feel safe to experiment, share ideas, and collaborate, driving continuous improvement and adaptation.

Ans.3. While process, tools, and people play important roles in an Agile transformation, the primary driver of change in culture is the mindset and behaviours of the individuals involved.

In Agile transformations, the focus is on fostering a culture of collaboration, adaptability, and continuous improvement. This cultural shift requires a change in the mindset of the people involved, including leaders, teams, and stakeholders.

Process: The Agile approach emphasizes iterative and incremental development, with a strong focus on delivering value to customers early and frequently. Adopting Agile processes, such as Scrum or Kanban, can help create a foundation for a more collaborative and adaptive culture.

Tools: Agile transformations often involve the adoption of specific tools and technologies that support Agile practices, such as project management software, collaboration platforms, and communication tools. While these tools can facilitate Agile practices and enhance collaboration, they are not the sole determinants of cultural change.

People: The most crucial aspect of an Agile transformation is the people involved. Agile encourages self-organizing teams, empowers individuals to make decisions, and promotes a culture of trust and accountability. Creating an environment where people feel safe to voice their opinions, experiment, learn from failures, and collaborate with others is essential. This involves leadership support, fostering a growth mindset, providing training, and coaching, and encouraging cross-functional collaboration.

Ans.4. Some effective personal, team, and leadership development practices that we can implement to improve Agile performance and promote continuous improvement are as follows:

- Emphasize open and transparent communication.
- Empower individuals.
- Adapt and respond to change.
- Encourage continuous learning and growth.
- One minute praising
- One-minute reprimands (One minute redirect)
- Regular Feedback and Recognition
- Balanced Approach
- Solution-Oriented Mindset.

Ans.5. Informal communication and grapevine networks can play a significant role in Agile transformations by facilitating information flow, building relationships, and promoting a culture of collaboration.

Few of the effective ways to leverage informal communications and grapevine in Agile transformations can be:

- Encourage open and transparent communication.
- Establish communication channels.
- Promote cross-team collaboration.
- Embrace storytelling and narratives.
- Emphasize the role of influencers.
- Foster a culture of trust.
- Leverage Agile ceremonies.
- Lead by example
- Monitor and address rumours.
- Encourage continuous improvement.

Agile games are interactive activities or exercises that are designed to promote learning and understanding of agile principles, values, and practices. Agile games provide a hands-on and engaging way to learn and reinforce agile concepts, and they can be adapted to suit the specific needs and context of different teams and organizations. Hence these games can be used in agile teams and organizations to enhance collaboration, communication, problem-solving, and decision-making skills.

It's highly recommended to include Agile games as part of the trainings, enablement and team building activities.

Here are a few popular agile games that we can explore:

- The Ball Point Game
- Paper Airplane Game
- Lego Scrum Simulation
- The Marshmallow Challenge
- Kanban Pizza Game

.

Appendix-B

Bibliography

A.Parthasarathy , Choice Upanishads, A.Parthasarathy, 2016
A.Parthasarathy , Vedanta Treatise – The Eternities, A.Parthasarathy, 2015
Andrew S Grove, Only the Paranoid Survive, HarperCollins, 1998
Ken Blanchard and Spencer Johnson, The One Minute Manager, Harpercollins, 2006

https://agilemanifesto.org
https://danielgolemanemotionalintelligence.com/
https://digital.ai/resource-center/analyst-reports/state-of-agile-report/
https://en.wikipedia.org/wiki/Adi_Shankara
https://en.wikipedia.org/wiki/Jesus
https://en.wikipedia.org/wiki/Johari_window
https://en.wikipedia.org/wiki/Muhammad
https://en.wikipedia.org/wiki/Ramakrishna
https://en.wikipedia.org/wiki/Serena_Williams
https://en.wikipedia.org/wiki/Teachings_and_philosophy_of_Swami_Vivekananda
https://global.toyota/en/company/vision-and-philosophy/production-system/
https://jamesclear.com/first-principle
https://pecb.com/article/digital-transformation-challenges-and-how-to-overcome-them
https://penpoin.com/tall-organizational-structure/
https://startuptalky.com/kodak-bankruptcy-case-study/
https://vitalitychicago.com/blog/what-leaders-role-agile-transformation/#agile-leader-characteristics
https://www.britannica.com/topic/J-curve-hypothesis
https://www.digitalocean.com/resources/article/what-is-technical-debt
https://www.forbes.com/sites/forbescoachescouncil/2020/06/17/15-key-qualities-that-define-an-agile-leader/
https://www.gallup.com/cliftonstrengths/en/252137/home.aspx
https://www.ihhp.com/free-eq-quiz/
https://www.instinctools.com/blog/omg-erp-implementation-risks-challenges-you-hadn-t-thought-about
https://www.knowledgehut.com/blog/agile/agile-transformation-and-challenges
https://www.openaccessgovernment.org/top-5-challenges-when-migrating-to-the-cloud/162580/
https://www.pbslearningmedia.org/resource/nat37.sci.agility/cat-adaptations-agility/
https://www.productplan.com/glossary/agile-manifesto/
https://www.projectmanager.com/blog/lean-principles
https://www.scrum.org/resources/scrum-values
https://www.shortform.com/blog/fixed-mindset-examples/
https://www.stackscale.com/blog/legacy-systems/